FUNDAMENTALS OF RUMI'S THOUGHT
A MEVLEVI SUFI PERSPECTIVE

FUNDAMENTALS OF
RUMI'S THOUGHT
A Mevlevi Sufi Perspective

Şefik Can

Edited and translated by
Zeki Sarıtoprak

First edition in Turkish published by Ötüken as *Mevlana–Hayatı, Şahsiyeti, Fikirleri* 1999

18 17 16 15   6 7 8 9

Sixth reprint in 2015

Published by Tughra Books
345 Clifton Ave., Clifton,
NJ, 07011, USA
www.tughrabooks.com

Library of Congress Cataloging-in-Publication Data

Can, Sefik, 1910 - 2005
        [Mevlana. English.]
Fundamentals of Rumi's thought : Mevlevi Sufi perspective / translated by
Cuneyt Eroglu and Zeki Saritoprak ; foreword by M. Fethullah Gülen.-- 1st ed.
in English.
        p. cm.
"First edition in Turkish published by Ötüken as Mevlana : hayati, sahsiyeti,
fikirleri."
    Includes bibliographical references and index.
    ISBN 1-932099-79-4
    1. Jalal al-Din Rumi, Maulana, 1207-1273. 2. Mevleviyeh. 3.   Sufism.
I. Title.
BP189.7.M42C3513 2004
297.4'092--dc22

                                                                        2004018391

ISBN 978-1-932099-79-9

Printed by
İmak Ofset, Istanbul - Turkey

TABLE OF CONTENTS

SUPPLICATION

O Rumi, our master! Many books and articles have been written about your glorious life for centuries. Many words have been said. Thousands of people across the world have benefited from your works. Your works have been translated into many languages, and those who love you have devoted a lot of work to introducing your teaching to the world. Ignoring my weakness, I also wanted to be among those who have given their hearts to you. I wanted to write and speak to those who love you. I seek your spiritual support for this work.

Şefik Can

FOREWORD

Mevlana Jalal al-Din Rumi

There are some significant personalities who with the help of their voice and breath, their love and excitement, and their promise for humanity always remain fresh and alive over the course of centuries. Time evidently fails to make these characters obsolete. Their thoughts, analyses, explanations, and spiritual messages, which never will be lost, represent ever new, alternative solutions and prescriptions for today's social problems, in great variety and diversity.

Rumi is one such personality. Despite the centuries that separate his life from ours, Rumi continues to hear and to listen to us, to share our feelings, to present solutions to our problems in a voice that is without equal. Despite the fact that he lived some seven centuries ago, he remains absolutely alive among and with us today. He is a man of light—one who receives his light from the spirit of the Master of Humanity (Prophet Muhammad, peace and blessings be upon him), distributing this light in various ways to just about everywhere. He was chosen to be one of the world's saints and to be pure of heart; a blessed one whose words are outstanding among those heroes of love and passion. He was and continues to function as Israfil, blowing life into dead spirits. He continues to provide the water of life to the barren hearts of many, a spiritual irrigation. He continues to provide light for the travelers on their paths. He was and continues to be the perfect heir of the Prophet.

Jalal al-Din Rumi, a man of God, hastened toward God on his own spiritual journey, but in addition to this he evoked similar journeys in countless others—journeys marked by an eager striving toward God. He was a balanced man of ecstasy who sprang alive with love and excitement; he did this to such an extent that he inspired in others these significant feelings, and he continues to do so. In addition to his passion for God and along with his knowledge and love of Him, Rumi further is renowned as a hero in terms of both his respect and fear of God. He was and continues to be one who beckons, one whose powerful voice invites everyone to the truth and the ultimate blessed reality. Rumi was an inclusive master whose joy was a direct consequence of His joy, whose love and passion were the result of His special favors to Rumi. His life provides real evidence of the Truth. While he spoke to those of his own times in an effective manner, Rumi has become even more influential in that he made his voice and breath, which reflected the voice and breath of Prophet Muhammad continue to be heard for centuries after. He spoke with such an enchanting voice that he was able to guide not only his blessed contemporaries, but also people of our time, centuries removed from his physical existence. God bestowed upon him this important duty. For this purpose, God blessed him with impeccable inner and outer qualities so that he would prove successful in this undertaking. His heart was full of the Divine Light. As such, his essence is marked by his wisdom, which shines like a light reflected through a precious gem. His innermost self was enveloped with Divine mysteries. His inner eyes were enlightened by this special light.

On this horizon, Jalal al-Din Rumi represents the North Star, the heart of the circle of guidance for his time. He embodies the characteristics of the lamp of sainthood, taking its light from that of the truth of the Prophet. Many of God's blessed creatures instinctively are attracted to light; Rumi's light has attracted hundreds of thousands of spiritual butterflies; they are drawn to the light. He represents a guide for humanity's quest for the perfection of human qualities. Rumi was a careful exegete of the truths presented in the Qur'an. A fluent interpreter of love and zeal for Prophet Muhammad, Rumi was able to use a mysterious language to guide others to a love of God. Those who enter his sphere are able to reach an ultimate sense or feeling in the presence of God. Those who examined the Qur'an by his guideposts underwent changes (and continue to undergo changes) similar to those witnessed by the people who lived in the era of the Prophet himself. When the verses of the Qur'an were interpreted by Rumi's closest associates, all hearts benefited from the illumination provided by his wisdom; it was as if all of heaven's mysteries were opened by his wholehearted recitation of that one word—God.

Rumi's love for God was a fiery one, with a constant longing for the mysteries of God. He experienced love and passion both in his solitary asceticism and his activities in the community. It was in his solitariness that he became most open to the truest union with God, and it was during separation from all things except God that his heart burned with fire. And while such a sense of burning would prove difficult for many to bear, Rumi never showed any signs of discontent. Rather, such burning was considered a requirement for passion, and refraining from complaint was seen to be in the tradition of loyalty. For Rumi, those who profess a love of God necessarily must accompany their statement of "I love" with a sense of furious burning—this is the price one willingly must pay for being close to or in union with God. Additionally, one must engage in behavior that is to a large extent ascetic, such as moderate eating, drinking, sleeping, and a constant awareness and orientation toward God in one's speech, and one inevitably must experience bewilderment when endowed with God's bounties.

Rumi cannot understand how a lover can sleep in an immoderate way, as it takes away from the time that can be shared with the Beloved. For him, excessive sleep is offensive to the Beloved. As God instructed David, saying, "O David, those who indulge in sleep without contemplating Me and then claim to be in love are liars," so too did Rumi state, "When the darkness falls, lovers become intense." Rumi continually recommended this not only in words, but also in his actions.

The following quotation from his *Divan-i Kabir* best represents several droplets from the ocean of his feelings and excitement, erupting like a volcano:

> I am like Majnun[1] in my poor heart, which is without limbs, because I have no strength to contest the love of God.
>
> Every day and night I continue in my efforts to free myself from the bonds of the chain of love; a chain that keeps me imprisoned.
>
> When the dream of the Beloved begins I find myself in blood. Because I am not fully conscious, I am afraid in that I may paint Him with the blood of my heart.
>
> In fact, You, O Beloved, must ask the fairies; they know how I have burned through the night. Everyone has gone to sleep.
>
> But I, the one who has given his heart to You, do not know sleep like them. Throughout the night, my eyes look at the sky, counting the stars.
>
> His love so profoundly took my sleep that I do not really believe it ever will come back.

If the spirit of the anthology of Rumi's poems—which are the essence of love, passion, divine presence, and excitement—were to be wrung out, what would result are the cries of love, longing, and hope. Throughout his life Rumi expressed love, and in turn, he believed he was beloved because of this. Accordingly, he spoke of his love and relationship with Him. When he did so, he was not alone—he took along with him many blessed individuals who were his audience. He assumed it to be a requisite of loyalty to offer, cup by cup, the drinks presented to him on the heavenly table to others who were in his circle of light.

Thus, the following quotation represents the ambiguous chanting that is reflected in his heavenly travels:

The Buraq² of love has taken my mind as well as my heart, do
not ask me where.
I have reached such a realm that there is no moon, nor day.
I have reached a world where the world is no longer the world.

Rumi's spiritual journey was an ascension in the shadow of
the Ascension of the Prophet, which is described by Süleyman
Chelebi (the author of the Turkish Mevlid—recited in commemo-
ration of the birth of the Prophet)—in these words: "There was no
space, Earth, or heavens." What his soul heard and watched was a
special reflection of His courtesy, which cannot be seen by the eyes,
heard by the ears, or comprehended by one's mind or thought.
Such reflections are not attainable by all. Rumi spiritually ascend-
ed, and he saw, tasted, and knew all that was possible for a mortal
being. Those who do not see cannot know. Those who do not taste
cannot feel. Those who are capable of feeling in this manner generally do not divulge the secrets that they have attained. And those
who do reveal these secrets often find them to be above the level of
the comprehension of most people. As the famous Turkish poet
Shaykh Ghalib said, "The Beloved's candle has such a wonderful
light, and its light does not fit into the lamp glass of Heaven."

The love, relationship, and warmth toward all creation
expressed by Rumi are a projection of a deeply-rooted divine love.
Rumi, whose nature was intoxicated by the cup of love, embraced
all of creation with a projection of that love. He was involved in a
dialogue with every creature, and all this was a result of nothing
but his deep love of God and his relationship with the Beloved.

I believe that these disordered and somewhat confused explanations are far from adequate to describe Rumi. This disorder is an
inevitable result of my search for a relationship with him. A droplet
cannot describe the ocean, nor can an atom describe the sun. Even
so, since his light falls once again on this earth, I would like to say,
in a few sentences, some words about Jalal al-Din Rumi.

Rumi was born in the city of Balkh in 1207, at a time when all of Asia was suffering from social, political, and military problems. His father, Muhammad Baha al-Din al-Siddiqi, was in the tenth generation of the descendants of Abu Bakr al-Siddiq, the first caliph of Islam. According to Tahir al-Mevlevi, Rumi's mother was also a descendant of the Prophet. He was the blessed fruit of a hallowed family tree. Being known as the Sultan al-Ulama (the Leader of Scholars), his father was a man of truth and an heir of the Prophet. Like many friends of God, he was persecuted and eventually compelled to migrate. Accordingly, he left the land of Khawarzm, where he was born, and undertook a lengthy journey that encompassed various destinations. First, he and his family visited the Holy Land, the cities of Makka and Madina. From here, he traveled and remained for some time in Damascus, where he met many pious persons, such as Ibn al-'Arabi, and exchanged spiritual enlightenment with them. Accompanying his father, the young Rumi, six or seven years of age, witnessed these and other events; his inquisitive senses enabled him to experience all of these with remarkable clarity. The young Rumi understood his environment even at such a tender age, and he was able to penetrate into the secret world of Ibn al-'Arabi. As an endowment of his presence with Ibn al-'Arabi, the child received kindness and favors. Despite the unfortunate circumstances surrounding their migration and the many difficulties that accompanied them, the family's journey provided them with a variety of favors and inspiration. Like Abraham, Moses, and the Prophet of Islam, may God's blessings be upon all of them, Rumi was able continuously to find these blessings and favors. Welcoming what fate gave him, he became a receiver of numerous bounties provided by God.

The journey took this blessed family to the city of Erzincan, and later to Karaman. It was during his time in the latter city that Rumi studied, for a short period, in the Halawiyye madrasa. In addition to this school, he studied Islamic sciences in several religious schools in Damascus and Aleppo. After graduating, he returned to the city of Konya, which he considered his hometown and a place of special regard. It was there that he married Gevher Khatun, the daughter of Shams al-Din Samarqandi. After some time, Rumi's father, Sultan al-Ulama, died and returned to God. Under the supervision of Burhan al-Din al-Tirmidhi, Rumi began his long spiritual journey. After several years, at the suggestion of Rukn al-Din Zarqubi, Rumi met with Shams-i Tabrizi who was then on a visit to Konya. It was through his meeting with Shams that he furthered his spiritual journey and eventually developed into the person who now is known the world over for his spiritual depth. What has been mentioned so far, in fact, represents an attempt to open a few small windows on the life of an exceptional personality in this creation, one whose capacity is open to the lofty world. This is also an attempt to present the life of an important representative of the Muhammadi spirit (i.e., the practice of the *sunna*)—displaying several snapshots of a man determined to dedicate his existence to the afterlife.

It is not my intention to stir the waters that comprise the lives of such remarkable and pure personalities with debates and questions that ultimately only will agitate and obscure. However, one must wonder whether Rumi opened the horizon of Shams or whether Shams took Rumi to the world of the unseen. Who took whom to the reality of realities—the peak of love and joy? Who directed whom to the real Besought and the real Beloved? Answering these questions is beyond the capacity of most ordinary people. One can say, at least, the following: During this period of time, two skillful and acute spirits came together, like two oceans merging into one another. By sharing the divine bounties and gifts received from their Lord, they both reached peaks that most people would not be able to reach easily on their own account. Through their spiritual cooperation, they established camps on the peaks of knowledge, love, compassion, and joy for God. As much as they enlightened those of their own times, they also influenced all centuries to follow, an effect that is still present today. The spring of sweet water that they represent continues to nourish the thirsty. They have been remembered continuously over the centuries for their beautiful contributions to countless lives. Here it is important to note that Rumi was informed by numerous sources in the flow of ideas, including his father, the great master of scholars. During his journey, he seemed to leave many of his contemporaries behind. His love and compassion flowed like the waters of the world's oceans, so much so that while continuing to live physically among humans, he managed to become ever closer to God. It seems he never elevated himself above others except through his writings, both during his life and after entering eternity; he provides a guiding star that echoes the spiritual life of the Prophet of Islam. Accordingly, he is among the few people who have exerted a great influence through both space and time.

Rumi, the Master, was not a pupil, a dervish, a representative, or master as is known among traditional Sufis. He developed a new method that was colored with revivalism and personal, independent reasoning by taking the Qur'an, the *sunna*, and Islamic piety as his points of reference. With a new voice and breath, he successfully brought to a new divine table both those of his generation and those of later times. As far as his relationship with God is concerned, he was a man of love and passion. As for those who turn to him for the sake of God, he represents a compassionate bearer of God's divine cup of love. Yes, as the rains of mercy fall forth from the clouds of the sky, and if the collections of his poems were to be wrung out, God's love and the love of His Messenger would gush forth in showers. His *Mesnevi*, exuberant with his spirit, a book that is in part didactic and was put in book form by his disciple, Husam al-Din Chelebi, represents his largest, most monumental treatise. While it stems from his involvement with the floods of a high level love and passion, it was presented in smaller waves so that their essence might be understood by a larger part of humanity who did not share the same capacity. His other work,

Divan-i Kabir, is both informed by and presented in this higher level of love and passion and better represents his own abilities.

In the *Mesnevi*, feelings and thoughts are put in such a way that they do not confuse our intelligence and in such a style that it does not surpass our understanding. As for the *Divan-i Kabir*, everything is like an erupting volcano. Its meaning is not understood easily by most. A careful investigation will show that this great book of Rumi's thought will explain such concepts as *baqa billah maallah* (to live by God with God) and *fana fillah* (annihilation in God) in the context of a larger understanding of the world of the unseen. Those who are capable of realizing this excitement in Rumi's *Divan* will find themselves in extreme bewilderment before a flood of love and ecstasy that is comparable to an erupting volcano. In these poems of the master, which are not easily accessible for most people, the limits of reason are surpassed, the meanings of the poems are elevated above the norms for humanity, and the eternal nature of the unseen world shadows the ephemeral colors and forms of what one encounters in their physical being.

Jalal al-Din Rumi was nourished by the fruit of numerous sources of ideas, including religious seminaries, Sufi lodges, and Sufi hermitages associated with strict Sufi asceticism. Rumi attained an understanding of the Ultimate Reality. He cultivated the heavenly through his own methods. Eventually, he became a central star, the North Star, in the sky which houses sainthood. He was like a bright moon that rotates on its own axis. He was a hero who reached the places where he should have reached and stopped where he should have stopped. He read carefully what he saw and evaluated well what he felt. He never displayed or participated in any improper behavior during his journey to God. Even though the numbers were vast, Rumi never lost any of the bountiful gifts he received from the world of the unseen, not even to the weight of an atom. Like many of his predecessors, he voiced these divine bounties through his poetry in an impressive manner. He often voiced his love and excitement in seemingly magical words that resembled the finest of precious gems. Within the vagueness of the poetry, he mastered the art of explaining his ambiguous statements in ways that opened their meaning to friends, but remained obscured to outsiders.

These statements that were at times both clear and ambiguous are the voice and breath of his own horizon—he was not acquainted with other pens or the wells of ink which supplied them. Although one can find a few foreign words or works falsely attributed to him, Rumi's anthology represents a warmth, the music of his own heart, a music that brings all who hear it under its influence with a captivating control.

Rumi possessed a very delicate disposition, often appearing more compassionate than a mother to her child. In short, he was an exceptional personality, particularly in his projection of the spirit of God's Messenger in his own time. This is illustrated in his collected works, including the *Mesnevi*, *Divan-i Kabir*, some collected letters associated with familial relations, and his special behavior with friends. Those who witnessed this were greatly excited to see the perfect heir of the Prophet and would say with great humility and respect, "This is a grace from God. He gives it to whom He wants."[3]

Rumi was a man of genuine sincerity and loyalty. He lived by what he felt in his heart as long as it did not contradict the teachings and laws of religion. While making his faith the focus of his life, while showing others the way of life, while blowing into the *ney*, and while dancing like a butterfly, his heart was burning with love and longing; it always ached and sang like the plaintive *ney*. Those who were not aching could not understand him. Those who were rude and tactless could not feel what he felt. He said, "I want a heart that is split, part by part, because of the pain of separation from God, so that I might explain my longing and complaint to it." Saying this, he searched for friends who had similar longings and complaints.

Throughout his life Rumi witnessed and experienced many difficulties. Yet, he never acted in a harsh manner or tried to hurt others in response. While proclaiming the bounties of God, Rumi roared and was fearless. In his personal engagements, he was always meek and humble, willing and ready to embrace everyone with great compassion. Bad characteristics, such as selfishness, pretentiousness, arrogance, or aggressiveness, found no quarter with him; they could not even come close to him. He was extremely respectful to all, especially those with whom he had the closest associations: he referred to his friend, Shams-i Tabrizi, the man from whom he lit his own candle, as his "Master"; he called his pupil and spiritual representative, Salah al-Din Faridun, "Spiritual Leader," "Master," and "Sultan"; he always mentioned Husam al-Din Chelebi with great respect. His behavior toward his family members mirrored the behavior of the Prophet toward his own family. His community of followers was open to everyone, like that of the Prophet—and he was close to even those who were farthest from him, so much so that his greatest enemies were compelled, unwillingly, to throw themselves upon his compassionate embrace. Once having entered this circle, no one ever abandoned him.

On the one hand, Rumi, the Master, had a specific intimate relationship with the world of the unseen, but on the other hand, especially as far as his relationship with people was concerned, he never promoted any sense that he was greatly different; this was because of his utmost sincerity and humility. He lived among the people as one of them. He would listen to them, eat, and drink with them; he never would disclose the secrets cultivated between him and God to those who could not truly appreciate their value. Being a guide, he lived by what he believed and always tried to find a way to penetrate the hearts of those around him. He would call his gatherings "Talks on the Beloved," thus making an effort constantly to draw attention to Him. He would say, "Love," "Longing," "Ecstasy," and "Attraction" to try to share with others the gushing excitement and feelings that were inherent in his spirit. He would show everyone who passed within his sphere the horizon of real humanity. He never allowed his eyes to rest on worldly possessions but rather would distribute any accumulated possession or any money that was beyond his own needs among those who were in need. When food was scarce in his house, he would say, "Thank God as today our house resembles the Prophet's house." Accordingly, it was through thankfulness and patience that he made his spiritual flights into the world beyond. Rumi did not accept charity or alms; in this way he was able to avoid a feeling of indebtedness—he suffered from hunger, lived modestly, and yet never would let others be aware of such situations. He did not want to stain his service of guidance for God by accepting gifts or presents.

In addition to his ascetic life, his fear of God, his chastity, his divine protection from sinfulness, his self-sufficiency, and his pure life that was directed toward the world of the unseen, Rumi's knowledge of God, his love of God, and his utmost longing for God kept him, throughout his life, rising as one of the moons that illuminates the sky of sainthood. His love for God was one that surpassed the normal bounds of love—it was a transcendental love. He thoroughly believed that he was also loved by Him. This security did not result, for him, in losses—neither in a lack of fear nor in a loss of respect for God. This was the horizon of faith and accountability, and Rumi would hint at this balance between fear and hope as an expression of the bounties offered by God. We rightly can call this sense of balance "The Declarer of the Gifts of the Eternal Sultan."

In his inner world, the various waterfalls of love flowed out at a variety of volumes and distances. His sincere approach toward the Divine and his fidelity were rewarded with divine ecstasy and attractions. He was privileged with the greatest closeness to God, and he frequently sipped from the cup of divine love, cup by cup, becoming intoxicated. He wanted to see, to know, to feel, and to speak only of Him and to relate all of his work and words only to Him. He was so earnest in this regard that if his eyes turned to outsiders for even a brief moment, he would sit and cry a great many tears. He strongly desired to live in the spacious environment of togetherness with Him. He convulsively struggled to be both a lover and a beloved and spent the minutes of his life in an intoxication that emanated from both.

Many were the lovers who felt these spiritual joys in a similar way and preceded Rumi in life and death. Yet Rumi's superiority is revealed by the way in which he spoke out so courageously about his feelings and thoughts in his *Divan-i Kabir*. In fact, since the time of the Prophet and through the periods that followed, there have been many great heroes who have been afforded superiority over Rumi by common consensus. However, Rumi's superiority lies in a special merit, whereas theirs are more general merits. Therefore, in this regard we can perceive Rumi as the leader of this field, the finest among the fine. Rumi is an outstanding guide in leading people to the Most Beautiful of the beautiful on the path of love.

It is a lofty rank for a human to be able to love God from the depth of his heart and always to remember Him with deep love and passion. If there is a higher rank than this, it is the awareness of the fact that all love, longing, ecstasy, and attraction in human beings are the result of His kind treatment and favor. Rumi breathed God's Beautiful Names and Attributes every time he inhaled and exhaled. He was aware that his disposition was a direct result of the grace and favor bestowed upon him by God. Those whose horizon fails to achieve this unique level may not be able to understand this. According to the following anonymous poem, there is no doubt that just as words represent the shells of meanings encompassed within, the abilities and capacities of humans are simply factors and conditions that are invitations for the receiving of divine gifts and:

The works of His grace are based on the ability of creatures.

From the rain of April a snake makes poison while an oyster makes a pearl.

Some people do not consider it proper to use the phrase "love of God" in the Islamic tradition. Like many of God's lovers, Rumi, in a way that is appropriate to the holiness and exaltedness of God, courageously defended the concept of love for God as being above all human concepts of love and relationships. He left a legacy of ambiguous divine love that was open for interpretation to the generations that followed him. Some Sufis and scholars of Islamic law questioned the use of musical instruments, such as the *ney*, and the music performed in the lodges, because of this ambiguity. These groups frequently criticized the performances of the whirling dervishes. However, Rumi, the master, had no doubts about the truthfulness of his interpretations. If he had, he would have broken the instruments and surely given up all such activities. In fact, I think Rumi's heart-felt relations with the spirit of religion and his being a faultless representative and living interpretation of the way and etiquette of Muhammad forbid others to say anything against him. Furthermore, these two concepts have been more than enough for a majority of people to accept his ways.

In fact, it was not initially my task to write on this invaluable subject; there are many others who are prepared better to address it. However, this request came from someone whom I have respected for a very long time and therefore I could not refuse. I took on this topic, which is, in reality, beyond my capacity. Hundreds, even thousands, have written about Rumi. It is their job to write—and if something important is to be said, it is their job to say it. Despite this, there is nothing that prevents simple people like me from uttering a few lines—I think that this is what I have done. It probably would have been better if I had stopped earlier and directed the reader to Şefik Can's *Fundamentals of Rumi's Thought*, so that a meaningful engagement with the actual text could have begun. Even if it is too late now, I do not want to limit or shadow the treatment any longer with my own limited understanding. And so now I stop and bring my comments to an end.

M. Fethullah Gülen

ACKNOWLEDGEMENT

Mevlana Jalal al-Din Rumi is currently one of the most influential Islamic mystics in the world despite the fact that seven hundred years have passed since his death. Rumi is the most widely read poet in the United States; his passionate and inspiring poetry has attracted many people from various backgrounds. Because of this, Rumi's ideas have become a bit ambiguous. There is no doubt that Rumi uses the elusive language of Islamic mysticism, leaving room for misinterpretation. He speaks of wine and drunkenness, but these are not meant to be taken literally. Therefore, those who are not familiar with mystical language may not be able to understand Rumi fully. His great love for Shams cannot be understood without a thorough knowledge of the concept of love within the Islamic mystical tradition; in particular, the love between master and disciple, or among friends. While Rumi's love for Shams is emphasized, his greater love for Prophet Muhammad is not as well-known. In some circles, Rumi is not known as a Muslim mystic though he is still considered a Sufi. And some groups believe him to be a great master who does not have any relation to the Islamic tradition. This work attempts to present Rumi to the English-speaking world and to shed light on his life as seen from within the Islamic mystical tradition. The knowledge presented in this work comes from Şefik Can, a great expert on Rumi and the highest authority, *ser-tariq*, of the Mevlevi Sufi order in Turkey.

This work originally was published in Turkish as *Mevlana: Hayati-Şahsiyeti-Fikirleri*, in 1999. It has been a great honor for me to edit this book and translate parts of it, making it available to the English-speaking world. In addition, I have annotated and referenced many Qur'anic verses and Hadith not previously documented in the original version. I have found it difficult to find references to some stories related to Rumi in the book, yet I consider these stories as a valuable part of the oral tradition in the Mevlevi order. I have updated some of the information that was not available to Şefik Can at the time he wrote the book, especially that on the cosmos and books that had not yet been published. For the sake of the reader, I decided to place the background information on Rumi and his works at the beginning of the book, as opposed to the end. I have used the Turkish version of the *Mesnevi* translated by Şefik Can as my primary reference for the Persian works of Rumi, as the point of this book is to convey Şefik Can's understanding of them. In some cases, I have incorporated R.A. Nicholson's translation of Rumi's poetry, making minor changes so that it corresponds with Şefik Can's version. Rather than adding a glossary, I explain most Sufi terms within the text, either in parentheses or brackets. Longer explanations or definitions are footnoted. I use the modern Turkish alphabet for Turkish terms and names, but for Arabic terms and names I have avoided a complete transliteration in the interest of the general readership. I have reorganized the structure of the book by dividing it into four chapters, removing the section on Rumi's contemporaries in order not to draw attention away from Rumi. I have to thank my colleague Cüneyt Eroğlu, who translated several sections of this work, for allowing me to revise and edit his translation. In addition, a number of people must be thanked for their assistance in the preparation of this book: Osman Şimşek for his valuable assistance with my request for the foreword from M. Fethullah Gülen; Allison Bramblett for providing helpful editorial support; and my Graduate Assistant Eric N. Abercrombie for his assistance at various stages in the preparation of the manuscript.

Two aspects of this work make it unique. The first is that the book originally is authored by a man who just recently passed away at the age of ninety-five and who dedicated his entire life to the teachings of Rumi. Such a Mevlevi's view of Rumi makes this work greatly valuable. The second important contribution to the book is the foreword, which I have translated from the original Turkish, written by M. Fethullah Gülen, a prominent Muslim thinker and interfaith activist in Turkey.

I hope that this book will bring a better understanding of Rumi worldwide. I trust that this work will please Şefik Can, who has been waiting a long time for the English version to be published. The Qur'an tells us, "Say: My Lord, Increase my knowledge!" (20:114). My wish for the readers of this book is that it will increase their knowledge of Rumi.

Zeki Saritoprak
Cleveland, OH
May 12, 2004

CHAPTER 1

The Political and Philosophical Situation of the Anatolian Seljuk Empire During Rumi's Life

B efore beginning our foray into Rumi's life, we first must review briefly the political and philosophical environment of the Anatolian Seljuk Empire during the twelfth century. This will help us to understand the time when Rumi migrated from Balkh with his father and under what circumstances he lived his life in Konya, produced his works, and guided his followers. Great poets and distinguished artists always emerge during magnificent ages. The artists need financial and spiritual support as well as peace. The famous Turkish poet Baki, called "Sultan al-Shuara," or king of poets, emerged during the most glorious era of the Ottoman Empire, the era of Süleyman the Magnificent. So when did Rumi, "Sultan al-Urafa" (the king of gnostics), live? Rumi lived in the thirteenth century, the most troubled and restless period of the Anatolian Seljuk Empire. Shortly after enduring devastation, massacre, and looting by the crusaders, the Islamic lands faced the Mongol invasion from the east. At the same time the Seljuk kings were further weakened by internal conflicts over the control of power. The soldiers of Jalal al-Din Muhammad Khawarzmshah (reigned 1220 – 31) who came to Anatolia to escape the Mongols also were inciting conflict in the region. Although these soldiers were also Muslims, they joined forces with the Mongols, the enemies of Muslims, and captured, burned, and devastated cities. Seljuk Sultan Ala al-Din Kay Qobad I[1] was forced to mobilize his forces for a major campaign in the east. He defeated Jalal al-Din Khawarzmshah's army in Yassı Çimen, near Erzincan in eastern Turkey. This, indeed, was a tragic event because Seljuk Sultan Kay Qobad had first proposed that Khawarzmshah join his forces against the Mongols. But the fight between these two Turkish sultans played to the advantage of the Mongols. Adding to the difficulties, the fact that the Seljuk sultan in Konya gained power and was temporarily relieved worried the Ayyubi sultan, ruler of another Muslim state. In 1232, the Ayyubi sultan began to move his forces toward the Seljuks. Sultan Ala al-Din's army of 100,000 stopped this occupation attempt. In the era of Kay Qobad I, the Anatolian Seljuk Empire experienced a short period of political, economic, and military triumph, yet the empire weaked and ultimately collapsed. The poisoning of Sultan Ala al-Din in Kayseri in 1237 became a turning point for the Anatolian Seljuks. As the Mongols approached and under the rule of Seljuk Sultan Ghias al-Din Kay Khosrau (reigned 1237 – 1246), the weak successor of the powerful and capable Sultan Ala al-Din, the collapse of the empire accelerated.

At the same time, the revolt of the Turkmens, who had come to Anatolia to escape the Mongols, caused major problems for the Seljuks. This uprising, which historians call the Babai Movement, was initiated by Baba Ishak, a successor of Baba Ilyas, who had migrated from Khorasan, a city in modern Iran, and settled in Amasya in modern Turkey. Baba Ishak first devoted himself to asceticism, gathering many followers and allowing his fame as a saint to grow.

The revolt of Baba Ishak was followed by another Mongol invasion. In 1241, Mongols captured Erzurum and massacred the inhabitants. The Mongol army under Bayju Noyan's command met the Seljuk army at Mount Kose, east of the provinceof Sivas. On Friday, July 23, 1241, the battle that was to determine the fate of the Seljuk Empire commenced. The Seljuk army suffered a terrible defeat. Sultan Ghias al-Din did not know what to do with an army defeated in chaos. He barely saved his own life by disguising himself and escaping to the city of Tokat. After dividing the immense spoils, the Mongols moved on to Sivas. They looted Sivas for three days then marched to Kayseri. They executed the entire male population in the town then left the city, taking the women and children with them. On the way, they mercilessly killed anyone who could not walk and keep pace with them. Recognizing that they did not stand a chance of defeating the Mongols, the Seljuks agreed to pay them a heavy annual tax. At this point, the Anatolian Seljuk Empire had become a Mongolian state.

After the death of Ghias al-Din II in 1246, the power struggle between his three young sons and state officials along with Mongol oppression and destruction weakened the state even further. Internal unrest spread throughout the whole country. The heavy tax did not suffice for the Mongols, and in 1256 the Mongol commander Bayju marched to Anatolia with his army and defeated the Seljuk army near Konya. Ghias al-Din Kay Khosrau's imprisoned son, Rukn al-Din Kılıçarslan, was enthroned, and Muin al-Din Süleyman Pervane became the new vizier. While Bayju Noyan was residing in Kızılviran, west of Konya, Sultan Rukn al-Din was held as a captive with him, subject to the Mongols' every whim. In 1277, the Mongols executed Muin al-Din Süleyman Pervane. This event coupled with internecine struggles removed any possibility for the Seljuk Empire to recover. The Anatolian Seljuk government, thoroughly weakened under the Mongol pressure, finally collapsed. Turkish beys, or commanders, instigated local resistance movements, marking the beginning of the emergence of the Anatolian beyliks. In 1308, the Anatolian Seljuk Empire was buried in history.

The period in which Rumi lived was a turbulent period in which people had grown weary of war and civil unrest. Rumi lived by the love of the magnificent King of Kings who was never to decline, collapse, and cease to exist. The divine poems he composed with the infinite power and inspiration he took from the beyond gave hope to the hopeless and bestowed joy, faith, and love on the troubled and saddened people. In those turbulent times, he was a source of comfort to the people, and with love and faith he freed the believers from sorrow and fear.

INTELLECTUAL ENVIRONMENT OF THE ANATOLIAN SELJUKS DURING RUMI'S TIME

To comprehend the un-Islamic beliefs and philosophies against which Rumi fought in the thirteenth century, it would be beneficial to return to the origins of these beliefs and to examine briefly how they emerged and grew. This way, we also will come to know the differences and various sects among Muslims. But before beginning this discussion, I would like to mention the following point: When some respected persons in their writings about the life of Rumi explain the philosophical and ideological environment of the Islamic world during the thirteenth century, they have a tendency to include views that contradict the Islamic faith. Furthermore, some Western thinkers who do not understand Islam fully liken religions of Divine revelation, according to the Muslims, to philosophical movements. This view is incorrect because Islam was not founded by Prophet Muhammad. The Prophet who could not read or write was not a scholar or a philosopher who could have been influenced by the ideas and books of the prophets before him and, according to these, establish a religion. Prophet Muhammad was a messenger, a prophet, a bearer of revelation from God. The Prophet did not establish Islam by his own will; God made him establish it. Thus, it is a fatal mistake to think that religions of Divine revelation like Judaism, Christianity, and Islam have taken ideas from each other just because one sees similarities in the practices and the truth of these religions. Since God loves human beings whom He created and wants them not to follow their physical desires but to walk on the true path of humanity, He has sent the same truths at different times through different religions and prophets, from the Prophet Adam to Prophet Muhammad. It is for this reason that the Qur'an says, "We do not make a distinction between any of His prophets."[2]

Let us now briefly review the philosophical milieu of the Anatolian Seljuks during the thirteenth century as well as the diverse sects and groups that spread among Muslims in that age. Accordingly, we will be able to understand the origins of the views, ideologies, and philosophies that Rumi fought against in his writings.

Pre-thirteenth Century Conceptual Differences within Muslim Communities

The first conceptual differences among Muslims emerged after the passing away of the Prophet. When Prophet Muhammad passed away, the question that occupied Muslims' minds was who was to assume his position. The Prophet was neither a king nor a president. He was a messenger who had made people aware of God. With the help of God, he had completed his duty and reunited with God, Whom he loved very much and by Whom he was loved very much. How would the person to replace him fill the gap? Since Prophet Muhammad was the last of the prophets, the person to replace him was simply going to be the leader of the Muslims, like a religious president. Who was the going to assume his position? While some of the notable Companions of the Prophet suggested that the person to replace him should be distinguished by his virtue and service to Islam and loved by the Prophet and his Companions, others argued that Ali, who belonged to the family of the Prophet and who was Prophet's son-in-law as well as his cousin should succeed him.

The Companions of the Prophet selected Abu Bakr as the first caliph, or successor.[3] Following the caliphate of Abu Bakr, 'Umar, 'Uthman, and Ali were selected as caliphs, all within approximately thirty years after the death of the Prophet. Although Ali was appointed by the majority and was a member of the Hashimi dynasty, Mu'awiyah, the governor of Damascus, did not recognize the caliphate of Ali. He dared to fight Ali's supporters for the sultanate of this world, causing the shedding of many innocent Muslims' blood on both sides. During these wars a third faction appeared among Muslims, the Kharijites, literally, "those who remain outside the main groups." The Kharijites were opposed to one individual holding the position of both caliph and head of state, a disagreement that caused chaos and bloodshed. They were fond of neither Ali nor Mu'awiyah. Like the terrorists of our day, they were a separatist group with destructive ideas who refused to recognize the authority of the government. As Islam spread, the former beliefs and philosophical views of the nations that had embraced Islam intermingled with the pure Islamic beliefs. Accordingly, different beliefs and different groups formed under the influence of the pre-Islamic traditions.

The ancient Greek, Indian, and Iranian books that were translated into Arabic during the time of Caliph Ma'mun, around the beginning of the ninth century, and those translations under his successors increased the philosophical current. When the ancient Greek, Iranian, Indian, Christian, and Jewish philosophical views spread throughout the Islamic world, the Mu'tazilah used these foreign views and theories more efficiently to defend their own views. The influence of ancient Greek philosophy can be seen clearly during Ma'mun's era in such grand masters of the Mu'tazilah movement as Ibrahim al-Nazzam (d. 835 CE) and Abu al-Huzayl (d. 840 CE).

In the face of the Mu'tazilah's efforts regarding these issues, the Sunni scholars did not remain idle. A new field of knowledge that the Sunnis called *kalam* was born out of the efforts of great scholars like Abu al-Hasan al-Ash'ari (d. 935 CE), a former Mu'tazilah scholar who returned to the Sunni path. However, while the Sunni *kalam* showed some inclination toward Mu'tazilah thought in a number of areas, the Mu'tazilah view had become removed further from its origins and now was saturated with Greek philosophical thought. At this stage, a new day dawned for Sunni *kalam* with the great scholar Abu Hamid al-Ghazali (d. 1111 CE).

The attention paid to the philosophical works translated into Arabic during the Abbasid Caliphate is due only to Islam's strong advocacy of knowledge. According to the holy order of the Prophet, "Wisdom is the lost property of the believer. He takes it wherever he may find it."[4] Thus Islamic scholars carefully read those works and interpreted and refuted what contradicted Islamic precepts.

They reflected on what was in accordance with Islam and wrote commentaries on these works. A Muslim must acquire knowledge even if it were in China. A Muslim must read Aristotle, Plato, and Confucius. If there had not been the commentaries written by Islamic scholars, the Greek works would not have been so well known by the Europeans. Those books are the reason behind the Enlightenment of Europe after the Renaissance.

The Origins of Sufism before Rumi

The different factions and beliefs that we have examined briefly weakened the holy joy and enthusiasm of faith and damaged the unity of the Islamic community. Sincerely devout Muslims who were disturbed and saddened by this situation retired to lonely places and devoted themselves to worship. They ate little, they drank little, as if turning their backs to the world. Those who behaved in this fashion eventually came to be known as Sufis. However, in the early stages of Islam, those who devoted themselves to this kind of worship were called *abid* (worshipper) or *zahid* (ascetic). Sufis took their name because they wore clothes made of rough wool, and the Arabic word for wool is *suf*. According to historical sources, the first person to be called Sufi and to build the first *zawiyyah* (retreat house of mystics) in Syria was Abu Hashim of Kufah (d. 767 CE). After him came many great saints like Sufyan al-Thawri (d. 784 CE), Dhu al-Nun al-Misri (d. 859 CE), Abu Yazid (Bayazid) al-Bistami of Khorasan (d. 874 CE), Hallaj al-Mansur (d. 921 CE), and Junayd al-Baghdadi (d. 910 CE). Despite all obstacles, all accusations, all insults and allegations of heresy and blasphemy, the Sufis' views and way of life spread to every corner of the Islamic world.

Due to the efforts of Abu al-Qasim Abd al-Karim al-Qushayri (d. 1072 CE) to show that the beliefs of Sufis did not contradict the Islamic and Muhammadi way and along with al-Ghazali's (d. 1111) very well-founded works, Sufis, who previously were looked upon with suspicion and less than admiration by the scholars of Islamic law, gained great regard and respect among the public and even among the scholars of Islamic law. Many famous scholars dedicated themselves to great shaykhs; the sultans and statesmen promoted Sufism, built dervish lodges and religious retreats, and facilitated the appearance of many shaykhs and dervishes in all corners of the Islamic world. From the eleventh century to the thirteenth century, the century of Rumi, Sufi orders began to be founded in the Islamic world, and from the thirteenth century onward, this network of Sufi orders expanded and gained importance in all areas.

In the ninth century, in which Sufism began to spread rapidly, the social and ideological environment was very suitable for the expansion of Sufism. The welfare and economic situation during the first century of the Abbasid caliphate provided a comfortable life for the public. The conditions necessary for a Sufi current to settle and grow among Muslims were now ripe.

It is erroneous to accept as true that the beliefs of different creeds and groups, philosophical ideas that started to spread with the translation of the ancient Greek philosophers' works, beliefs migrating from India and Iran, and especially the Neo-Platonic view of the Alexandria School, caused Sufism to emerge among the Muslims. Indeed, the main issue that led to the emergence of Sufism is the fact that popular un-Islamic beliefs had forced the believers to turn inward, to be absorbed in their religious beliefs, and to reject all views outside the Qur'an. Therefore, just as Islam was not influenced by the previous religions, Sufism was not inspired by Indian or Greek ideas. As in every religion, there is a mystical current within Islam that is unique in itself. Islamic mysticism, or Sufism, belongs to Islam. The source of Islamic mysticism is the Holy Qur'an and the Noble Prophetic Traditions. In this regard, if we remember the following, it will save us from remaining under the influence of this idea.

At the time of Abu Hashim (d. 767 CE), the first Sufi of Islam and founder of the first *zawiyyah* in Syria, Indian and Greek texts had not yet been translated into Arabic, and thus the Sufis of Islam could not have come under the influence of foreign beliefs. The oldest book written about Sufism that has remained today is that of Abu Abd Allah al-Harith bin Asad al-Muhasibi (d. 837 CE).

RUMI'S LIFE

Mevlana Jalal al-Din Muhammad was born on September 30, 1207 in the city of Balkh, in modern Afghanistan. There are different opinions regarding the date of his birth. While Aflaki (d. 1360 A.D.), author of *Manaqib al-Arifin*, gives the above date, Rumi, in his book *Fihi Ma Fih* writes, "We were in Samarqand. Khawarzmshah had surrounded the city, deployed his forces around the city, and was fighting. In that neighborhood there was a very pretty girl. She was so beautiful that there was no girl like her in the city. I heard her praying, 'O God, don't leave me in the hands of these tyrants.'"[5] These short remarks suggest that Aflaki's date is incorrect because Samarqand was surrounded by Khawarzmshah in 1207, the date given as Rumi's birth year. For Rumi to remember the surroundings and the beauty of the girl, he must have been at least five or six years old. Probably for this reason, historian Will Durant shows Rumi's birth at 1201, while Maurice Barres fixes it at 1203. The city of Balkh, in those days before being captured by the Mongols, was a center of learning. It was famous for its mosques, seminaries, and palaces. It was a capital on the Silk Road, economically developed, and full of traders.

Titles

His name is Muhammad and his title is Jalal al-Din. All historians know him by this title. Besides the name Jalal al-Din, he is also called Hudavendigar. In some commentaries on the *Mesnevi*, he is referred to as the Mevlana Hudavendigar. The term Hudavendigar is often used in the book of *Manaqib*, which was written by Faridun bin Ahmed Sipehsalar, who served Rumi and his father for nearly half a century. This work was translated into Turkish by my teacher and my master, the forgiven,[6] Midhat Bahari as well as Ahmed Avni

Konuk and Tahsin Yazıcı. As far as the expressions Mevlevi and Mevlana are concerned, today by Mevlevi, in general, we mean people who have given their hearts to Mevlana. However, in the old days among Sufis, this title was reserved for lovers of God, people of truth, and people whose hearts were awake. Therefore, there have been people who remembered our Mevlana, Rumi, by Mevlevi. Among them, the great Sufi poet Qasim-i Envar of Tabriz (d. 1432) recalls Rumi as Mevlevi in his couplet: "O Qasim, if you desire to seek and find the spirit of meanings, read Mevlevi's *Mesnevi* that is the source of meanings." Rumi also is called "Mevlana Jalal al-Din" by preceding his name with Mevlana, meaning "our master," and sometimes just Mevlana, the most common title for saints.

Since Rumi spent most of his life in Anatolia, which was the land of the Romans at the time, he also is called Mevlana Rumi, Mevlana Jalal al-Din Rumi, or just Rumi. Rumi's surname in poetry is "Shams-i Tabrizi." He also uses the word "khamoosh" or "khaamoosh" (silent), though seldom.

Ancestry

Rumi's ancestry reaches back to Abu Bakr, the first caliph of Islam. Sultan Valad writes in his *Ibtidaname* about his grandfather Baha al-Din Valad, "His title became Baha al-Din Valad. His devotees are countless. His ancestry reaches back to Abu Bakr. Therefore, he attained the highest spiritual level just like Hadrat Siddiq Abu Bakr." Aflaki agrees with this position. He determined Baha al-Din Valad's chain of ancestry as follows: Baha al-Din Valad – Huseyin Khatibi – Ahmed Khatibi – Mahmud – Mavdud – Husayyib – Mutahhar – Hammad – Abdurrahman – Abu Bakr.

Parents

Rumi's father was Muhammad, son of Huseyin Khatibi. He is known as Baha al-Din Valad. He was given the title Sultan al-Ulama, the king of the scholars. There is another account in which it is related that the Prophet gave the title Sultan al-Ulama to Baha al-Din Valad. One night, Rumi's father had a dream: The Prophet was sitting and talking with his closest Companions in a majestic tent set up on a battle ground when suddenly Baha al-Din Valad comes in. He approaches the Prophet's presence with respect. The Prophet compliments him and shows him a place to sit on his right side. Then, addressing the group present, he says: "In our eyes, Baha al-Din Valad's value is very high. From now on, call him by the title Sultan al-Ulama." The next day three hundred scholars who had seen the same dream came to Baha al-Din Valad's school. They wanted to disclose their dream. But before they could begin telling the dream, Baha al-Din Valad narrated the dream to them. They were astonished completely. It is because of the Prophet's love for Rumi's father that he will be called the king of scholars until Judgment Day.

In fact, Baha al-Din Valad was not only the king of scholars, but also the king of all virtues. He was a perfect role model and a perfect human being. In addition to breadth of knowledge, he also had Muhammadi morals and virtues. He used to do good for everybody and would abstain from evil. He lectured those around him, warning them in order to protect them from faithlessness and going astray. He was an eloquent orator, and those who listened to him would be ecstatic with love and faith.

He was not a cowardly scholar. He even pointed out the mistakes of sultans to them. Just as Shaykh Sadi shouted, "You are a tyrant!" to the face of Hulagu who had devastated Baghdad completely, Sultan al-Ulama said to Khawarzmshah's face that the path he was on was not that of Muhammad. He was not a scholar who kept his opinions to himself because of fear, and he never praised the sultans and behaved hypocritically because of material interest. He warned scholars as well as sultans who were under the influence of Greek philosophy. Therefore, the faithful people treasured him. The people of the city of Balkh, which was a center of learning and gnosis at that time, showed great love and respect for Baha al-Din Valad, which frightened Sultan Khawarzmshah. Most of the scholars who could not appreciate him and who did not recognize his faith envied him. But he did not hesitate at all to express his opinions freely. According to Aflaki, Sultan al-Ulama's father Huseyin, son of Ahmed Khatibi was one of the most well known scholars and most virtuous of men of his time. Razi al-Din Nishaburi, a prominent twelfth-century scholar of law, was taught by him. Muhammad Baha al-Din Valad's mother was a member of the Khawarzm dynasty.

Baha al-Din Valad's Migration from Balkh

Sultan al-Ulama migrated from Balkh due to differences of opinion and belief. Khawarzmshah's relationship with the members of the Kubrawiyyah order was not good, and Baha al-Din Valad was devoted to Najm al-Din Kubra (d. 1221). In his sermons, he openly proclaimed that the scholars who were taken by philosophy and overvalued reason were not following the way of the Prophet. Thus the scholars who did not agree with him turned the sultan against him. Meanwhile, Majd al-Din Baghdadi, a deputy of Najm al-Din Kubra, was thrown into the river Jeyhun by the order of Khawarzmshah and drowned. On one hand, Sultan al-Ulama was envied, but on the other hand, he was kept under psychological pressure. As a matter of fact, Sultan Valad wrote that his grandfather had migrated because the people of Balkh offended him and broke his heart. On the other hand, Sipehsalar and Aflaki wrote that the great scholar of the time, Fahr al-Din Razi (d. 1210) had caused Sultan al-Ulama's migration. But since Fahr al-Din Razi had passed away a few years before Baha al-Din Valad's departure from Balkh, it is apparent that Fahr al-Din Razi did not personally cause Sultan al-Ulama to leave Balkh. However, although he had passed away, Khawarzmshah and other scholars who had adopted Fahr al-Din Razi's opinions and philosophical views flinched at this great scholar who fearlessly criticized Razi's philosophical views. It was in this situation that Sultan al-Ulama decided to migrate in order not to cause any instigation. It is not known precisely, however, when Baha al-Din Valad migrated from Balkh.

Baha al-Din Valad left Balkh together with his closest disciples, deputies, and family, including his wife Mumine Khatun, daughter of the sultan of Balkh, his older son Ala al-Din Muhammad, and his younger son Jalal al-Din Muhammad. Some of his relatives remained in Balkh. Sipehsalar wrote that after leaving Balkh, traveling from one town to another, he went to Makka for pilgrimage, stopping over in Baghdad. He then proceeded to Anatolia, and after spending the winter in Akşehir near Erzincan, he came to Konya upon the invitation of the Seljuk Sultan Ala al-Din Kay Qobad.

How old was Rumi when this migration started? This is not known for a certainty. Although Rumi's date of birth is usually given as 1207, based on his statements in *Fihi Ma Fih*, it can be concluded that this year is not his real date of birth and that his actual date of birth must be around 1200. One can consider that Sultan al-Ulama's departure date for pilgrimage was again approximately 1221 and that when this migration started, Rumi was twenty-one years old. However, Sultan Valad states in his *Ibtidaname* that Rumi was fourteen years old at the beginning of the migration.

Baha al-Din's Meeting with 'Attar

The migrating caravan's first important stop was the city of Nishapur, another important gnostic center of that age. Moreover, Farid al-Din 'Attar (d. 1220), who was a disciple of the same Kubrawi shaykh as Sultan al-Ulama, lived in this city. Both were among the prominent deputies of Najm al-Din Kubra (d. 1221), the founder of the Kubrawiyyah or Zahabiyyah order who was martyred along with his disciples while fighting against the Mongols. When 'Attar heard of Sultan al-Ulama's arrival in Nishapur, he went to visit him. The two saints attained the secret of the Qur'anic verse, "He has let free two seas meeting together."[7] It is said that during this meeting Farid al-Din 'Attar, sensing the spiritual greatness of young Rumi, said to his father, "It is hoped that this son of yours will soon set on fire the hearts that burn with divine love." And he took great pleasure in presenting his book *Asrarname* as a gift to the spiritual boy in his early youth, the boy who would indeed set fire to the hearts that burn with love and who would become familiar with the divine secrets. Rumi liked *Asrarname* a lot. He always kept it with him. Years passed, and when he was dictating his *Mesnevi*, he not only included tales from the *Asrarname*, but he also expressed his love for 'Attar at every occasion. In his *Divan-i Kabir* Rumi writes: "'Attar was the spirit. And Sanai was his two eyes. We came to the realm of truth after 'Attar and Sanai. We followed them."

Baha al-Din in Baghdad

The second important stop of Sultan al-Ulama was Baghdad, which was the capital of the Abbasid state. As Jami narrates, when the caravan of Baha al-Din Valad arrived in Baghdad, people asked, "Who are these people? Where are they coming from? Where are they going to?" Sultan al-Ulama answered, "We came from God. We again are going to Him. We have no strength except for God." When they related this answer to Shaykh Shihab al-Din Suhrawardi (d. 1235), the author of *Awarif al-Ma'arif*, he said, "Nobody except Baha al-Din Valad of Balkh could have made this statement." He immediately went to see him. When he saw him coming with his caravan, he got off his horse to show respect, approached the caravan, and kissed the knee of Baha al-Din Valad. He asked them to stay and honor his dervish lodge. But Sultan al-Ulama stayed in a seminary, saying, "It is more appropriate for scholars to stay in a school." Suhrawardi did not leave this honorable guest alone, stayed with him and served him.

The caliph of Baghdad wanted to make a donation to this great saint. He sent three thousand golden Egyptian dinars. Baha al-Din Valad did not accept this gift, stating, "It is unlawful and dubious." The caliph wanted personally to welcome him and to have him as a guest in his palace. Rumi's father rejected this wish of the caliph as well because he had heard that the caliph continuously drank and engaged in illegitimate activities, inconsiderate of the spiritual significance and value of his position. It was not appropriate for a Sufi to stay in such a person's palace and accept the gold that he sent.

The sermon he gave in the biggest mosque of Baghdad was magnificent. Countless believers, including the caliph, filled the mosque. It was so crowded that it was impossible to find a place to sit. Everybody was standing and listening to this great saint. The entire congregation was excited, and people shed plenty of tears. This luminous and faithful saint who migrated from Balkh and was going to visit our Prophet in the Hijaz with his family and disciples spoke perfect Arabic and fascinated everyone, including the caliph. This holy man, who practiced what he believed and voluntarily migrated and endured the pain of being separated from his home, conquered the hearts of all the people of Baghdad with his conduct and speech. Before visiting the Ka'ba, he had visited the *Ka'ba of hearts* of countless believers; he had addressed them from his heart and made them aware of the calamities that Islam faced, and he had warned them. He mentioned that the beautiful city of Balkh, which he had left, had been crushed under the feet of the Mongols and that the Khawarzmshah ruler Sultan Tekish had been overthrown. The caliph as well as the believers who listened to him became his admirers. They asked him to settle in Baghdad, but he did not stay for more than three days. He continued on his pilgrimage. After performing the rites of the pilgrimage, Sultan al-Ulama touched his face to the holy shrine of the Prophet in Madina, the luminous city of the Prophet. The father, along with his sons and deputies, shed tears of love in the tomb (*Rawdha al-Mutahhara*—the Pure Garden) of Muhammad Mustafa, who was sent as a mercy to all the worlds. Then continuing on their way and passing through many places, they reached Jerusalem. There they visited Masjid al-Aqsa, the first *qibla* of Islam. Then they came to Damascus. Upon hearing that a great saint was about to enter their city, the people of Damascus gathered outside the city to welcome Baha al-Din Valad. After meeting some well-known scholars in Damascus, they continued on their way to Anatolia.

Leaving the city of Damascus behind, the caravan went to Aleppo. They stayed there a few days before continuing on their way. Soon they set foot in the land that in those days was called the "land of the Romans." The caravan proceeded without staying for more than a few days at any place. Arriving in Malatya, they headed to Erzincan. In those days, Erzincan was the capital of the Mangujak dynasty. When the Mangujak Sultan Fahr al-Din Bahramshah (d. c. 1218) and his wife Ismati Khatun learned that Sultan al-Ulama was coming to their city, they traveled to Akşehir near Erzincan to welcome him and his caravan. The sultan desired to take them to his palace and host them there, but Baha al-Din Valad stayed in a learning center, as he had done everywhere else. He remained there for some time.

Sultan Fahr al-Din Bahramshah appreciated knowledge and scholars, and therefore he supported scholars and poets, appreciated their works, and as an incentive, he donated money for the books dedicated to him. In fact, Nizami, the famous poet of Ganja, dedicated his book *Makhzan-e Asrar* to the shah of Mangujak, and in return the shah awarded him with one hundred thousand gold coins and five valuable horses. Such a generous and scholar-cherishing dynasty wanted to devote their lives to the saint from Balkh. But, as everywhere else, he did not want to live here under the favor of others. After staying in Erzincan for a while, he came to Larende, or Karaman as it is called today, traveling through Sivas, Kayseri, and Niğde.

Baha al-Din in Larende

In that age in which there was no telecommunication equipment like telephones or telegrams, the approache of great saints and highly esteemed scholars to cities was known far in advance, and the people would gather at the outskirts of the city and welcome them with love and great anticipation, an expression of the value attributed to gnosis and knowledge at the time. The glad tidings would spread from mouth to mouth, and it was as if the news would reach its destination by the blowing wind and flying birds. In those times there was no telephone, but respect, feelings, and love lay in the hearts of the believers who loved knowledge, humanity, and God. As in other cities, in Larende the coming of Baha al-Din Valad was heard of a few days in advance. The sultan of Larende, Amir Musa Bey, who was a lover of God and a man of virtue, along with the other high ranking officials of town came out of the city on foot. They welcomed "the King of the Scholars" with respect and excitement. The sultan insistently invited him to his palace. But as in other places, he politely refused Amir Musa's offer: "We need to sit in a seminary, not in a palace." His request was accepted, and he was hosted in a seminary. However, Amir Musa immediately ordered that a new learning center, or madrasa (an institute of higher education) be built for this great saint who had come to his city. At an appropriate location, a beautiful madrasa was built, and Sultan al-Ulama settled at this college campus in a short time with his family and disciples. There he began lecturing and preaching.

The Sultan of the Scholars was happy in Larende. Amir Musa and the public loved this great saint very much. His sermons were a source of abundant spiritual benefit and faith. Meanwhile, Mevlana Jalal al-Din Rumi, as a young but very knowledgeable dervish, attended the lectures of his father and never missed any of his sermons. He also spent his time reading other scholars' works and expanding his knowledge of Islam.

Rumi's marriage

Sharaf al-Din Lala of Samarqand, who had migrated from Balkh with Sultan al-Ulama and who was one of his favorite disciples, had a very beautiful daughter named Gevher Khatun.[8] Besides possessing a unique beauty, this young lady's character and morals were unlike any other. God had combined physical and spiritual beauties in Gevher Khatun's person. Baha al-Din Valad considered marrying this beautiful girl to his younger son Jalal al-Din Muhammad. What was the reason behind finding a wife for his younger son before taking into account his older son Ala al-Din Muhammad? Of course, there was wisdom in this. Up to the age of seven, Gevher Khatun had been a student of Sultan al-Ulama. The character of his younger son and that of his beautiful student were very much alike; thus he believed this marriage would be very appropriate. When he revealed his thoughts to the girl's father, Sharaf al-Din Lala became glad and said, "This marriage brings us nothing but honor and happiness." And so the two fathers agreed on the marriage.

In the spring of the year 1225, these two beautiful and peerless personalities got married in a very modest and simple wedding ceremony. A short time after this marriage, Mumine Khatun, Sultan al-Ulama's wife, noble in blood and spirit, and faithful as her name, passed away. Since they had come from Balkh to Karaman, Mumine Khatun had endured the pains of being away from home and had been a source of consolation to her beloved husband in those troubled days. In her sensitive heart, she had kept alive the sorrow and longing for their beloved, devastated, burned, and ruined hometown (Balkh), and for their relatives they had left there. The happiness she felt at the magnificent welcome Sultan al-Ulama received in big cities and the spiritual enrichment and joy of their visit to Makka and Madina had made her a Mumine Khatun,[9] which was her living name.

The death of Mumine Khatun was followed by that of Ala al-Din Muhammad, Mevlana Jalal al-Din Muhammad's brother. Losing first his faithful and loyal wife and then his beloved son drew Baha al-Din Valad into indescribable sorrow. Not much later, Mevlana Jalal al-Din Muhammad's mother-in-law, that is, the wife of Sharaf al-Din Lala of Samarqand died. She was buried in Karaman next to

Mader Sultan (Queen Mother), Rumi's mother, and brother. So Rumi, who already had lost his beloved mother and brother, also lost his wife's mother. After three of his loved ones had been buried in the soil of Karaman, God gave him two precious baby boys. Both Sultan al-Ulama and Mevlana Jalal al-Din were very happy about this favor and blessing of God. Rumi named his first son after his father, Sultan Valad. He gave his second son his brother's name, Ala al-Din Chelebi. These two boys consoled them and made them forget their sorrows. Sultan al-Ulama stayed in Karaman for approximately seven years. He educated many students. He guided many people on the path of Truth. The number of his disciples increased constantly and his sermons and moral efforts circulated.

The Seljuk ruler in power during this period was Sultan Ala al-Din Kay Qobad. At a time when the Anatolian Seljuk state was on the verge of collapsing, this valuable sultan provided remarkable leadership with his elevated ability, virtues, and courage and enabled the state to experience a bright period in history. Though temporarily, he achieved military successes and served knowledge and gnosis by calling scholars and other great personalities to Konya. He was also a learned and poetic sultan, and he could not accept that a great personality like Sultan al-Ulama had settled in Karaman, far from him. He sent a message to Amir Musa, whom he loved and admired very much, that he was somewhat offended because Amir Musa had blocked the way of the great saint of Balkh and had kept him in Karaman. When Amir Musa informed Baha al-Din Valad of the sultan's offense, Baha al-Din Valad advised Amir Musa to go immediately to Konya and explain everything to the sultan truthfully.

Amir Musa, who was devoted to the sultan and who was loved very much by the sultan, hurried to Konya. He immediately went to the palace and explained that Sultan al-Ulama had settled in Larende according to his own wishes. The good-hearted sultan carefully listened to the amir, reassuring him that he had not insulted him. Then he invited the king of the scholars to Konya, saying, "If Sultan al-Ulama cares to honor our Konya, this would make me very happy. I would become his servant and disciple and walk on the path of Truth that he shows. The city of Konya is awaiting him with all its sultans and amirs." With this intention, gifts were given to Amir Musa, and he was sent to Larende.

Family and children

Rumi had married Sharaf al-Din Lala's daughter Gevher Khatun (d. 1229) while they were in Karaman before they came to Konya with his father. Rumi's oldest son Sultan Valad and his middle son Ala al-Din were born from Gevher Khatun. After Gevher Khatun passed away, Rumi married a widow, Karra Khatun (d. 1292). Karra Khatun, whose name resembles a Roman name but who was a Turk, already had a son, Shams al-Din Yahya, when she married Rumi. The name of her first husband was Muhammad Shah. Rumi had a son and a daughter with Karra Khatun. His son's name was Muzaffar al-Din Amir Alim Chelebi, and his daughter's name was Malika Khatun. Thus, Rumi had three sons and one daughter. Of these his middle son, Ala al-Din Chelebi, died in 1262 and was buried to the right of his grandfather Sultan al-Ulama's grave. We do not know with certainty whether Ala al-Din Chelebi had any children. Although Aflaki writes that Ala al-Din Chelebi had children, since there is no such record in other books, the Chelebi's of Rumi's descent have all descended from Sultan Valad's grandchildren.

Rumi's youngest son from Karra Khatun, Muzaffar al-Din Amir Alim Chelebi (d. 1277), worked at the Seljuk palace and advanced to the position of treasurer. He was buried in front of Rumi's blessed grave. Rumi's daughter, Malika Khatun, married a businessman named Shihab al-Din of Konya. Malika Khatun passed away and was buried next to the grave of her brother, Amir Alim Chelebi.

Dwelling in Konya

The king of the scholars accepted the invitation of the Seljuk ruler Ala al-Din Kay Qobad. He asked his family and friends to begin travel preparations immediately. He was going to leave Karaman, where he had been living for seven years. On a spring day in 1229, they set out on a journey to Konya accompanied by the tears of the people of Karaman. Baha al-Din Valad had accepted the sultan's invitation in order to be more beneficial to the people. Were it not for this calling, he never would have left Karaman, where his loved ones were buried. He was not unaware of how much the people of Karaman loved him. The tears of separation were not shed in vain. He saw how the lectures and sermons he had given and the knowledge he had transmitted had induced the people of Karaman to change. Now he was going to a larger city, to the capital of a great sultan who loved and respected scholars. Konya was to be the last destination for him. A stronger saint, the king of the scholars was coming to Konya, the gathering point of the saints who were rushing here from Turkistan, Iran, and other Islamic lands. The mature-spirited, young Rumi was again at the side of his beloved father, his greatest guide and teacher. He had buried his mother and brother in Karaman. But now he had with him his faithful wife, two sons, and his father who was his everything.

The little caravan proceeded slowly toward Konya. The people of Konya were preparing to welcome not only Sultan al-Ulama, the king of the scholars, but also the king of the gnostics (Sultan al-'Arifin), the king of the saints (Sultan al-Awliyya). This small caravan of five to ten people that had left Balkh years ago and traveled to cities like Nishapur and Baghdad, that had not settled in cities like Aleppo or Damascus, this small but spiritually great caravan that could not fit in any city, not even Baghdad, the fortress of the saints, would fit in Konya and settle there. The people of Konya had heard that this great saint was going to honor their city, and therefore were filled with great joy and excitement. Led by Sultan Ala al-Din Kay Qobad, all notables of Konya, high-ranking state and religious officials, scholars and shaykhs, along with the people of Konya went to welcome the king of the scholars.

On a beautiful spring day outside Konya's city walls on the Karaman road, two great sultans were going to meet. One was the greatest sultan of his time, Ala al-Din Kay Qobad, who had revived the great Anatolian Seljuk State at a time when it was collapsing. The other was king of the scholars and sultan of the gnostics, Baha al-Din Valad, who was fighting against ignorance and un-Islamic innovations; he was an example of humanity, virtue, and faith who was enduring voluntary separation from his home for the sake of his ideas and faith. Ala al-Din Kay Qobad had grown tired of never-ending battles and understood the nothingness of being a sultan in this rewardless world. He had decided that he would kneel in front of a sultan of spirits in hopes of becoming his dervish or disciple. It is for this reason that the great sultan Ala al-Din Kay Qobad of noble spirit was more excited than everyone else as he waited for the great saint Baha al-Din Valad.

The modest caravan became visible on the horizon. Sultan al-Ulama with his white beard and luminous face appeared riding on his horse in front of the caravan. Rumi was following his honorable father. His dervishes, disciples, and family, and behind them a few camels carrying loads of book also could be seen. When the caravan came near, the sultan, who was waiting on his horse, dismounted immediately. He ran and grabbed the reins of Sultan al-Ulama's horse and helped him dismount. The two sultans greeted each other with respect, and Sultan al-Ulama was helped back onto his horse. The Seljuk ruler, great Sultan Ala al-Din Kay Qobad, however, did not ride his horse next to Baha al-Din Valad. Instead he walked next to the great saint's horse, at times pulling the reins, at times holding the saddle. The sultan of the world had become the servant of the sultan of the spirits. The people who saw this were amazed. They were fascinated by the modesty of their sultan, and they loved and admired him more. As they entered the city, the streets were filled with people. The spectators watched this unique scene from their windows and rooftops. The Seljuk sultan wanted to take his cherished guest to the room in the palace he had prepared for him. He requested that he stay and live there. Baha al-Din Valad replied, "O mighty sultan, I understand your intentions. But madrasas are for imams, dervish lodges for shaykhs, palaces for kings, caravanserai for tradesmen, and hostels for the poor. With your permission, I would like to stay in a seminary." The sultan complied with this request. They were hosted in the greatest seminary of the city, Altun Aba. As was the custom among sultans, amirs, and men of high positions at the time, Sultan Ala al-Din showered his cherished guest with many gifts. Although he sent money, food, and many other offerings, Baha al-Din Valad politely returned all of these gifts. Just as in the other cities, in Konya he did not accept any gifts from anybody including sultans, and said, "We have no aspirations for worldly wealth. Whatever worldly possessions we inherited from our grandfather are enough for us. The sultan should not give himself the trouble of sending us things we do not deserve."

Years later when Sultan al-Ulama's grandson would discuss in his book *Ibtidaname* his grandfather's arrival in Konya, he would write, "All people, men, women, young, old, all turned to him. They saw his *karamat* (a saint's miraculous powers). They heard many secrets from him. From his favor and abundance they progressed spiritually. They continuously spoke of him and his greatness. A few days passed in this manner. Then young, old, men, and women all became his disciples. Not long afterward, Sultan Ala al-Din respectfully came to visit him with his commanders. When Sultan Ala al-Din saw his luminous face, with love and utmost sincerity, he became his disciple. When he heard his sermon he became his admirer and in his heart he reserved a place for him. And in his heart he found many signs from him."[10]

Baha al-Din Valad occupied a few rooms in the Altun Aba seminary assigned to him and settled there with his sons and grandsons. He preached in the Ala al-Din Mosque that is still to be seen in Konya. Wherever he went, a great crowd of locals followed him. And the sultan frequently came with his commanders to listen to his sermons.

Baha al-Din Valad had decided to settle and stayed in Konya as the greatest of the "saints of Khorasan" who had come to the "Roman land." After a few days, Sultan Ala al-Din Kay Qobad arranged a big ceremony in the palace. He invited to this ceremony, along with Baha al-Din Valad, the foremost scholars, shaykhs, viziers, and commanders of Konya. The great Seljuk sultan welcomed Baha al-Din Valad at the gate of the palace. He led him to the great ceremony room himself. Everybody in the room stood up and greeted the two sultans. The mighty sultan who was the head of a great empire and the sultan of the spiritual world were standing next to each other. All eyes were on them. Sultan Ala al-Din Kay Qobad addressed Sultan al-Ulama by raising his voice so that those present could hear him, "O sultan of religion. I have been thinking and have come to a decision. From today on, I shall leave this throne that I inherited from my forefathers to you. From now on, you will be the sultan and I shall be your servant. The sultanate of the physical world that is seen and the other world that is not seen is with you." He said this and gave the crown to him. Upon hearing these words, the sultan of the scholars stood up, hugged the sultan and kissed him on the eyes and said, "O sultan of angelic character and great state! You have acquired the wealth of this world and hereafter. Nobody doubts that. You sit on your throne comfortably. We long since have closed our eyes to this world's wealth. Now we are worshipping God and trying to follow His commandments."

The quarters of the Altun Aba madrasa were not spacious enough for Rumi, who was married with two children, nor his dervishes and disciples. Because of his humility, Sultan al-Ulama could not let Ala al-Din Kay Qobad or others know about this situation, so he prayed in his heart. One day as he was preaching in the Ala al-Din Mosque, the sultan, his commanders, and all of the notables in Konya attended. Amir Badr al-Din Govhartash, the building master of the palace and tutor of the sultan, was also there. He had become one of Sultan al-Ulama's disciples. He was fascinated by his sermons. That day, while listening to the great saint, he became ecstatic and had the urge to be of service to him. Was he not the architect of the palace? He decided to build a madrasa for the family of Baha al-Din Valad and his son Rumi and their children. Soon afterward, the construction of the madrasa began in the most beautiful area of the city around the sultan's palace. This college-style madrasa was completed within a few months. Sultan al-Ulama along with his son Rumi and his family moved to this new residence. They resided in this madrasa until the end of their lives.

It is narrated that the Seljuk sultan had dedicated the rose garden of the palace, east of the Konya Fortress, to Baha al-Din Valad. They say that one day Sultan al-Ulama pointed to this small hill and said, "My tomb and the tombs of my grandchildren will be there. From now on, that place is the garden of soul and heart, a firm standing place of saints." In fact, after his passing away, Baha al-Din Valad was buried there. The shrine of Rumi also was built there.

Rumi's works

Rumi's works consist of the *Mesnevi*, *Divan-i Kabir*, *Fihi Ma Fih*, *Majalis-i Sab'a*, and *Maktubat*. There are other books attributed to him, like *Tirashname*, *Ashqname*, *Rasail-i Afaq wa Anfus*, and *Risala-i Aqaid*. But both their styles and their themes show that these are not Rumi's.

The Mesnevi

The honorable *Mesnevi* contains 25,618 couplets in six books. The name of this book was taken from its form. The *Mesnevi* form is a lyrical form in Islamic literature in which the two lines of each couplet rhyme internally, and all verses share the same meter. This book is one of the masterpieces of Sufi literature. Hence, Abdurrahman Jami says the following about Rumi and *Mesnevi*: "The *Mesnevi* is sign enough to show the value of that peerless king of the spiritual world. How can I describe the qualities of that great person? He is not a prophet but has a (holy) book." Muhammad Iqbal agrees with Jami: "The *Mesnevi* of the master of the spiritual world is virtually the Qur'an written in Persian." Also, "Mevlana (Rumi), whose creation was blessed, appeared to me. That Rumi has written a Qur'an in the Persian language."[11]

These words have been said due to the love and admiration felt for Rumi. But Rumi's spirit was very uncomfortable with these excessive praises, especially with the comparison of the Qur'an and the *Mesnevi*. We find evidence of Rumi's view in his statement: "I am the slave of the Qur'an as long as I shall live. I am the soil under the feet of Prophet Muhammad." The following is a quatrain by Ibn al-Kamal, the head of Ottoman religious authority at the time of Sultan Yavuz Selim: "In my dream I saw the Most Honorable Messenger. He held the *Mesnevi* in his hand and said, 'There have been many Sufi books written but among them there is none like this one.'" Indeed, there are countless books in Sufi literature that prepare for those spirits who are in love with the heavens, ladders to escape the prison of body, leave this dirty world, and rise to a place beyond. These books serve as subsistence for hearts and spirits. But the *Mesnevi* has features that other Sufi books do not have. In the *Mesnevi*, there are medications for our spiritual ailments, bad habits, and un-Islamic beliefs. These bitter pills have been hidden in stories and tales so that they are presented sweetly to spiritually sick humans.

Rumi wrote the first eighteen couplets of the *Mesnevi* with his own hand, but he dictated the rest of the *Mesnevi* to Husam al-Din Chelebi. When the writing of each volume was complete, Husam al-Din Chelebi recited it back to Rumi, and Rumi made the necessary corrections. Then Husam al-Din Chelebi would produce a clean copy of the corrected text. Rumi described the *Mesnevi* in many ways such as *Sayqaal al-Arwah* (Polish of the Spirits) and *Husamname* (Book of Husam al-Din). But these are not the name of the book itself, only descriptions. Contrary to common misconceptions, the *Mesnevi* is not merely a didactic book. It contains sections very similar to the ardent poems in *Divan-i Kabir*, which touch the reader very deeply. One is amazed by such deep thoughts and emotional expressions in the *Mesnevi,* expressions that the holy saint recited without taking a pen in his hand, without working on the meter or the rhyme of the verses, and reciting very comfortably as it came to his heart and mind. Defects of meter and rhyme are very rare in the *Mesnevi,* although it was written without deep reflection and study. This is not a quality to be found in any other poet. Rumi's ability is a gift that God bestowed upon him.

Rumi was very skilled at associating ideas. He had a very strong memory. He had at least a basic knowledge of every area of study of his time. In addition to his mother tongue, Rumi spoke Arabic, Persian, and even Greek and read books written in these languages. Therefore, the *Mesnevi* is like an exhibition of a very rich collection of ideas and feelings. One reads views on many different subjects in the *Mesnevi.* Rumi's metaphors, sensations, expressions, joy, and fantasy fascinate the reader. Rumi's sharp intelligence, sensitive spirit, and ardent love and faith take the reader to a different world.

But one should note that the tales in the *Mesnevi* do not conform to today's storytelling techniques. When Rumi explains a subject, he begins by telling a story in order to clarify his point. Then in the middle of the story, he relates certain wisdom and truths. He produces such peerless couplets that the reader is astonished. These couplets that he recited in a state of ecstasy remind him of another story. So he begins a new story and then finally returns to complete the first story. This way, stories within stories follow each other. If we are patient and read the stories carefully, we shall see that each of these stories tells us about deeply meaningful subjects, human thoughts, divine love, the unity of God, and Islamic faith; and they remove marginal beliefs and un-Islamic views from the reader. These stories carry those readers who are able to understand their deep meanings from our material world to the spiritual world. They raise the reader spiritually, morally, and emotionally. In other words, they make the reader a "true human being."

Today's living conditions force people to engage in excessive struggle mercilessly. Our day turns people into robots. It blinds the feelings of mercy and kills the spiritual side of humans. The average modern human has become submerged so deeply in making a living that he seems to have forgotten where he came from and where he eventually will go. People do not listen to the truths conveyed by the prophets, saints, great philosophers, scholars, and real poets. They follow their egos, and hence they almost lose their human aspects. The stories in the *Mesnevi* will comfort the pessimistic individual in pain in this material world by telling him of the eminence and beauty of the spiritual world. With the permission of God, these stories will return humankind to the lost paradise even while they are in this world. Those who read the *Mesnevi* or listen to it will receive spiritual joy and holy signs from the deeply meaningful truths found in the *Mesnevi* in accordance with their own abilities and capacities. When they read this blessed book, they will be touched by it and obtain holy light from its light. They will be saved from spiritual illnesses, bad behavior, and un-Islamic beliefs. But there is a prerequisite for obtaining the full benefit of the *Mesnevi*: The eye of our hearts should be opened, and the deafness of our spirits should be removed by the blessing of Rumi. Indeed, Sultan Valad writes the following on this matter: "Know that Rumi is the head of saints. Do whatever he tells you to do. His words are the mercy of God. If spiritually blind people read his writings, their spiritual eyes will be opened and they will see the truth." God willing, when we read the *Mesnevi*, our spiritual eyes will be opened with the help of God, and we shall understand the truths in the *Mesnevi*.

Rumi's *Mesnevi* is for both well-educated people and people with little education. The *Mesnevi* guides the new initiate on the Sufi path, one who is advanced on this path, and even one who has reached the highest levels on this path. Rumi takes the walker on the path of God and brings him to God by means of the *Mesnevi*. Rumi says, "After us (when we pass away), the *Mesnevi* takes on shaykhdom, guides the seekers of Truth, leads them to high levels and to the attainment of their Ultimate Goal."[12]

Some people wonder where Rumi heard and from where he took the tales of *Mesnevi*. Certainly Rumi heard most of the stories from his father, Sayyid Burhan al-Din, or from Shams, and he probably read some of them in books. But as mentioned above, stories in the *Mesnevi* are not intended for amusement but are analogies from spiritual truths and messages that Rumi wanted to convey. At every stage of the stories that he selected, Rumi conveys a moral. Some stories reminded Rumi of certain truths, and sometimes Rumi told stories to explain his message better. Among the stories in the *Mesnevi*, some of them are funny and some are even obscene. Some *Mesnevi* stories come from sources as diverse as Indian mythology, Greek, and even Roman literature. There are fables from *Kalila and Dimna* as well as stories from the Roman poet Apolla. Rumi borrowed these stories because he followed in the footsteps of our great Prophet who commanded, "Wisdom is the lost property of the believer. He takes it wherever he may find it." Therefore, Rumi took stories that were appropriate to educate the faithful. These stories are not for making people laugh or to amuse them but for wisdom and advice. Rumi says the following regarding a few obscene stories in the *Mesnevi*: "My couplets are not couplets but climates (of truth). My obscenity (obscene stories in the *Mesnevi*) is not intended as obscenity but for teaching."

In order to obtain full benefit from the *Mesnevi*, we have to read it slowly and very carefully as one reads a deeply meaningful book. One also should record the beautiful couplets or passages of the *Mesnevi* in a notebook and review them from time to time to remember them easily. In order to understand the passages that symbolically explain *wahdat al-wujud* (unity of existence), we have to refer to reference books that have information on *wahdat al-wujud*, commentaries on the *Mesnevi*, and experts on this subject. We have to read the stories in the *Mesnevi* not with the intention of reading a story but with the intention of hearing the voice of Truth hidden behind the story and attaining Divine Love. Those thirsty for Truth have named the *Mesnevi* the "essence of the Qur'an." Rumi says, "Our *Mesnevi* is a store of unity. Whatever you see there other than God is seeing an idol." When one comprehends the deep meanings of this couplet, one understands that those who see a difference between Rumi and Muhy al-Din Ibn al-'Arabi are mistaken. Both saints explain the doctrine of *wahdat al-wujud* in their works in their own words. It is for this reason that Ahmed Avni Konuk, a recent *Mesnevi* commentator, has relied on the *Mesnevi* in his commentary on *Fusus al-Hikam* and on *Fusus al-Hikam* in his commentary on the *Mesnevi*.

Rumi dictated the *Mesnevi* under the strong influence of Hakim Sanai and Farid al-Din 'Attar. 'Attar's *Ilahiname* especially influenced Rumi. But because striking elaborations, deep meanings, and eloquent descriptions in the *Mesnevi* lead its readers to spiritual joys and explain its subjects very well, it has been customary for the authors of books on Sufism to use couplets from the *Mesnevi* after excerpts from the Qur'an and Prophetic Traditions to explain Sufi concepts. Let us now see how Rumi himself describes the *Mesnevi* in the foreword: "The *Mesnevi* is a path for those who want to attain the Truth and be aware of the secrets of God. The *Mesnevi* is the essence of the essence of the essence of religion. It is the most infallible Law of God and His enlightened path to Truth. Undoubtedly, the *Mesnevi* is medicine for hearts of pure people. It removes sorrow. It helps one to understand the Qur'an better. No one is permitted to touch the *Mesnevi* other than those who love the truth." The expression "no one is permitted to touch the *Mesnevi* other than those who love the truth" should not be misunderstood. It is known that our brethren in faith have different approaches. Those who dislike some of the subjects in the *Mesnevi*, who cannot penetrate the inner meaning of the stories and hence cannot see the truth will not enjoy this blessed book. Because of differences in the ways of interpretation, they may not comprehend completely the messages contained in some stories in the *Mesnevi*.

God revealed in the Qur'an to the Prophet many examples and analogies so that the people would not believe blindly, but rather they would believe through thinking and understanding the Creator's power. Let us carefully read the following Qur'anic verse: "God does not hesitate to put forth a gnat or something larger as an example to explain the truth. The faithful know that this example is a truth coming from their Lord. But the infidels say, 'What does God mean by this example?' God misleads many of them with this example and guides many of them to truth with this example. Only the sinners are misled by it."[13] Rumi points to this Qur'anic verse and says, "Just like the Qur'an, our *Mesnevi* also misleads some people from truth and guides some to the truth." In the above-mentioned Qur'anic verse and the couplet from the *Mesnevi*, the concepts of "guidance" and "misguidance" should not confuse us. We have to know that God is the Creator of guidance as well as misguidance. If God had not created misguidance and guided everyone to truth, misguidance would not have existed even if people wanted it. But misguidance is deserved and chosen by people. God creates guidance and misguidance and people choose either of these with their own free will and responsibility. It is not logical to think that God, who created humankind with all the potential for guidance, would force them in to misguidance.

To return to the main topic, the *Mesnevi* is an enlightened path for pure people thirsty for the truth. It is a medicine for hearts. Especially in our day in which true saints and great spiritual guides rarely exist, the *Mesnevi* is not only a book but also a spiritual guide. The following is said about the *Mesnevi*: "Surely, one can call this blessed book a spiritual guide without a tongue in the flesh. But in reality it is a spiritual guide with one hundred tongues." Aflaki writes, "In order to understand properly the secrets and subtleties of the *Mesnevi* and the affiliation among the stories, the cited Qur'anic verses, and the Prophetic Traditions, it is necessary to have a strong faith, a continuous love, uncompromising ethics, a pure heart, a sharp mind, and at least a basic understanding of sciences. If you are a true lover of God, then your love can guide you to understand the *Mesnevi*, and you can reach your goal. God is the Grantor of Success. He is the Guide to the True Path and is the True Helper."

It is related that the following was written on the cover of an old copy of the *Mesnevi*: "I have not dictated the *Mesnevi* to be memorized. But I intended the *Mesnevi* for the lovers of God to be a spiritual ladder that raises them to the heavens. So the *Mesnevi* is not meant to be a ladder carried from town to town on the shoulder. This is because one cannot climb to the heavens by means of the ladders we know and achieve the desire of the hearts." In the epilogue at the end of Book Six of the *Mesnevi*, Sultan Valad writes, "The *Mesnevi* is the ladder of the hearts. Whoever climbs this ladder reaches the roof. But this roof is not the roof of the blue skies. This roof is superior to the heavens. It is higher than the heavens."[14]

Since the *Mesnevi* is a much loved book from which readers can benefit spiritually, it has been translated into many languages and many commentaries have been written on it. As mentioned in an earlier section, the whole world knows Rumi and reads his masterpiece, the honorable *Mesnevi*. In order to keep this section short, we shall mention only the Turkish translations and commentaries:

Commentaries on the Mesnevi

1. Commentary by Sururi: This is an unprinted commentary by Mustafa Sururi Efendi (d. 1561) who lies in the garden of the mosque that he built in Kasımpaşa, Istanbul. Mustafa Sururi Efendi also wrote commentaries to the *Divan* of Hafiz and the *Gulistan* of Sadi.

2. Commentary by Sudi: Sudi Efendi (d. 1595), who was originally from Bosnia, wrote commentaries on the *Mesnevi* of Rumi and the *Divan* of Hafiz. His *Mesnevi* commentary has not been published.

3. Commentary by Sham'i: This *Mesnevi* commentary, which was started during the reign of Sultan Murad III, took a long time to be completed. The commentator began the commentary on the

sixth book of the *Mesnevi* in 1600 but it is not known when he finished it. This *Mesnevi* commentary, which was favored by Esrar Dede, has not been published.

4. Commentary by Ahmed Rusuhi Ismail Dede: Ismail Dede was a shaykh of the Bayrami order in Ankara. Due to his admiration of Rumi, he entered the Mevlevi order and was appointed the shaykh of the Kulekapisi Mevlevi Lodge in Istanbul. He passed away in 1631 and is buried in the garden of the Mevlevi lodge where he had served as shaykh. This commentary is seen as the best Turkish commentary, and its author therefore is called the "Revered Commentator." The famous English orientalist R. A. Nicholson used Ismail Dede's commentary extensively while writing his own commentary on the *Mesnevi* in English. Since Ismail Dede was a great scholar and a shaykh who practiced what he preached, for centuries his commentary has been a great help for those trying to understand the difficult verses in the *Mesnevi*. Unfortunately, since he used a language full of Arabic and Persian words, not everyone can make use of his commentary today. The "Revered Commentator" was deeply influenced by Muhy al-Din Ibn al-'Arabi and Ibn al-Farid. His commentary was published both in Egypt and in Istanbul (1872). In addition to writing a commentary on the six volumes of the *Mesnevi*, Ismail Dede wrote a commentary on a fabricated seventh volume for some unknown reason, but the commentary on this fabricated seventh volume is not printed. Professor Furuzanfar of Tehran University has proven empirically that this seventh volume has nothing to do with Rumi.[15] The fact that some Mevlevi shaykhs have written commentaries on this fabricated seventh book of the *Mesnevi* (for example, Ferruh Efendi d. 1840, Mevlevi shaykh of Tokat, Hafiz Mehmed Emin Efendi, Shakir Mehmed Efendi d. 1836), believing that this book was written by Rumi should be considered as a sign of their deep reverence for Rumi and their attachment to Rumi in their hearts. If they had examined this book impartially, they never would have accepted it as Rumi's. When they heard Rumi's name, they immediately accepted this seventh book because

of their love for Rumi and became blind to the flaws in this fabricated volume. Like the "Revered Commentator," they smelled the thorns of a rose garden thinking that they were roses.

5. Commentary by Abdulmajid Sivasi: Abdulmajid of Sivas (d. 1639), who was a prominent Sufi of the Khalwatiyyah order during the seventeenth century, wrote a commentary on only a portion of the first book of the *Mesnevi*. This incomplete commentary has not been published.

6. Commentary by Sarı Abdullah Efendi: Sarı Abdullah Efendi (d. 1660), who was a Bayrami shaykh, wrote a commentary on the first book of the *Mesnevi*. His commentary was printed in five volumes (Istanbul, 1871) and was entitled *Cevahir-i Bevahir-i Mesnevi* (Pearls from the Oceans of the *Mesnevi*). The Turkish National Library would have gained a Sufi masterpiece if Sarı Abdullah Efendi, who was a learned person and a true lover of God, had been able to complete his commentary.

7. Commentary by Ismail Hakkı of Bursa: This great saint (d. 1725) of Bursa wrote a well known, ten-volume commentary on the Qur'an entitled *Ruh al-Bayan* (The Spirit of Proclamation), making extensive use of the *Mesnevi*. In his *Mesnevi* commentary, he completed only up to couplet 738 of the first book. His commentary is printed in two volumes in Istanbul.

8. Commentary by Shaykh Murad Buhari: Shaykh Murad Buhari (d. 1848) wrote a commentary on all six books of the *Mesnevi*. This commentary, which has not been published, is now preserved in the manuscripts section of the Istanbul University Library.

9. Commentary by Abidin Pasha: Abidin Pasha (d. 1907) wrote a commentary on the first books of the *Mesnevi* which was printed in six volumes in Istanbul.

10. Commentary by Ahmed Avni Konuk: Ahmed Avni Konuk (d. 1938) was a prominent commentator on the *Mesnevi* of our time. He wrote a commentary on *Fusus al-Hikam* as well as a very comprehensive and well prepared commentary on the *Mesnevi*. A

manuscript of this very valuable commentary, which has not been published yet, can be found in the library of the Konya Mevlana Museum and another manuscript in Koca Ragıp Pasha Library in Istanbul.

11. Commentary by Kenan Rufai: Kenan Rufai (d. 1950), a well-known Rufai shaykh, wrote a commentary on the first book of the *Mesnevi* which was revised by his eminent disciples and published in 1973 in Istanbul under the title *Şerhli Mesnevi-i Şerif*. This commentary is the most widely read commentary to date. The couplets have been translated with additional phrases to help the reader to understand the material better. The style used is especially elegant. Unfortunately, like the commentaries by Sarı Abdullah Efendi and Abidin Pasha, this commentary is only on the first book of the *Mesnevi*.

12. Commentary by Tahir al-Mevlevi: Tahir Olgun (Tahir al-Mevlevi) (d. 1951), a prominent figure within the Mevlevi community, wrote a commentary on the first four books and some of the fifth book of the *Mesnevi*.[16]

13. Commentary by Abdulbaki Gölpınarlı: Abdulbaki Gölpınarlı (d. 1960), a well-known scholar who wrote countless books and a complete translation and commentary of the *Mesnevi*. This commentary has been published by the Turkish Ministry of Culture in six volumes. Abdulbaki Gölpınarlı, whom I knew very well, was an adherent of the Shi'ite-Jafari creed, and, as in many of his books, in his the *Mesnevi* commentary he promoted his creed.

In the above list I have included thirteen known Turkish commentaries on the *Mesnevi*. These are the known ones. Only God knows how many more have been left to collect dust on a shelf or have been burnt or otherwise destroyed by neglect. I could not conclude this section without including the following opinion of Professor Furuzanfar on the commentators and commentaries on the *Mesnevi*:

"Since it is difficult to understand the secrets and subtleties of the *Mesnevi*, scholars and Sufis have made a lot of effort to explain the *Mesnevi*'s somewhat complex parts and have written Arabic,

Persian, or Turkish commentaries either on the whole *Mesnevi* or parts of it. This is a criticism of all of the commentaries: The commentators use their own knowledge and understanding to explain and analyze Rumi's views. Some of them even refer to philosophical books to explain parts of the *Mesnevi* and use philosophical methods. Instead of all this endeavor, if they had explained the *Mesnevi* by carefully studying the *Mesnevi* itself, they could have written better commentaries."[17]

Turkish Translations of the Mesnevi

1. The first Turkish translation of the *Mesnevi* in verse was written by Muini Chelebi under the title *Mesnevi-i Muradi*. Muini Chelebi translated most of the *Mesnevi* tales in verse and dedicated his work to Sultan Murad II (1438). The original manuscript of this work is preserved in the Orhan Gazi Library in Bursa.

2. Dede Ömer Ruşen (d. 1478) of Aydın is said to have made a *Mesnevi* translation entitled *Neyname*.

3. The *Mesnevi* was translated into Turkish by Mevlevi Nahifi Süleyman Efendi, an eighteenth-century poet. This translation was printed in Egypt by Bulaq Publishing House in 1851. In 1967, Professor Amil Çelebioglu rewrote this translation in modern language and published it with its original text. Nahifi also translated the fabricated seventh book of the *Mesnevi* which unfortunately is included in the Bulaq edition.

4. Tahir Bey of Bursa, a historian of Turkish literature, writes that Abdullah Salahi (d. 1782), a prominent Ushshaqi shaykh, translated the *Mesnevi*.[18]

5. Kütükçü Süleyman Hayri Bey (d. 1891) attempted to translate the *Mesnevi* in verse but could only finish a portion of the first book. This incomplete and unsuccessful translation was printed in Istanbul in 1890.

6. Avni Bey of Yenişehir (d. 1892) translated the *Mesnevi* in verse up to the fourth book.

7. Feyzullah Sacid Ülkü translated the first book of the *Mesnevi* into Turkish in verse. This translation was published in 1945.

8. Valad Chelebi, a descendant of Rumi, translated the six books of the *Mesnevi* into Turkish in prose. This translation was published in 1942 by the Turkish Ministry of Education as the first of a series of Eastern-Islamic classics.

9. Dr. Abdullah Öztemiz Hacitahiroğlu translated the *Mesnevi* into Turkish with its original meter. In the first volume of this translation, published in 1972, there are 2,108 couplets.

10. Feyzi Halıcı, a contemporary poet, has started translating the *Mesnevi* with its original meter. His translation has been published in two small volumes of 1,001 couplets.

Divan-i Kabir

Divan-i Kabir (the great collection of poems) is the name of the book that contains Rumi's poems. *Divan-i Kabir* contains Rumi's poems in several different styles of Eastern Islamic poetry (e.g., odes, eulogies, quatrains, etc). Although most of the poems are in Persian, there are also Arabic and Turkish poems. *Divan-i Kabir* also is called *Kulliyat-i Shams-i Tabrizi*, or *Divan-i Shams* because unlike other poets who mention their pennames in the last couplet of each poem they compose, Rumi used Shams' name. In none of his poems did he use his name, "Mevlana" or "Jalal al-Din Rumi." In some of his poems he used the names of Salah al-Din Zarqubi or Husam al-Din Chelebi. The odes with these two names number around one hundred. Rumi occasionally used nicknames, such as *khamoosh* (silent) or *khamoosh kon* (be silent). Rumi used Shams' name in his poems because they were friends of the heart. Those who do not know this think that these poems were composed by Shams. However, we have no historical record of Shams having written any poetry.

However, in an edition of *Divan-i Kabir* printed in India in 1885 under the title *Kulliyat-i Shams-i Tabrizi*, there are many poems that are not Rumi's. These poems were composed mainly by Shams-i

Tabasi and Shams-i Mashriqi, who used similar nicknames to Shams. Likewise, in some editions of *Divan-i Kabir* printed in Iran, there are poems that are not Rumi's. For example, in *Divan-i Shams al-Haqaiq*, which is a selection from Rumi's poems by Rıza Kuli Khan, there are many poems that are not Rumi's. These poems do not conform to Rumi's faith, personality, and ideals. Those poems which deify Ali, for example, confuse the readers. Some of the readers who know little about Rumi are misled into believing that Rumi was Shi'ite. Unfortunately, this selection of Rumi's poems, *Divan-i Shams al-Haqaiq*, contains the most beautiful of Rumi's poems translated by Midhat Bahari Beytur, without removing the poems that are not Rumi's. This translation was published by the Turkish Ministry of Education in three volumes.

The most reliable edition of *Divan-i Kabir* has been prepared and published by Professor Furuzanfar of Tehran University who studied the oldest ten manuscripts of the *Divan*. In this edition, there are no poems that are not Rumi's but there may be a few poems by Rumi which have been left out. Nevertheless, this edition of the *Divan* is the best and the most elegant of the *Divans* printed in India or Iran. This edition, which was printed in 1957, displays differences between manuscripts and contains short explanations. It has been typeset carefully as a large size book, apt for its name. May the publisher's soul be blessed. Abdulbaki Gölpınarlı translated into Turkish *Divan-i Kabir's* oldest manuscript preserved in Konya in the Mevlana Museum. This translation has been published twice.

The exact number of poems and the number of couplets in the poems of *Divan-i Kabir* are not known for certain since there are variations in different editions and manuscripts. The oldest manuscript in Konya contains 2,073 odes and 21,366 couplets. The exact number may be found by comparing all the different editions and manuscripts. In addition, there are thousands of Rumi's quatrains, the exact number unknown. Beginning in Konya's libraries in 1964, I collected all the quatrains that were attributed to Rumi. I searched manuscripts and leaflets in libraries in Istanbul. I scanned the *Divans* printed in Iran, Afghanistan, and India and compared the quatrains in them with those that I had collected. Thus, *Rubailer Divanı* (Collection of Quatrains) was born. The Turkish Ministry of Culture published *Rubailer Divani* in two volumes that contain the originals and the translation of the quatrains as well as explanatory notes.

The poems in *Divan-i Kabir* are lyrical poems. They are products of love and excitement. Friends and disciples wrote down these holy, gnostic poems that Rumi sometimes composed in a state of ecstasy. Just as with the *Mesnevi*, Rumi recited these poems as they came to his heart without taking a pen in his hand. He would recite them sometimes while whirling and other times during a walk through the gardens of Meram in Konya. In these poems, which were composed without forethought or a conscious concern for meter and rhyme, there is an effect of burning in the heart, ecstasy, and love. There are inspirations and messages from the beyond. In some editions of the *Divan*, especially in some of the published ones, there are poems that are not the product of Rumi's ardent nature, love, and excitement. Those who are familiar with Rumi's style and feeling recognize these poems instantly. They enrapture the reader and grant him indescribable joys and ecstasy. In those poems Rumi exists. In those poems we find Rumi's love. In most of this great saint's poems, the reader feels the pain of separation, tears, aching hearts, longing for the Beloved, laments, and pleas, as well as joyful, hopeful, and grateful prayers. Some poems have a meter appropriate to their theme. You feel that the leaves are falling in autumn, the trees are shaking, and the seasons are coming to an end. A sensitive person can understand what Rumi means through the harmony and spiritual atmosphere of the poems even if one does not know Persian. These poems sometimes make the reader shed tears. Sometimes they enrapture, and sometimes they take one to the other world.

In the foreword to Professor Furuzanfar's edition of *Divan-i Kabir*, Rumi presents his poems to the lovers of God with the following lines:

"These poems are spiritual secrets (subtle meanings). For those who have given their hearts to God, they are Noah's ark. They are holy breaths, pleasant breezes for the spirit, and inspirations from the Lord. They open up the eye of the heart during dawn. They are inspirations from God, Who is pure from all imperfections and deficiencies. They are unique signs, surprising phrases. They are lights from the sea of the Unity of God. They are large pearls from the sea of the Unseen. This *Divan* is the Divan of Lovers of God. It is the spring of spiritual joy and the light of hearts.

"It is true words accepted by lovers of God and gnostics and the key of the people of Presence (peace). They are the places of free people in the unseen world. It is the heart of the hearts of people who have a heart. It is the flower of the garden of heart. The words in this *Divan* are the rivers that bring blessings and spiritual joys to assemblies of true servants of God. They are accounts mentioning the saints. They are the alchemy of bliss for mature people. They are a sermon for the people of strong faith. They are ornaments for those who love God and abstain from evil. These words are God's sword against the hypocrites.

"They are an elixir for great and good people. They are a gift for the traveler of the path of God. They are the language of the birds of *jabarut*.[19] They are the praises of angels in the unseen world."

Fihi Ma Fih

This book is composed of Rumi's speeches on different subjects. Rumi himself did not prepare or write these discourses. They were written down by his son Sultan Valad or some other disciple of Rumi and put together as a book. Some of the discourses are addressed to Muin al-Din Pervane. Some portions of it are a commentary on the *Mesnevi*. There are also references to Shams-i Tabrizi, Burhan al-Din Tirmidhi, and Salah al-Din Zarqubi. *Fihi Ma Fih* was first translated into Turkish by Ahmed Avni Konuk, but this translation was not published and now is preserved in the Konya Mevlana Museum. Later, it was translated again by Meliha Ülker and published in the Turkish Ministry of Education's series on Islamic classics in 1954.

Majalis-i Sab'a

As the name implies, this books contains seven sermons given in seven different assemblies. As Aflaki relates, after Shams-i Tabrizi, Rumi gave sermons at the request of notables, especially Salah al-Din Zarqubi. Seven of these sermons are collected in this book. This work was translated into Turkish by Hulusi Efendi and was published by Feridun Nafiz Uzluk with its master copy in 1937. Another translation of this book by Adbulbaki Gölpınarlı was published in Konya.

Maktubat

This book is composed of letters that Rumi sent to state officials. Like all of his other books, Rumi did not write these letters himself. He dictated them. This book, which contains 147 letters, was published in Persian by Feridun Nafiz Uzluk in Istanbul in 1937. These letters were translated into Turkish by Abdulbaki Gölpınarlı.

THE DEATH OF RUMI'S FATHER

Sultan al-Ulama was already over eighty-five years old. It had been two years since he had come to Konya. He became suddenly ill in the winter of 1231. On the morning of the third day of his illness (January 12, 1231), he closed his eyes to this mortal world. The next day an immense funeral was held for him. Commencing with Sultan Ala al-Din Kay Qobad, all commanders, scholars, and shaykhs were present at his funeral. Sultan al-Ulama, who had held a place in the hearts of the people of Konya for the past two years, now was proceeding toward his holy destination on their shoulders and above their heads. Everybody was crying. People of sensitive hearts were very sad about his leaving. They had become the orphans of a spiritual father.

In describing Sultan al-Ulama's passing away, Sultan Valad wrote in his *Ibtidaname*, "When Sultan al-Ulama's coffin was being carried it was like the Judgment Day. Men and women, everyone was shedding tears of anguish. Scholars and commanders, along with the sultan, fell in front of the coffin with nothing on their heads. Because of his sorrow, the sultan could not sit on his throne for a week." The mourning in the Seljuk palace lasted for forty days. The sultan and his officials did not ride their horses for forty days in the Seljuk palace.

The following was written on his tombstone, which was erected after some time: "God is Eternal. This is the resting place of our Master, High Office of the Law, Source of Wisdom, Rejuvenator of the Prophetic Tradition, Remover of un-Islamic Beliefs, one loved and followed as an exemplary Muslim, Man of God, Learned Man, one who Practiced what He Knew and Believed In, King of All Scholars, Mufti of the East and West, the Value of the Law and the Religion, Shaykh of Islam and Muslims, Muhammad, son of Huseyin, son of Ahmed of Balkh. May God be pleased with him and his ancestors. He passed away on the eighteenth day of the month Rabi' al-Akhir of the year six hundred twenty-eight (after Hegira) in the late morning. May God have mercy on him."

One year later a simple shrine of sun-dried bricks was built over Sultan al-Ulama's tomb. Later, in place of this modest shrine, the Seljuk vizier Muin al-Din Pervane (d. 1277) asked Rumi about building a large shrine and a high dome appropriate for the glory of the king of the scholars. Upon this offer, Rumi asked Vizier Pervane this question: "Can you build a bigger and higher dome than the one encompassing the universe?" The vizier answered, "No." And Rumi replied, "Then do not bother to build a new one." The magnificent shrine seen today was built after Rumi's death, and it contains the tombs of Rumi's loved ones including Sultan al-Ulama. The tall wooden sarcophagus on Sultan al-Ulama's tomb, regarded as one of the most beautiful examples of wood carving from Seljuk era, was placed on Rumi's tomb until the time of Süleyman the Magnificent. In the time of Süleyman the Magnificent, this tall wooden sarcophagus was taken from Rumi's tomb and put on his father's tomb; a shorter sarcophagus made of marble with a *puşide* (cover) on top of it was constructed for Rumi. Contrary to common misconception, Sultan al-Ulama did not stand up to show his respect for Rumi's knowledge and virtues when he entered the room. Neither the father nor the son needed to exalt each other by standing up. However, those who have given their hearts to them stand up in their presence with excitement, love, and respect, and they will continue to stand till Judgment Day.

Sultan al-Ulama Muhammad Baha al-Din Valad wrote a three-volume book in Persian called *Ma'arif*.[20] It is said that *Ma'arif* was compiled from Sultan al-Ulama's sermons or lectures given in various places. Aflaki relates that Rumi recounted what he remembered from his father's sermons and lectures while others wrote these down, and even Shaykh Mahmud Sahib dried the manuscripts over the oven. No matter how it came to be, Rumi benefited very much from the work of his father, who was a great public speaker. In fact, the greatest work of the sultan of scholars was his son Rumi. He was his father, teacher, and spiritual guide. After his father's death, Rumi lived without a spiritual guide for one year. Then Sayyid Burhan al-Din Tirmidhi became his spiritual guide.

RUMI'S SPIRITUAL GUIDE AFTER HIS FATHER'S DEATH

The loss of his father left Rumi feeling emotionally and spiritually empty. That was because he had lost not only a father but also a spiritual guide, a friend of heart, an example of knowledge and virtue, and a perfect man. As much as he was recognized as a shaykh, the head of the order, and a great scholar at his young age, and surrounded by many people, after Sultan al-Ulama's migration to the realm of eternity, Rumi could not consider himself a replacement for his father and suffered from spiritual loneliness. But one year after Sultan al-Ulama's death, one of his deputies, Sayyid Burhan al-Din Tirmidhi (d. 1245), came to Konya to see him. He saw that his shaykh, whom he loved very much, had passed away and his son Jalal al-Din was in his place. Who was this Sayyid Burhan al-Din who came to Konya? When Baha al-Din Valad was in Balkh, Sayyid Burhan al-Din was there, too, and he was one of Sultan al-Ulama's disciples. When Jalal al-Din Muhammad was a child he had taken the responsibility for raising him. Rumi was very glad that Sayyid Burhan al-Din had come to Konya. He kissed the hand of his former teacher and father's friend. They remembered the good old days that had passed in Balkh. It then became clear to Sayyid why he had come to Konya. Once he had been the tutor of his dearly beloved shaykh's son, now he was going to be his spiritual guide.

After explaining the coming of Sayyid to Konya and his meeting with Rumi, Sultan Valad writes that he said the following to his former student: "You are peerless in knowledge. You are a superior and outstanding individual, but your father possessed spiritual states. You also should leave mere words and concern yourself with acquiring spiritual states. Work hard in this so that you may be his heir not only in knowledge but also in spirit. Enlighten the universe like the sun and show the true path to those who remain in the dark and stray from the Muhammadi path." Rumi accepted these words that came straight from the heart as if they were his father's words. He submitted to Sayyid Burhan al-Din, who said, "I want you to receive the truth from me that I received from your father who was my shaykh (spiritual guide). Without wasting any time you need to set out on the path of dervishes. The knowledge of *ladun*, the knowledge of knowing and finding God, is the knowledge of the prophets and saints. Now it is time for you to advance in this knowledge."

From that day Rumi became a disciple of Sayyid Burhan al-Din, and he started to recite regularly the prayers and praises of the Kubrawiyyah order taught to him by his shaykh. First, Sayyid locked Rumi in a room for forty days and had him perform a *khalwat* (seclusion). Rumi was released from spiritual loneliness when he found his father's friend Sayyid Burhan al-Din and enthusiastically and ardently recited prayers and other recitations given to him by his shaykh. Although Rumi had learned much from his father and teacher, Sultan al-Ulama, Sayyid Burhan al-Din advised him to go to Aleppo and Damascus to enhance his knowledge of religion and the law. Thus, following the order of his shaykh, Rumi went to Aleppo with a few of his dervish friends. When he sent his student and disciple to Aleppo to deepen his knowledge, Sayyid did not stay in Konya but returned to Kayseri. This was only temporary. When his dear disciple would come back, he too would return to Konya.

In Aleppo, Rumi studied for two years in a Halawiyye madrasa, the most famous of that time. He learned Islamic Law from Kamal al-Din, the most renowned scholar of the region. This famous scholar had met Rumi's father. Therefore, he took great care of the son of Sultan al-Ulama, whom he knew and loved very much. He attended to him intensively. He was amazed by Rumi's talent and intelligence and helped him to advance his knowledge in every area.

Rumi went from Aleppo to Damascus. Damascus was bursting with scholars and Sufis escaping the Mongol invasion. It was as if the Hand of the Most Powerful had prepared everything for the education of Rumi who was going to be a peerless Sufi and provide a service to the knowledge of *ladun* (gnosis) with his work the *Mesnevi*. In fact, in those days, Damascus was a city where saints gathered, almost a city of saints. Muhy al-Din Ibn al-'Arabi (d. 1240), who was to be called the most distinguished Sufi of all times, was also in Damascus during this time. Rumi stayed in the Maqdisiyyah madrasa in Damascus. He benefited greatly from the scholars and Sufis there. He read with love and enthusiasm, frequently visited scholars and Sufis, attending their lectures, asking them questions, and receiving answers. He gained deeper knowledge of the views of Ibn al-'Arabi. Rumi stayed in Damascus for more than four years. He had a wide circle of friends. Everybody who knew him showed him respect. Everybody was amazed by his intelligence and spiritual insight.

The time for his return to Konya came. It would not be correct to restrict Rumi's educational experience to the two years he studied in Aleppo and the four years in Damascus because historical events show that Rumi deepened his already broad knowledge in both cities. In fact, his education began in Balkh, a city full of scholars and Sufis. Although from the disputes about his year of birth one might consider him to be very young at that time, the fact that he was at an age where he could understand the book presented to him by 'Attar shows that he had not come from Balkh without any education. His real teacher was his father and he was always with him. What a great gift and a divine grace it was for Rumi to be with a father who was the Sultan al-Ulama, to benefit from his lectures, ideas, suggestions, and advice, and to be raised by his manners. When Rumi came back to Anatolia, he first went to Kayseri and visited Shaykh Sayyid Burhan al-Din. From there they went back to Konya together. The shaykh was very pleased with this situation. He found Rumi very changed. Rumi's knowledge, maturity, and attachment to Islamic Law were clearly remarkable. He had fulfilled his duty of guiding his shaykh's son to perfection on the path of knowledge and faith. Now he was attending to him personally, trying to advance him to an even more perfect state by his suggestions and views.

We do not know much about the life of Sayyid Burhan al-Din who contributed so much to Rumi's development. Like the lives of many saints, the life of Sayyid Burhan al-Din remains beyond parables. It is said that his ancestors go back to Huseyin, the grandson of the Prophet, may God be pleased with him.[21] It also is written that he possessed saintly miracles and knew what was in everybody's heart, and even that he foretold the coming of Shams to Konya without revealing his name and was therefore called by the nickname "Sayyid-i Sirdan" (Sayyid who knows secrets).

Rumi was raised by the hands of this spiritual guide and teacher. Sayyid went to great efforts to educate Rumi. He instructed him to read his father's book *Ma'arif* over and over again for months and years. Every year that passed made Rumi even more mature. The days of fasting and asceticism passed. Now he had educated Rumi as he wanted. He had the inner comfort of a spiritual guide who had accomplished his duty.

According to Sayyid, the *insan al-kamil*, or the perfect man, must be knowledgeable, a gnostic, a lover of God, a friend of God, and a beloved of God. He explained the most advanced issues of Sufism in a very simple and clear way. He spoke about philosophy, Islamic Law, natural sciences, chemistry, and Prophetic Traditions. He was truly a great scholar and at the same time a great mystic. We know that after his return from Damascus, Rumi brought his shaykh to Konya. According to Sipehsalar, although Sayyid Burhan al-Din had asked Rumi's permission to go back to Kayseri, Rumi did not want to be separated from his shaykh. Contrary to Rumi's request, Sayyid Burhan al-Din attempted to go to Kayseri, but on the way his horse's hoof slipped. Sayyid Burhan al-Din fell from the horse and injured his foot. He returned to Konya and asked Rumi why he was blocking his way and would not let him to go to Kayseri. To this question Rumi replied with the question: "O my Shaykh, why do you want to leave us?" Sayyid Burhan al-Din replied to this question, "In Konya a strong lion appeared. I am a lion, too. Two lions cannot be in the same city. We cannot get along with each other anymore. Therefore, I would like to go." Upon hearing this, Rumi kissed the hands of his shaykh and with a few of his disciples sent him to Kayseri.

When Sayyid Burhan al-Din arrived in Kayseri, he was welcomed enthusiastically by the governor of the city, Sahib Shams al-Din Isfahani. He was hosted in a dervish lodge. The notables of the town came to his presence and kissed his hands, welcoming him and presenting gifts they had brought. Sayyid Burhan al-Din ordered them to be distributed to the poor and the *majzub* (mentally unstable because of divine love) without even touching the gifts. At this point, he went into complete seclusion. Rumi pleased his shaykh by visiting him several times. The people of Kayseri showed great respect to Sayyid Burhan al-Din. They invited him to serve as the imam in a local mosque. He sometimes stood for hours in prayer, reciting long praises as he bowed and prostrated. The congregation could not carry this heavy burden, so when Sayyid Burhan al-Din noticed this, he asked to be excused from this duty, "Count me as excused. I am an anxious man. When in the presence of God I lose myself. I cannot be an imam. You find yourselves a different imam." And once again he returned to his little room of seclusion.

It was less than a year since Sayyid Burhan al-Din had come back to Kayseri, and this holy man felt that he was living the last days of his life. One day he asked his servant to prepare hot water. When the water was ready he took a full body ablution (*ghusl*). He said to his servant, "Go close the door tight and to those whom you see outside call out, 'The poor Sayyid has migrated from this world.'" Retiring to a corner of his room he said his last prayers: "O my great God, O Friend, accept me and take my life. Take me from me. Take me from the two worlds. I want you. Take from me everything which is not with you."

The servant ran to Sahib Shams al-Din and gave him the news. The news of Sayyid's passing away was soon heard in Kayseri and a big crowd gathered in front of his little room. While preparing the funeral, Sahib Shams al-Din informed Rumi about the death. The funeral was performed with prayer and remembrance of God. When Rumi received the news of his shaykh's passing, he became very sad and immediately went to Kayseri. When he arrived, he went directly to Sayyid's tomb and prayed there for hours.

Sahib Shams al-Din submitted his shaykh's books to Rumi. Rumi returned to Konya with these books, saddened and broken-hearted. Among these books there was also Sayyid Burhan al-Din's famous book *Maqalat*. Sayyid Burhan al-Din Tirmidhi passed away in 1241.

RUMI'S MEETING WITH SHAMS

After Burhan al-Din Tirmidhi passed away, Rumi began lecturing in the madrasa in Konya and training students. He had taken his first lessons from his father, the king of scholars. On the one hand, Rumi lectured in the seminary, held conversations with those seeking the truth, and answered their questions; on the other hand, he guided the lovers of God and warned them. In this way Rumi became the sultan of scholars in the religious sciences and other sciences, like his father, and he also became the sultan of gnostics in the area of Sufism. The public admired Rumi very much. In the view of the sultan, notables, and the common folk, he was known as a most elevated Muslim, an *insan al-kamil*, because of his devotion to worship, dedication to fasting and praying, virtues, humanity, graciousness, modesty despite his great knowledge, abstinence from the world, his commitment to the Muhammadi path just like his father, and his crystal clear life.

It was around this time that an event occurred that was going to change Rumi's life. Shams al-Din of Tabriz came to Konya. This poor person who came, Shams of Tabriz, enraptured Rumi, the great scholar, busy with his lectures, and cautious great Sufi and spiritual guide. He made him into an ardent lover of God.

Who was this Shams al-Din of Tabriz who brought about such a big change in Rumi's life? Aflaki writes that Shams' father was Ali, son of Malikdad. Since he was born in Tabriz, he may have been of the Azeri Turks. It is clear from the *Maqalat* that he was very well educated and familiar with all the sciences of his day. Since he never stayed in one place for a long period of time and traveled to many places, he was given the nickname "Shams-i Perende" (Flying Shams) He is also called "Kamil-i Tabrizi" (the perfect one of Tabriz) since he was a perfect man. Although he was a great saint, he concealed himself and his saintly miracles from everyone. He lived in towns anonymously, and whenever he became known, he would depart that town. During his travels, he never would stay at dervish lodges or seminaries. He would lodge at inns, and closing his door tightly, he kept nothing inside except for a rush mat to sleep on. He dressed as an ordinary tradesman, never wearing the glamorous clothing of shaykhs. Faridun bin Ahmad Sipehsalar (d. 1284) describes him as one who attained the bliss of closeness to God while still being alive, the sultan of the saints, pole of the gnostics, heir of the prophets, the crown of those loved by God; and he writes that Rumi was an *insan al-kamil*, possessor of clairvoyance, and possessor of spiritual states. Shams was like Moses, in his close connection with God, and like Jesus, in his secluded and solitary lifestyle, may peace be upon them.[22] If he had not possessed those attributes how could he have befriended Rumi? How would those two saints, lovers of God, have united like two seas? In his *Ibtidaname*, Sultan Valad likens the meeting of Shams and Rumi to the meeting of Moses and Khidr. As is commonly known, although Moses was a prophet who attained the station of *kalim Allah* (one who has spoken with God), he admired the lovers of God and sought them out. Similarly, although Rumi had attained the highest levels of madrasa teacher and spiritual guide, he still admired and loved the lovers of God. Contrary to the misconception of some, he was not looking for a spiritual guide. He was reared by the knowledge and gnosis of a peerless father, Sultan al-Ulama, and became a spiritual guide passing through the levels of spiritual journey under the guidance of the greatest spiritual guide, Burhan al-Din Tirmidhi.

Shams also was a great personality. He too loved God like Rumi. He also had traveled to many locations and seen numerous scholars and shaykhs, and in his own words, he was unable to find what he was looking for in any of them. No one really could understand his spiritual state. No one could comprehend the truth of his secrets. Rumi had attained levels of perfection, settled in Konya, and become a teacher and a spiritual guide by the time he reached fifty years of age. He no longer needed to go anywhere or search for anything. Shams, however, had passed sixty years of age and was still wandering around looking for a spiritual guide, yet unable to settle anywhere. In his book *Maqalat*, Shams writes, "I left Tabriz in order to find a spiritual guide, I left the town but I could not find a spiritual guide. The universe is not empty, so there must be a spiritual guide somewhere . . . I had a shaykh in Tabriz called Abu Bakr. He would weave baskets and make his living from this. I benefited from him very much, but I had something that my shaykh did not see in me. In fact, nobody could see it."

We do not know for sure to which Sufi order Shams belonged. According to some scholars, he was devoted to Baba Kamal, one of the deputies of the great saint Najm al-Din Kubra, Sultan al-Ulama's spiritual guide who was martyred while fighting against the Mongols. Others say he was from the Ahbariyya branch of the Khalwati chain. However, as mentioned above, Shams himself states that he was the dervish of Shaykh Abu Bakr of Tabriz. In fact, Shams was not a dervish who would stick to the basket-maker Abu Bakr who could not see what was in him and boasted that he was a shaykh. He confesses, "I left him and he was very sorry." Who knows, he might have confronted his shaykh with his mistakes and left. No one knows for sure. Shams could not see anything in the shaykh who could not see anything in him.

In those days, Shams was unable to find what he was looking for in the famous shaykhs whom he met in different places, got to know, and whose lectures he attended. He found himself unable to devote himself to them. He was looking for a perfect spiritual guide. In his mind, there was the image of a pure, untarnished shaykh living like a Companion of the Prophet, completely on the Muhammadi path. However, since he saw flaws in the persons he met who claimed to be shaykhs, he could not devote himself to them. He was saddened whenever he could not find the Islamic way of life in those whom everybody respected greatly and whose hands everybody kissed. He said in his *Maqalat*, "It is only yesterday that he left his mother's womb and today he is claiming, 'I am the Truth.' How can someone born from such and such a woman say he is the Truth. Most of these shaykhs are the bandits of Muhammad's religion. They block people's ways."[23] Shams always stayed away from the shaykhs who were after ostentation and reputation, and until he met Rumi he did not devote himself to any guide. When Shams-i Tabriz met Rumi, when he saw the truth in him, he said, "I found what I was looking for in my Hudavendigar, Rumi," and he stayed in Konya.

Aflaki relates that prior to their meeting in Konya, Rumi and Shams met in Damascus. He writes that one day while Rumi was in the market place someone dressed entirely in black with a conical hat kissed Rumi's hand and told him, "O judge of the realm of meanings! Find me! Understand me!" and then vanished into the crowd. He narrates that this man was Shams. Shams arrived in Konya on Saturday morning October 23, 1244. As was his habit, he directly went to an inn. It is said that he went to the Pirinçciler (rice farmers) or Şekerciler (sugar farmers) inn and rented a room. It is also narrated that for the public to think of him as a rich tradesmen, he put an expensive lock on his door worth three dinars and tied the key to an end of his turban and let it hang from his shoulder. However, there was nothing in Shams' room other than an old rush mat, a broken jug, and a sun-dried brick he used as a pillow. There is no record of how long after he came to Konya he met Rumi.

The accounts of his meeting with Rumi are numerous. According to Aflaki's account, one day Rumi came out of the Iplikçi madrasa accompanied by his students and disciples and riding his donkey. At that moment Shams al-Din of Tabriz ran into Rumi. Holding on to the reigns of the donkey, he stated the above. However, Sipehsalar narrates the meeting of Rumi and Shams like this: Shams al-Din of Tabriz arrived in Konya at night. He went to the Pirinçciler inn. There was a decorated sofa in front of the inn gate. Usually notable people would sit on that sofa. Shams sat on that sofa in the morning. It became clear to Rumi that Shams had arrived through the holy light of sainthood. Coming out of their home of happiness, he went in that direction. On the way, people tried to approach him and to show their respect for him. At that moment Rumi's glance sud-

denly lighted on Shams. He understood that the holy person foretold to him in his dream was this person. He said nothing.

Mevlana Hudavendigar came and sat on the other sofa facing
Shams. For a while they kept quiet. Then they began to converse:

> Shams: Is Prophet Muhammad greater, or Bayazid Bistami?
> Rumi: What kind of a question is this? Of course, Prophet
> Muhammad is greater.
> Shams: Yes, but Muhammad says, "Sometimes my heart gets
> veiled. Therefore, seventy times I seek refuge in my Lord and
> ask for forgiveness," while Bayazid says, "I dissociate myself
> from all imperfect attributes. How great an event is my cre-
> ation and appearance" and "there exists nothing under the robe
> I wear other than God." And he sees himself as superior. What
> do you think in this matter? What do you say?
> Rumi: Muhammad was advancing seventy levels every day. And
> every time he advanced to a higher level he was ashamed of his
> state in the lower level and asked for forgiveness. On the other
> hand, Bayazid was amazed by the greatness of the first level he
> reached. He lost himself and said these words.

After this conversation, Rumi and Shams both left the sofas
they were sitting on and shook each other's hands and hugged each
other. Then in Jalal al-Din Zarqubi's small room, they held conversations for six months.[24] In *Ibtidaname*, Sultan Valad expresses their
closeness and admiration: "When Rumi saw Shams' face, the secrets
opened up for him. He saw unseen things. He heard things that he
never heard from anyone. It was almost as if Rumi's shadow disappeared in Shams' holy light."

In this closeness, in this true friendship, in this divine love, one
cannot claim superiority or emphasize a difference by saying who
became whose spiritual guide, or who became whose disciple. This
couplet of Amir Khusrau Dahlavi describes the situation of the two
lovers of God: "I became you and you became I. I became the flesh
and you became the soul. After this nobody can claim I am separate and you are separate." The fact that these two great saints met,
loved each other as true friends of God, and continuously spent

time together was not well received by those around them. Rumi's students, disciples, notable imams, and religious men, even members of his own family hated Shams because they could not see and sense the truth, love, and power of faith in Shams who had such an influence on Rumi.

Rumi's wife Karra Khatun related that before Shams arrived, Rumi would read his father Baha al-Din Valad's book *Ma'arif* under a tall candle till the dusk. Shams not only kept him from reading his father's book, but he also did not let him read the *Collected Poems of al-Mutanabbi* that Rumi loved very much or any other book. This was because he gave importance to the knowledge of heart, Divine Inspiration, and Divine Attraction but not to the knowledge that was going to be forgotten, that was going to be a burden to the human being, and that was going to inflate one's ego. The knowledge of heart is not learned from books. He was convinced that even if a man lives six thousand years, even if he were given six times Noah's lifetime, what is obtained by struggling for thousands of years would not equal Divine Inspiration gained through being united with God for one moment. Shams took conversation and God's Attraction as fundamental. He held that knowledge was not an end in itself but a means of letting us know of our inadequacy in realizing the truth and understanding God. Therefore, by separating Rumi from the things he loved very much, Shams was trying to bring Rumi even closer to God, to whom Rumi was already close.

He distracted Rumi, who had been spending most of his time reading books in the meeting hall of the madrasa, from full devotion to those books. He also did not allow everyone to see him. Sitting at the gate of the seminary, he asked of those who came to see Rumi, "What did you bring as a gift of pleading and gratefulness? Show me that and I shall show you Rumi." One day when someone got angry with this strange man and asked, "What did you bring so that we also need to bring something?", Shams replied, "I brought myself, I sacrificed my head for his sake."

In *Ibtidaname*, Sultan Valad describes how close Shams was to Rumi and how much he influenced him: "When the public saw this attachment, this loyalty, this rapture, and this love, they were envious and began criticizing. Shaykhs and other important people openly started rumors saying, "What kind of a man is this that he changed Rumi so much? While none of us see goodness in Shams, why does Rumi view him as a superior man and honor him? He has neither spiritual state nor knowledge. Is it possible that we might call him a man of the Divine Glance and conclude that the eye of his heart is open?" When Shams saw that things were getting out of control and everyone was turning against him, he suddenly vanished one day. After fifteen months and twenty days, Shams left Konya on February 15, 1246.

In *Ibtidaname*, Sultan Valad writes that Rumi was very sad about Shams' departure and would not even look into the faces of those who had caused him to leave. He also reports that these people regretted what they had done, and Rumi forgave them.[25] While Sultan Valad writes that Shams went directly to Damascus, Sipehsalar relates that it was not known where Shams went first. After some time, Shams sent a letter to Rumi from Damascus, and in this way it became clear that Shams had gone to Damascus.

When Shams wrote a letter to Rumi from Damascus, Rumi replied. In those days since there was no postal service as there is today, letters were carried by special messengers, and it took a long time. In Aflaki's *Manaqib al-Arifin*, there are four letters to Shams written by Rumi in verse. From these poetic letters, I have taken some couplets as an example of their conversation:

> O light of my heart, come! O the aim of my struggles, come! You know that our lives are in your hands. Don't make the sweet life difficult. Don't torment your slaves, come! O love, O beloved, overcome the obstacles, leave stubbornness and come!
>
> O graceful person of the world! I send my greetings to you. Know that my health and illness are in your discretion. Even if

I am not physically with you and serving you, my spirit and
heart are most surely with you.

May the life of our honorable master be long. May God be
his protector and cherisher. May there be nobody deprived of
love and with frozen hearts in his joyful and warm assembly full
of sweetness and beautiful conversation.

After receiving a letter from Shams, Rumi called Sultan Valad.
He gave him some money and said, "You go as a messenger. Spread
this money under his feet. And ask him for a favor on my behalf.
Those who treated him badly are remorseful. Let him do us a kindness and come back." Sultan Valad eagerly accepted this mission. He
also loved Shams very much. He had seen the greatness of Shams
and understood his truth. In describing his travel to Damascus, Sultan
Valad relates, "I ran without getting tired, I crossed the mountains
without regarding them as anything more than a piece of hay. The
thorns of the way appeared to me as roses."

Aflaki writes that Sultan Valad went with twenty people. They
found Shams in Damascus. Sultan Valad did as he was told. He
spread the money at Shams' feet. When Shams saw the money, he
smiled and replied, "Why does Rumi of Muhammadi character busy
us with money? His request is more than enough." He then accepted the request to return to Konya. Sultan Valad and his friends stayed
a few days in Damascus. Whirling ceremonies were performed. They
rested and then set out for Konya with Shams.

When the caravan from Damascus approached Konya, Sultan
Valad sent a bearer of good news to his father. When Rumi received
the good news, he came out of the city to welcome them with dervishes, important officials, and Rumi's employees. On May 8, 1247 Shams
honored Konya once more with his arrival. When Shams saw Rumi,
he got off his horse and they hugged each other. Two seas of the
realm of meaning reunited once more.

When Shams returned to Konya, his adversaries were initially
remorseful for what they had done. Like Rumi, Shams forgave them
all because both Rumi and Shams were of Muhammadi character. It

is well known that the Prophet forgave those who stoned him in Ta'if and wounded him on his feet. Rumi had already forgiven those who worked against Shams and spread rumors about him before Shams returned. Shams followed the same path. He was lenient with those who mistreated him and forgave their misdeeds. Whirling ceremonies began to be arranged, and both Rumi and Shams received invitations from various people. But the days that passed in joy and enthusiasm with whirling ceremonies did not last long. Grudge and hate surfaced once more. Rumors against Shams flared up again. Lies and instigations soon followed and spun out of control. This time the instigations were more intense. In Sultan Valad's account, Shams, who could not stand insults and threats, said, "This time when I leave, I will leave in such a way that nobody will find my trace. I will vanish such that time will pass and even the dust of my trace will not be found. They will say, 'Definitely an enemy of his must have killed him.'" Shams had left Damascus with Sultan Valad and his friends with such hopes and such great longing, crossing mountains and rivers. Now these immature people who envied him, his devotion to Rumi, and Rumi's respect and closeness to him were harassing him continually. Since Shams was a very good person, he buried the attacks and gossip of the ill-intentioned who envied him and did not let Rumi know. Shams' wife Kimia,[26] whom he loved very much, died shortly after their wedding. No matter how great a person, Shams was also human, after all. The death of his wife on the one hand and the gossip on the other had worn him out. He had no power to stand against the insults and threats. His attachment to Rumi and the truth he saw in him was keeping him alive. On a Thursday in December 1247, Shams disappeared.

According to Sipehsalar, on the morning that Shams disappeared, Rumi went to the madrasa; unable to find him, he became very sad. He immediately went to the room where Sultan Valad was sleeping and called out to him, "Baha al-Din, why are you still sleeping? Get up and look for your shaykh. Our spirits once more are deprived of his pleasant smell."[27] However, Aflaki relates two different accounts about Shams' disappearance. According to the account from Sultan Valad, when Shams and Rumi were sitting together, someone from outside called Shams. Shams told Rumi: "They are calling me to death." After a short silence Rumi recited the following Qur'anic verse: "Know that creation and command is His. How great is the Lord of the Worlds."[28] Upon hearing this Shams went outside; seven people waiting for him in hiding jumped on him and martyred him with knives. Shams screamed and all of them fainted. When Rumi heard Shams' cry he said, "God does as He wills and judges what He wills." When Shams' attackers came to themselves, they saw a few blood drops on the ground but Shams was gone.

Aflaki's second account is as follows: Shams was martyred and his body thrown into a well. One day Shams entered the dream of Sultan Valad and showed him the well in which his body had been thrown. He then went with a few friends and removed the body from that well and buried it near Rumi's madrasa next to Amir Badr al-Din Gowhartash, who had built it.

In the light of these accounts decorated with fantasies, we must wonder if Shams disappeared as he had said: "I will leave in such a way that nobody will find me." Did he go on a journey with no return, or was he martyred? Only God knows the truth. When we consider Aflaki's accounts, we can draw this conclusion from these accounts: When Shams was with Rumi, he was called outside, but he never returned and was never seen afterward. Did those who called him kidnap him? Did they kill him? Did they help him go somewhere outside Konya? Did Shams go to Damascus where he had gone before? The answers are not known for certain. The only thing to know is that Rumi did not know anything about Shams being martyred. Did they keep such a tragedy secret from Rumi? Did such a tragedy occur at all? How can truth be kept secret from a great saint? Just as he had noticed the first arrival of Shams in Konya by the holy light of sainthood, as Sipehsalar writes, just as he came to the Pirinçciler Inn where Shams lodged and found him, he would have known that Shams had been martyred and would not have gone twice to Damascus in search of him. As Abdulbaki Gölpınarlı (d. 1982) writes, "The Qur'anic verse recited by Rumi, Shams' cry, the fainting of the assassins, and the few drops of blood on the ground are epic components such that mystical thinking was involved in this event."[29]

RUMI AFTER THE DISAPPEARANCE OF SHAMS

Sultan Valad describes Rumi's state after Shams' disappearance as follows: "After his departure, Rumi almost lost his mind. The shaykh who issued religious rulings became an ardent poet of love. He was an ascetic and became a bartender, but not a bartender that drinks and sells the wine made of grapes. The spirit that belongs to the holy light does not drink anything but the wine of light."[30] Rumi whirled day and night, and his crying was heard by all, young and old. Whatever gold and silver he received, he would give to the musicians; he gave everything to charity. On those who claimed to have seen Shams, he would bestow his garment if he did not have money. As Sultan Valad writes in his *Ma'arif*, "Someone told Rumi that he saw Shams ad-Din. Rumi gave him the garment he was wearing. They said to Rumi, 'This man is lying. The news he gave has no substance. Why did you give your garment to him?' Rumi said, 'Whatever I gave him was indeed only for this lie. If what he told had been the truth, I would have given my life.'"[31]

In *Ibtidaname*, Sultan Valad writes that Rumi went to Damascus to look for Shams, and in Damascus many people became his disciples. The people of Damascus had not seen such love since Adam, and they admired Shams as a great saint since such a unique person as Rumi was looking for him. Sultan Valad goes on to say, "Rumi could not find Shams in Damascus, but he saw that Shams' truth and secret rose like the moon in his existence and said, 'Physically we are far away from each other, but beyond soul and body we are one light. See him or see me, O seeker, I am he and he is me.'" In *Ibtidaname*, Sultan Valad writes about the oneness of Rumi and

Shams in spirit: "Shams of Tabriz and my father—may God bless the secrets of both— were among the elite of the most beloved servants of God. They were one person, one holy light. Separate in appearance but one in truth." He relates that after a few years, Rumi went to Damascus for a second time with his disciples. He stayed there for months. The date of Rumi's first as well as second Damascus trips are not known. Sultan Valad says that his father took his first trip to Damascus a few days after Shams' disappearance but fails to report how long he stayed in Damascus on his first trip. His second trip was made a few years later.

Rumi gave up hope after he failed to find Shams in spite of all of his searching. He had also heard the rumors about his murder. Now he was also aware that his son Ala al-Din Chelebi was involved in this. He found consolation in expressing his feeling through poetry filled with love and longing. I will share one from among many of these poems of longing:

> O Friend of Heart, what a pity, you left us with sorrows and longing, and went away.
>
> I know you didn't want to leave us. You complained and lamented. But this was not good. You obeyed the unchangeable judgment and walked away and left.
>
> You ran in all directions. You sought remedies (to change the situation and) to stay with us, you made up excuses. But you couldn't find a remedy and you went without having a remedy.
>
> What happened to your lap full of roses, to the luminous face like the moon? How did it happen that you went under the soil lowly and in shame?
>
> How did you leave the assemblies of friends and the ranks of friends that were with you all the time and go under the ground among ants and snakes?
>
> What happened to those meaningful words and beautiful speeches? What happened to the mind that was familiar with divine secrets?
>
> What happened to those hands that were holding our hands? What happened to those feet that walked to the gardens of Meram, to the rose gardens?

You were graceful and gracious; you knew how to win people's hearts and how to love people. Now you have gone to the
soil which doesn't like people and swallows them.

What happened? What kind of an idea came to your mind so
that you would take a curved and difficult road?

When you set off on that road crying, the heavens, too, started shedding tears and the moon scratched its face.

My heart has been filled with pain. What do I know? What
should I ask? You tell me, did you go awake?

Now that you have left us, have you chosen the company of
lovers of God and saints? Or have you been deprived of love?
Or did you go in denial?

What happened to those sweet answers you gave to the questions you were asked? Now you have stopped talking and given
up on speaking.

What kind of a fire is this? What kind of a longing is this?
Like a guest, you never let anybody know and went away.

Where did you go? Even the dust of your way cannot be
found. The road that you took this time is indeed a road full of
blood.[32]

Of these two great saints, who saw the truth in each other,
admired each other, which one was superior?

It is a mistake to compare saints who have effaced their selves
in divine love. These holy personalities who are cleansed from all
human contamination, released from physical desires, blessed with
the manifestation of God, submerged in the ocean of Unity, and
self-effaced cannot be superior to one another. Is it not the same
sunshine that is reflected by many mirrors that are free from dust
and dirt? Can these be distinguished from one another?

When Rumi was looking for Shams in Damascus with his heart
burning with the fire of longing, the gnostics of Damascus were fascinated by Rumi's knowledge, gnosis, and love. Those whose eyes
were dazzled by Rumi's holy light were surprised to see a spiritual
guide looking for a spiritual guide. Just as Rumi was looking for
Shams, Shams had been looking for Rumi. Shams had not been able
to find what he was looking for in the famous shaykhs and spiritu-

al guides in the towns he had visited, but when he found Rumi, he said, "Ever since I left my home town I have not seen any shaykh other than Rumi. I found what I was looking for in Rumi." What had these two seen in each other? What had they found? They became mirrors for each other. They transcended the levels of shaykh, spiritual guide, deputy, and disciple and saw what was inside them. Therefore, there is no use in considering either of them the spiritual guide of the other. Why should we keep ourselves busy with these thoughts? Why should we say that there is a difference between them? We should know that both of them were among the most advanced scholars, gnostics, and spiritual guides of their time. There were many similarities of opinion and understanding between them. It is also a huge mistake to think of Shams only as an unconventional dervish who excited the great scholar Rumi and brought him to spiritual ecstasy and not to see Shams' knowledge and gnosis.

Shams was a great scholar just like Rumi. As can be seen in his *Maqalat*, one clearly notices from his elaborations on issues that he was familiar with *tafsir* (Qur'anic commentary), *hadith* (Prophetic Tradition), poetry, and all sciences of his day. Like Rumi, he also did not like philosophy. According to Shams, it is possible to attain the truth only by adhering to the Prophet's way, refraining from ostentation, becoming a person of spiritual states, practicing what one believes in, and by divine love. Like Rumi, Shams was a lover of the Prophet. Just as Rumi declared, "I am the soil under the feet of Muhammad Mukhtar," Shams also pronounced, "I would not exchange even an issue seeming to be of the least importance from the Sunna for a book like Qushayri's *al-Risalah*[33] or other such important texts. Compared to the Prophetic Traditions, all those books are tasteless and dull."

Rumi and Shams's views were unified in terms of abiding by the Law, advancing religious practice from imitative to a conscious level, and walking on the path of faith and love far from ostentation. There might have been small differences between them in terms of methodology. Rumi was cautious; Shams was ardent and enthusiastic. But if Shams had not come, Rumi would have been a second Sultan al-Ulama. Maybe he would have written tales in the *Mesnevi* similar to those found in *Mantiq al-Tayr* of Farid al-Din 'Attar (d. 1220 A.D.). Ardent love poems would not, however, have been written. The *Divan-i Kabir* would not have come to be. As Abdulbaki Gölpınarlı writes, "If Shams had not come, Rumi would not have become Rumi and would have remained a shaykh from the ranks of many shaykhs, a Sufi among countless Sufis. But it is also a fact that if Rumi had not seen Shams, nobody ever would have heard of Shams. Rumi was already ready for ecstasy. He was like an oil lamp that was cleaned, filled with oil, its wick prepared. For this oil lamp to flare up, a spark was needed. Shams served that very purpose. And then Shams became like a moth to that flame. He gave his life to it and joined the light. Shams was a mirror to Rumi. Rumi saw in him the truth encompassing the whole universe and himself. And he fell in love with himself and praised himself.

> "Shams of Tabriz is just a pretext.
> We are the one praised in beauty.
> We are the one praised in grace.
> But to conceal this truth from the public, he said:
> 'He is the graceful King and we are the poor.'"

If people were able to see what was in themselves and the truth in each other like Rumi and Shams, the world would become a paradise. Human beings would live in constant peace, wars would disappear, all the weapons factories would close, and there would be no hunger in Africa or elsewhere. The world would live in comfort. Rumi says, "Our bodies that we see in this world are actually the shadows of our real existence. In fact, we live above these shadows."

In the world we live in today, in the age of the atom, in an age where people are chasing only after materialistic gains, are there no more Rumis or Shams? New saints are not coming from the Khorasan region to Anatolia. They are not coming, but the Islamic countries are not empty. How well spoke Baba Kamal Khojandi: "Do not think that the lovers of God, the saints have all gone and the city of love has become empty. The world is filled with people like Shams of Tabriz, but where are the men like Rumi to see the truth in them?"

Now Rumi gave up hope of finding Shams alive and stopped looking for him. He understood that he would not be able to find Shams in Damascus or elsewhere, but as Sultan Valad put it, he found him in his heart. He had found him but his eyes were still looking for a friend of heart like Shams. Although his family, sons, friends, students, and disciples surrounded Rumi, he felt an emptiness inside, and he felt alone. Surely the greatest friend of humans is God. Doesn't He say, "Wherever you are I am with you"?[34] Rumi expresses this truth as follows: "There is someone hidden here. Don't think that you are alone."

But Rumi was in need of a friend of God, a mirror, and a horizon of spirit like Shams who would share this feeling and let him sense what was within him. Without such a friend, he was unable to find peace. Yahya Kemal expresses this spiritual loneliness in his poem "Horizons":

> Spirit cannot live without horizons
> Spirit searches for a spirit horizon
> Those great prophets whose spiritual horizons were vast
> But they are the exceptions beyond our discussion
> They were very happy in this world
> Living with their disciples and companions
> What horizons and what nice spirits they had, O Lord!

Later on, Rumi would captivate the matter of the mirror of the spirit in a passage of the *Mesnevi*:

> The soul's mirror is naught but the face of the friend, the face of that friend who is of yonder country (the spiritual land).
>
> When your eye became an eye for my heart, my blind heart went and became drowned in vision.
>
> I saw that you are the Universal Mirror unto the everlasting: I saw my own image in your eye.

> I said, "At last I have found myself: in his eyes I have found
> the shining Way."
>   (But) my image gave voice from your eye (and said), "I am
> you and you are I in (perfect) oneness."[35]

After Shams, Rumi's friend of heart and mirror of spirit became
Salah al-Din of Konya. Rumi escaped spiritual loneliness with this
companion and friend of heart. He found peace and tranquility.

SHAYKH SALAH AL-DIN OF KONYA, THE ZARQUBI OR GOLDSMITH

Salah al-Din Faridun was born in a village near Konya. His father's
name was Yagi Hasan. Since their village was at the shore of Lake
Beyşehir, the family made its living by fishing. Salah al-Din had
come to Konya, learned the trade of goldsmithing, opened a shop,
and was making a living there. Salah al-Din who was a religious
and virtuous person had devoted himself to Rumi's father's dear
friend and deputy, Sayyid Burhan al-Din and had advanced consid-
erably on the path of Sufism with his manners, sincerity, and devotion to worship until he reached the position of shaykh by becoming a deputy of Shaykh Sayyid Burhan al-Din. His shaykh used to
love this pure person, this lover of God very much. According to
Aflaki's account, Sayyid Burhan al-Din said this about Salah al-Din
Zarqubi: "I attained two great things from my shaykh, Sultan al-
Ulama. One of them is articulate speech, and the other is beautiful
spiritual states. I gave articulate speech to Mevlana Jalal al-Din because
his spiritual states are very beautiful. I gave my spiritual states to
Shaykh Salah al-Din because he has no spiritual states." As a matter of fact, Salah al-Din was an illiterate but very pious, devout, and
luminous believer. He had given his heart to divine love and attained
many spiritual states.

When his shaykh Sayyid Burhan al-Din went to Kayseri, Salah
al-Din went back to his village, got married there, and had children.
He came to Konya on a Friday to perform his Friday prayer at the

Abu'l-Fazl Mosque. After the prayer, Rumi began to deliver his sermon, speaking very ardently and very beautifully. In that day's sermon Rumi talked about spiritual states, virtues, and the divine love of his shaykh Sayyid Burhan al-Din. As Salah al-Din, the goldsmith, listened carefully to Rumi, suddenly he saw his shaykh Sayyid Burhan al-Din in Rumi's person. It was as if Rumi had gone and Sayyid Burhan al-Din had come in his place, sat down, and was uttering these ardent, beautiful words. Salah al-Din could not control himself; he stood up and started shouting and running toward Rumi. He came under the place where Rumi was preaching and fell at Rumi's feet. This event happened after the passing away of Sayyid Burhan al-Din in 1239, and before Shams' coming to Konya in 1244.

Salah al-Din Zarqubi loved Rumi very much. He had a deep respect for him because both had received blessings from the same shaykh, Burhan al-Din Tirmidhi. Both were in the same Kubrawiyyah order. Both had effaced their selves in God. Rumi also loved Shaykh Salah al-Din very much and used to do favors for him. But since Rumi was occupied with a stronger friend of heart, at first he did not show much interest in him. When he gave up hope of finding Shams, he turned to Salah al-Din with all his heart and attention. He chose him as his deputy and called on his friends and disciples to follow him. Since Rumi never confined himself to the terms and methods of other great Sufis in explaining the truth or in matters like educating the disciples, discipleship, and mastership, he also did not follow a strict set of rules. He said, "I don't know much. I am intoxicated with the glass of divine love." Overwhelmed by divine love and ecstasy, he had no time to concern himself with "this and that."

Rumi did not occupy himself with people who wanted to join his order. After meeting Shams, he gave this duty to a mature shaykh from among his selected friends. When he gave the duty of spiritual leadership to Salah al-Din, he was doing the same thing. In this new friend of heart, the goldsmith shaykh, he saw the divine light of Shams and began viewing him as Shams. Sultan Valad tells us of Rumi's making Salah al-Din his friend of heart and companion as follows: "When he found the holy light and reflection of Shams in Salah al-Din, he said to his friends, 'From now on I have nothing to do with anybody anymore. I do not feel like being a shaykh anymore. From now on your shaykh is Salah al-Din. You all seek his pleasure and follow him.' He called me and said to me, 'Behold Salah al-Din's face; he is Shams himself. Now you follow him, too.'" After writing these accounts in his *Ibtidaname*, Sultan Valad continued, "I accepted my father's order eagerly, and I followed Salah al-Din." After seeing Shams' holy light in this old illiterate goldsmith, Rumi was very much attached to him. As Aflaki writes, Rumi used to say to those who loved him, "Don't talk of Shams in Salah al-Din's presence and don't talk of Salah al-Din in Husam al-Din's presence. There is no difference between them, but this is against good manners. Saints have Divine Jealousy."

Salah al-Din's attachment to Rumi was also infinite. One day he told Rumi: "There were springs of light in me, and I wasn't aware of that. You discovered them and brought them flowing fiercely." As Sipehsalar writes, one day when Rumi was walking in front of Salah al-Din's goldsmith's shop, from his regular and harmonic hammer strokes he became ecstatic and began whirling there. When Salah al-Din saw this he kept on hitting the gold without thinking that the gold under the hammer would be wasted. This encounter that Sipehsalar writes about, Aflaki relates in more detail: When Salah al-Din saw Rumi coming to his shop, he left the work to his apprentices and came out of the shop. When Rumi saw him, he embraced and kissed him and they started whirling together. But the old goldsmith Salah al-Din who was weakened by asceticism noticed that he couldn't whirl with Rumi. He excused himself and Rumi did not insist. Upon returning to his shop, Salah al-Din ordered his helpers to hit the gold not thinking of what was going to happen to the gold. This way Rumi whirled from noon until close to evening, and while whirling he recited an ode beginning with the following couplet:

A treasure of meaning appeared to me in this goldsmith's shop. What a luminous motive, what a pleasant meaning, what beauty, what beauty!

Those who were deprived of divine love, those who could not defeat their corporeal desires with worship and asceticism now envied Salah al-Din, the goldsmith, just as they had envied Shams because after Shams' disappearance, Rumi had selected this goldsmith as his companion and friend of God and asked them to recognize Salah al-Din as shaykh and to obey him. No book other than Sultan Valad's *Ibtidaname* could explain this situation better. Sultan Valad writes that the people of Konya who could not see his faith, divine love, and spiritual superiority decided to get rid of this virtuous goldsmith, Salah al-Din: "They all gathered in one place. They decided to eliminate Salah al-Din. They said, 'Let us prove our valiance. Let him not live.' They vowed this and said, 'Whoever changes his word has no religion.'" One of them left their ranks by deception. He brought the news to Rumi of what had happened and the decision that had been reached. This news reached the ear of Salah al-Din, the light and lamp of the eye of all those who see the path of truth. When he heard this decision, he smiled meaningfully and said, "Those blind, those faithless, those rough people do not know anything of truth that even a piece of hay will not move without God's command. Who can attempt to kill me, shed my blood without God's permission?"

Just as Rumi was very much devoted to this friend of God and mirror of heart, his true disciples and sons also took him as a spiritual father, following him on the path to knowledge of God. As Sipehsalar writes, during a discourse when Rumi pronounced the word "*khom*," which means jug in Persian, as "*khomb*," one of the people present tried to correct Rumi. Rumi said, "Yes, I know that the correct form of this word is '*khom*.' But since Salah al-Din always pronounces this word as '*khomb*,' I also pronounce it like that," silencing that pedantic person.

Although Salah al-Din the goldsmith was an illiterate person who had never attended school, he was a great gnostic and a great saint. In fact, any person whom such a great lover of God as Rumi loves and makes his companion is definitely a great saint and a perfect human being. Every friend to whom he gives a place in his heart is also holy and perfect. To think of them otherwise and seek their mistakes is nothing but sheer blindness and injustice. Unfortunately, the people of Konya did not understand these friends of God. While Shaykh Salah al-Din was illiterate, he had taken blessings from Burhan al-Din Tirmidhi. Shams-i Tabrizi had also loved him. Sometimes one can find people to whom God grants knowledge of the beyond without having to read stacks of books or to study in schools for years. Sometimes knowledge, books, gnosis, and talents can give one arrogance and selfishness. Salah al-Din, the goldsmith, who never studied in a school but enjoyed the company of gnostics, was blessed with God's grace. From his humble shop a spiritual treasure appeared to Rumi, and from his heart that was not kneaded with scholastic knowledge sprang the source of the knowledge of the beyond. With God's help he became the shaykh of shaykhs, as Rumi addresses him in one of his letters: "Salah al-Din, shaykh of shaykhs, sultan of shaykhs, saint of God on earth, God's light among human beings, Sayyid Burhan al-Din's son of spirit and heart, the only deputy of Sayyid, the spirit of gnostics, blessed with the holy light of God, possessor of heart and people of heart, pole of the two worlds, safety of truth and religion."

Shaykh Salah al-Din was a very soft spoken and cautious person. He was devoted whole-heartedly to worship and asceticism and was known as a person who would check and weaken himself. The fact that he received calmly the news that people wanted to kill him and was never afraid or anxious shows how worship and asceticism strengthened his will-power. Sultan Valad describes his caution and talent in guidance as follows: "Rumi's ardor calmed down with him. His guidance was of a different kind. His effect was more than anybody's. What was attained by saints in years was attained by him in a moment, in a breath. He would reveal secrets without tongue or lips. One would benefit from him without hearing a word or a sound as if he was talking to one's heart. His words would travel from heart to heart silently."

When those who could not understand the spiritual greatness and state of Salah al-Din Zarqubi saw the love and respect Rumi showed the goldsmith on every occasion, they were ashamed of the gossip they were spreading and regretted their envy. Furthermore, since these adversaries were not attending the gatherings, they were already in despair. Finally they could no longer bear this burden, and they again reached a unanimous decision. Together they went to Shaykh Salah al-Din and Rumi and expressed their sorrow and regrets. They cried, pleaded, repented, and then they were forgiven. From that point onward, the gossip ceased and unrest ended. Now whirling ceremonies were arranged, and time was spent in love and joy. Around this time Rumi arranged the marriage of his son, Sultan Valad, and Salah al-Din's daughter, Fatima Khatun. On the wedding day, Rumi was very happy. He whirled, reciting this poem:

> May our wedding be blessed in the world. God has arranged this wedding and marriage for us in the most appropriate fashion. The spouses suit each other very well. Because of this wedding, with the favors of our Lord, hearts rejoiced, two souls became a couple, they married.
>
> Sorrows and pain have left the hearts. O beautiful girl who beautifies our city, in the name of God you are going as a beautiful bride. You, too, are about to become a groom to a beautiful lady. How nice is your departure from our village. How nice is your coming to us. How nicely you are flowing and streaming to our river. O our river, O friend looking for us.
>
> Dance in the happiness of that king of the world, that king of ours who increases our livelihoods. O gnostics, O Sufis, whirl.
>
> Some people are enraptured in joy like the sea, some prostrate like the waves. Some fight like swords, drinking the blood of all our limbs. Be quiet, be quiet, because tonight the kitchen of our beautiful and blessed king is opened. How amazing, our Beloved who is as sweet as a dessert is cooking us dessert.

Rumi was very happy to have his son married to the daughter of his companion and deputy, Salah al-Din. Sultan Valad writes that his father and Shaykh Salah al-Din lived in joy and happiness for ten years. The people of Konya benefited from both of them, but after ten years Shaykh Salah al-Din became ill and passed away on December 29, 1258.

Rumi was very much saddened by the physical death of his dear friend. He said farewell at his funeral along with all the notables of Konya. Rumi expressed his pain of separation:

> O Beloved with whose separation the heavens and the earth are crying, my heart is breaking with your departure, the mind and the spirit are crying. There is nobody who could take your place. It is for this reason that this world as well as the other world are mourning for you.
>
> The wings of Gabriel and other angels are blue and all prophets and saints are shedding tears for your passing away. In this mourning I have come to a point where I can't utter any more words. Otherwise I would have shown the world how to cry. I would set an example in crying and wailing.
>
> When you left the house of this world, the roof of happiness collapsed. Even happiness started to cry for those tested with separation and death. O great being in reality, you were hundreds of universes appearing as one person. Last night I saw that this universe and the other universes were crying for you.
>
> When you fell out of sight, the eye followed you and went after you. This way the spirit became without eye and began to spill blood.
>
> If you wanted me to cry, I would pour tears like rain. But it is better for my heart to cry secretly, spilling blood. One should not cry for you, but one should shed sacks of tears over your separation, melt with blood at every moment, wail at every breath. What a pity, what a pity that these eyes are crying for those eyes that were seeing everything clearly with holy light and faith.
>
> O Shah Salah al-Din! O fast flying bird of happiness! You left just as the arrow leaves the bow. Now the bow, too, is crying for you.

> Nobody can cry enough for a superior personality like Salah
> al-Din. Only one who knows how to cry for human beings
> knows what that crying is. How would everybody know that
> crying?[36]

My dear readers, please pay attention to these feelings bursting
with deep meaning, to this pain and this subtlety coming from a
holy heart filled with love and faith. Can you feel the burning in this
sincere wail coming from seven centuries before our time? In this
elegy, under each word, we find Rumi's tears and hear his laments.
When Salah al-Din felt that the time of his passing was nearing, as
his last request, he said, "Don't ever cry for me. That day is my hap-
piest day, because that day I am being reunited with my Beloved.
Carry my coffin in a joyful manner, playing drums, tambourines, and
clapping your hands. Take me to my grave whirling."[37] Therefore,
Rumi says in the above elegy, "If you wanted me to cry, I would
pour tears like rain. But it is better for my heart to cry secretly by
spilling blood." He recited these words and did not cry openly, but
for his dear friend, he made the heavens cry, he made the earth cry,
he made the worlds cry, and he made angels, prophets, and saints cry.

Rumi carried out the last will and testament of his friend of
heart and companion completely. Drums, tambourines, and beautiful voices singing hymns accompanied the funeral procession of
Shaykh Salah al-Din. As the coffin was being carried with great joy,
Rumi whirled with his head uncovered. Shaykh Salah al-Din was
buried next to Sultan al-Ulama. It was the first day of the month of
Muharram of the Hegira year 657, which corresponds to 1258 CE.

That drums were played, hymns sung, and people whirled at a
gnostic shaykh's funeral, one who was very devoted to asceticism,
ate little, slept little, prayed all night until the morning, and who
followed the *sunna* very closely, and of his very own will, once
again surprised the people of Konya. They did not approve of Rumi's
whirling while the coffin was carried. Those who were devoted
excessively to law were very angry and critical about this. Those
who understood Islamic law as more than mere compliance with

its tangible aspects did not think that either Rumi or Shaykh Salah al-Din were deviating from the law even as much as a hair's breadth. They knew that Salah al-Din the goldsmith was very ascetic, taking the utmost care to follow the most subtle aspects of the law. In fact, during a very cold winter in Konya, Salah al-Din's only robe had been washed and spread on the roof to dry. The robe not only failed to dry but it also froze. At that moment, the call to the Friday prayer was made. Without hesitation, his holiness put on the wet robe and went to the Friday prayer. Some people from the congregation who noticed this situation asked him, "O Shaykh, wouldn't you get sick by wearing this robe?" Shaykh Salah al-Din replied to them, "To carry out God's commandment is more important than my getting sick."

Rumi continued to show his devotion to the goldsmith, both during his life and afterward. He not only took care of him but also his family. In fact, Salah al-Din's daughter, Fatima Khatun, learned how to read, write, and recite the Qur'an. When some occasional arguments and quarrels typical of all families occurred between Fatima Khatun and her husband Sultan Valad, Rumi would console Fatima Khatun and tell his son not to hurt his wife and to be nice to her. Rumi also shows his devotion to his second dear friend through his poetry; seventy-one odes in the name of Salah al-Din the goldsmith can be found in the *Divan-i Kabir*. Rumi used to visit Shaykh Salah al-Din every day during his long illness, and he would lift his spirit. Shaykh Salah al-Din had grown tired of this long illness, wanted to reunite with God, and requested Rumi's permission and prayers for his departure. Upon this, Rumi did not go to visit him for the next three days. However, he could not help but write this letter to the beloved Salah al-Din:

> Possessor of heart, possessor of possessors of hearts, blessed and superior man in this world and the Hereafter, Shaykh Salah al-Din, with this letter I declare that I never forgot you and I always remember you. May God give you health and welfare. Because the health and welfare of all believers depend on your health.

> O walking cypress! May the autumn wind not touch you. O
> pupil of the world! May an evil eye not target you. O holy being,
> the spirit of the earth and the heavens! May nothing but the
> mercy and comfort of God reach you.

Please turn your attention to the feelings, love, respect, and
wishes in this letter and prayer for a sick person.

Before ending this section I would like to add this: In his nature,
Shaykh Salah al-Din was a patient and quiet person who appreciated silence rather than talk. Therefore, Rumi found a certain amount
of peace in his spiritual friendship with him. The fireplace of love
that was burning with divine love did not go out but was covered
with ashes. Skin formed over the wound caused by the separation
from Shams. This was a transient state and a temporary calm because
Rumi was by nature not the kind of person to stay in a place or
remain in a state for too long. He was always in need of advancing,
always ascending, always burning, and always being burned in the
love of God. In fact, he separated not from his father, nor from
Sayyid Burhan al-Din, nor from Salah al-Din. For a limited time he
was burnt with their love and took from them what he was to take,
and then finding them in him, his blessed heart, he continued his
journey with them. All of these great personalities remained as a stage
of education, training, manners, morals, love, and faith in Rumi's
life. It was as if God had created all these distinguished people for
Rumi to grow spiritually because if Rumi had not honored these
famous people, he would not be so eminent himself.

Rumi continued to progress on the path of God, the path of
truth, with the beloved that he put in his heart as a servant of the
Qur'an and a lover of Muhammad Mukhtar and he did not remain
in any place. His ultimate purpose was not mortal friends. His aim
was to be with true friends who loved God, in order to attain the
True Friend, Friend of Friends. This great saint whose heart was
filled with the love of friend, love of humanity, and love of God has
been a torch of faith, a torch of love, not only for the faithful in his

day but for all believers and people who love God in the many, many centuries which followed.

HUSAM AL-DIN CHELEBI

After Salah al-Din, the goldsmith, passed away, Husam al-Din Chelebi became the companion and deputy to Rumi. The family of Husam al-Din Chelebi, who is described by Sipehsalar as the person in whom divine light is manifested, teacher of secrets of truth and knowing God, a personality of whom saints on the Muhammadi path are proud, was originally from Urumiyeh, but migrated to and settled in Konya. Husam al-Din Chelebi was born in Konya in 1225. One might think that Husam al-Din was related to Rumi since Rumi's descendents are also called Chelebi. Here "Chelebi" connotes a polite, sophisticated person, and it is a title used by the public for generally loved and respected people. Other than Chelebi, Husam al-Din also had the honorific "Ahi Türkoğlu" (The Son of the Turkish Dynasty). Husam al-Din Chelebi's real name was Husam al-Din Hasan. His father's name was Muhammad, and his grandfather's name was Hasan.

Husam al-Din Chelebi's grandfather was a great saint, Shaykh Taj al-Din Abu al-Wafa, who was Kurdish and died in Baghdad in 1107. Although this great saint was illiterate, he was a gnostic. Some members of the community who only valued educational levels, high positions, wealth, and physical appearances asked him to preach to them in order to embarrass this great saint. Shaykh Abu al-Wafa replied, "God willing, I shall preach tomorrow. Be present." That night he supplicated sincerely to God, performed the ritual prayer, and went to bed. In his dream he saw the Prophet of Islam. The Prophet gave good news to this illiterate Kurdish saint: "God manifested Himself to him through His names of *Alim* (All-Knowing) and *Hakim* (All-Wise)." The next day when he sat on the *kursi*, or chair, to begin his sermon in the mosque, his first sentence was: "I slept as a Kurd at night and rose as an Arab in the morning." He

gave a very beautiful, very scholarly, and gnostic sermon that surprised everybody.

Since Husam al-Din's father was the head of the *ahi* group living in and around Konya, he was called "Ahi Türk," and Husam al-
Din was called as "Ahi Türkoğlu." The institution of *ahis* was a
guild that embraced all small craftsmen and business people. The
way of *ahis* was called *futuwwat* (chivalry). Since Husam al-Din
Chelebi's father was the head of the *ahi* organization in and around
Konya, he was respected widely. All of the *ahis* in Konya were raised
under the supervision of his father and mother and were mentored
by them. Therefore, they were all in the service of Chelebi's father.

When Husam al-Din Chelebi's father passed away, they wanted him to replace his father as leader. But this great man, realizing
that fame, fortune, and high position really did not give anything
to a person, gathered all of his followers and intended to make Rumi
the new leader. He put his head on Rumi's threshold. Husam al-
Din Chelebi asked his men to continue whatever work, craft, or
business they were doing and to bring him his share, and he gave
away all his possessions to Rumi until he no longer possessed anything. His tutor complained to him, "No means of income or wealth
remained." Then he said to sell off everything in his house. A few
days later, his servants came to him and said that there was nothing left in the house except for them. Upon hearing this, Husam
al-Din Chelebi said, "Praise be to God. It became possible for us to
follow the Tradition of our Prophet at least in appearance. For God's
sake and for Rumi's love, I free you all. Go and find a new business."

Rumi, too, was just as attached to this very generous lover of
God who sacrificed his everything for Rumi. When Husam al-Din
Chelebi was not present, it was not possible for Rumi to be joyful
in an assembly. As Aflaki writes in his book *Manaqib al-Arifin*, one
day Muin al-Din Pervane arranged a big whirling ceremony in his
palace. Rumi, great shaykhs, and distinguished scholars were invited. Rumi was quiet in that gathering because Husam al-Din Chelebi
was not present in that congregation. When they realized this, with

Rumi's permission, they invited Husam al-Din. When Chelebi arrived, he stood up and greeted him saying, "Welcome, O my spirit and faith; welcome, O my light and my master; welcome, O the beloved of God and the Prophet." After this, Vizier Muin al-Din Pervane started showing great respect toward Husam al-Din Chelebi.

Whatever Rumi received he would pass it to Husam al-Din Chelebi without even touching a penny of it, and Husam al-Din Chelebi would distribute it to everyone according to how much they deserved. One day Amir Taj al-Din Mu'tazi Khorasani sent Rumi a large sum of money and asked him to hold a feast for dervishes with that money. Whirling ceremonies were to be held, and the dervishes were to pray for him. When Rumi gave all this money to Husam al-Din Chelebi, his son Sultan Valad was uncomfortable and complained, "There is nothing at home. Whatever comes you send it directly to Chelebi. What are we going to do?" Rumi replied, "Baha al-Din, by God, by God, by God, if hundreds of mature ascetics were facing death because of starvation and we had a loaf of bread, we would still send it to Chelebi." Thereby he wanted to remind his son Valad how reliable, how compassionate a person Chelebi was and how much he cared for the poor. One day Rumi saw a man with a basket on his back carrying food to Husam al-Din Chelebi's house. He told the man, "I wish I was in your place and you were in mine." He took off his robe and gave it to the man.

Husam al-Din Chelebi was such a noble-spirited and perfected human being that Rumi had not given love and compliments to anyone as much as he did to Chelebi. He held him in such high esteem that one would think that Husam al-Din Chelebi was Rumi's shaykh. The expressions of praise and love that Rumi uses for Husam al-Din Chelebi in the *Mesnevi* on every occasion are rather surprising. Just as the holy light, the light of love that manifested itself in these two *insan al-kamil* (perfect human beings), captivated them seven centuries ago, that same holy light that transcends centuries illuminates the hearts of poor servants like us who love Rumi and his writings, and it increases our admiration of them. If Rumi had not taken Husam al-Din Chelebi as a friend of God, if he had not seen the truth in him, if he had not been attached to that truth, today humanity would have been without a peerless work like the *Mesnevi*.

It is also true that if Rumi had not existed, neither Shams of Tabriz, nor Salah al-Din, the goldsmith, nor Husam al-Din Chelebi would have been remembered. As is the case in every age, who knows how many more Shams, goldsmiths and Ahi Turks came to this old world, lived, illuminated hearts, and educated disciples. Some of them were mentioned in the books about saints while others were never known, and no books cited them. A Prophetic Tradition to which Rumi refers is very interesting: "There are some saints of God who are concealed. Their hair becomes like felt due to lack of care, their faces dusty. When they want to see a person of high position, they are not allowed in. They are not seen in public, they are not sought after, when they are not present at an assembly, they are not called. When they get sick, nobody asks them how they are. Nobody comes to check on them. When they die, nobody attends their funerals. They are not known on the earth, but in the heavens, they are famous."[38] Similarly Yunus Emre mentioned such saints when he said:

> May they say a stranger has died
> May they hear it after three days
> May they wash (my corpse) with cold water
> Just a homeless wanderer like myself.

The most beautiful memento of Rumi's days of friendship with Husam al-Din Chelebi is without a doubt his work, the honorable *Mesnevi*. If Husam al-Din Chelebi had not been there, this great and peerless Sufi text would not have been written, and the Islamic world would have been deprived of the most read masterpiece after the Qur'an and Prophetic Traditions. People would not have been able to receive spiritual joy and abundant blessings from this divine wonder that has been translated into many languages. The only reason for such a great divine blessing and for the spiritual *Mesnevi* to be presented to the lovers of God is Husam al-Din Chelebi.

It is narrated that Husam al-Din Chelebi saw that Rumi's devotees and lovers of God were reading the *Hadiqa* of Hakim Sanai (d. 1131) and *Mantiq al-Tayr* of Farid al-Din 'Attar (d. 1230), and his heart was not content with that. He was regretful, as he believed that Rumi was reciting many beautiful odes, and his *divan* (collection of poems) was growing every day with new odes, but Rumi had not yet formulated books like those of Sanai and 'Attar that explained the Path, Truth, and intricacies of Sufism. One night Husam al-Din found Rumi alone. Mentioning to him the high number of his odes, he asked him to tell also Sufi tales to guide dervishes like the stories of Sanai and 'Attar. Rumi wanted to let the seekers know the truth through tales that everybody could understand, and so he reached a decision in this matter. Upon these words of Chelebi, he immediately took out a piece of paper from his turban. On this piece of paper, the first eighteen couplets of *Mesnevi* were written. "Chelebi," he said, "if you write it down, I will dictate it." Husam al-Din Chelebi agreed to this joyful suggestion enthusiastically. So the writing of the honorable the *Mesnevi* began. Exactly when did the writing of *Mesnevi* begin? We do not know exactly. However, Rumi continued to write the *Mesnevi* until the end of his life.

After Rumi reached the decision to write the *Mesnevi,* his days and nights were filled with this activity. Especially at night when everyone had gone to sleep, in the silence of the night, Rumi would dictate without taking paper or pen in his hand. And Husam al-Din Chelebi quickly wrote it all down. Around the time the first volume was finished, Husam al-Din Chelebi's wife passed away. Therefore, the second volume could not begin immediately. After two years, Rumi began the second volume, and the process continued in the previous way. Some nights, the writing of the *Mesnevi* continued until the morning. Chelebi kept on writing with joy and enthusiasm, without growing tired or bored. The spiritual joy and excitement Rumi felt during dictation allowed him to forget his tiredness. It was as if God created Husam al-Din Chelebi for the purpose of recording this holy book; he predestined him for this blessed duty. Rumi was also ready for this unique book to be created, recited, and written. No Sufi other than Rumi would have been able to produce such a vast and magnificent work because Rumi was educated by his father and his shaykh Sayyid Burhan al-Din. He had a deep knowledge from the countless books he had read, a strong memory, and a superior talent. He possessed a contemplative nature that was able to recognize subtleties that no one else would notice, and he expressed them in a very pleasant and sweet manner. His keen sense of observation and perception, his deep feeling of sorrow and sensitivity were among the rarest. Beyond all these attributes, he had a great faith and an infinite love. God had filled the heart of his dear saint with knowledge, love, and gnosis.

Beginning with the Prophet of Islam, he loved all saints and all human beings. He had an attitude of infinite lenience and tolerance that saw no fault in human beings created by God. Furthermore, for Rumi to become Rumi, God had bestowed on him friends of God and mirrors of heart beginning with Shams. When Rumi was a very ascetic Sufi, Shams of Tabriz removed this dry asceticism from him and threw him in to the realm of divine love and attraction. Salah al-Din, the goldsmith, took him from the world of transience to tranquility with his quiet nature and caution. Husam al-Din Chelebi helped Rumi to become a spiritual sun for all the lovers of God and for all humanity by spreading Rumi's knowledge and gnosis after he had become settled, had matured even more, and had attained perfection.

Husam al-Din Chelebi became Rumi's companion and his deputy five years after Salah al-Din had passed away. But Husam al-Din Chelebi was among the very close friends of Rumi even when Shams of Tabriz was there. I can not help but mention a few compliments that Rumi paid to his last friend of heart and the reason for the materialization of the honorable *Mesnevi* as he was dictating it to Husam al-Din Chelebi. In the second volume, he proclaims, "Husam al-Din, the light of God, once again changed the direction of his reins from the heights of the heavens and started the *Mesnevi* again." In the third volume, he writes, "O Husam al-Din, the light of God. Make this third volume come forth, because it is a Prophetic Tradition to do something three times . . . O Husam al-Din, your power leaks and comes from the power of God." In the fourth volume, Rumi reveals, "O Husam al-Din, the light of God. You are such a man that the *Mesnevi* was enlightened with your light." He also says: "You are the reason for the *Mesnevi's* writing in the beginning. If it increases and lengthens, it is you who is increasing and lengthening it. Now that you will so it means God, too, wills so. God grants the wishes of the pious . . . O Husam al-Din, spread holy light in the fourth volume because the sun rises in the fourth heaven and fills the universe with light."

In the fifth volume, he tells us, "Shah Husam al-Din, light of the stars, wants the fifth volume to begin . . . O light of God! The generous Husam al-Din, you are teacher to the teachers of those who rescue people from blurred vision and bring them to clarity. Had the people not been behind a curtain, were their hearts' eyes open and their understanding not limited, I would have begun to praise you spiritually, and I would open my mouth to utter words other than these words. It is not appropriate to praise you to those in prison. I shall praise you in the assembly of the spirituals (angels) and spread your praises there. It is unnecessary to tell the people of the world about you. I am keeping you secret as the secret of divine love."

In the sixth volume of his *Mesnevi*, Rumi praises his friend of God who was the reason for the *Mesnevi* to be written by calling the *Mesnevi* "Husamname": "O Husam al-Din, the life of hearts! Long have you wanted the sixth volume to be written. *Husamname* is rotating with the attraction of a learned man like you . . . O spiritual man! I am dedicating this sixth and last volume of the *Mesnevi* to you." The above praises and the fact that the *Mesnevi* was delayed for two years after the

completion of the first volume because Chelebi was unable to partici-
pate due to the passing away of his wife show us that if it had not been
for Husam al-Din Chelebi, the *Mesnevi* would never have been written.

RUMI'S MIGRATION TO THE WORLD OF ETERNITY

I could not dare use expressions like "death," "passed away," or
"reunited with God" for Rumi, who attained the secret of the
Prophetic Tradition "Die before you die" and who effaced his self
in God while he was still alive, so I choose to consider Rumi's
departure from this mortal world to the world of eternity as a
migration. Our master, Sultan al-Ashiqin (sultan of the lovers of
God), Hudavendigar's sixty to seventy years of blessed, holy, honorable life had come and gone. The counted breaths determined for
every mortal had almost expired. The honorable *Mesnevi* was complete, and Rumi was tired. The sorrow of his childhood with his
father Sultan al-Ulama, the years of migration in physical and spiritual difficulties, his years of education in Damascus and Aleppo
away from his family, the loss of his mother, his father, and his dearly beloved shaykh Sayyid Burhan al-Din all had an impact on him.
Furthermore, the loss of his friends of heart, Shams and Salah al-
Din, the disrespect he had seen from his son Ala al-Din Chelebi,
the criticism of some, the gossip that reached even his ears, his continuous endeavors, worship, and asceticism had all exhausted Rumi.
He was spending his last moments in continuous reflection. This
great saint was focusing on himself and he was finding the eternal
tranquility and inner peace he searched for in himself.

One day Rumi's wife said, "It is necessary for Hudavendigar to
fill this world with truth and meaning that a precious life of three to
four hundred years be given to him." Upon hearing this, Rumi
replied to his wife, "Why, why, we are neither Pharaoh nor Nimrod.
What do we have to do in this world of soil? How can we have
peace and stability in this mortal world, the world of soil? We are
put in the prison of the world for a few prisoners to be released. It

is hoped that we shall soon go back to the presence of God's dear friend, our Prophet."

> I remained in this prison of the world for the goodness of others. But where is prison? Where am I? What property did I steal that they put me in prison?

Rumi sensed that his precious life was coming to an end, and he recited moving poems about death from time to time, bringing those around him to tears. I could not continue without sharing some of these poems:

> O bird that has flown away from this tight cage of the body! You took all your possessions and ascended to the heights of the heavens.
>
> After this, behold a new and fresh rejuvenation, a new life will come; until when are you going to continue this disorganized life, this miserable life on this earth?
>
> Death in fact is the life of this world. Death that scares us is life itself, in fact. To think the opposite, that is, to consider death annihilation instead of being born to a different world is faithlessness.
>
> If God tears down the house of the body, do not lament, do not complain. Know this well: You are in fact imprisoned in the prison of the body. When death comes and that place collapses you will be free.[39]
>
> O my soul, there is a concealed joy, a hidden happy life beyond this cover of soil. Behind the cover concealing everything are hundreds of beautiful Josephs.
>
> When the material existence, this physical body, goes away, the spirit that is your real being remains. O spirit that is infinite, O body that is mortal!
>
> If you want to know how this happens, look at yourself every night. When you fall asleep your body seems as if dead. But your spirit is stretching its wings over the gardens of paradise.[40]
>
> How could the spirit not soar when it is being said, "O my servant, come!" with a very sweet appeal to the spirit from the Creator of this universe and every being, the Possessor of Majesty and Beauty?

When the sounds of waves reach the ears of a fish separated from the clear sea and fallen on dry land, would the fish not jump immediately back into the sea, its real homeland?

Under the sunlight of eternity that saves his soul from annihilation, how would a Sufi not shiver like an atom and dance?

How unfortunate, how bad, and how astray is the one who cannot find, know, and love the Supreme Being who is so Benevolent, so Beautiful, so Lovely, and so Life-Giving.

O bird of spirit! You have been cleansed from your ambitions and sins. You have been freed from the cage of your lower self (nafs). Your spiritual wings have opened up, come! Fly back to whence you came, fly to your homeland, fly![41]

O those who now are separated from their cages, show your face again, appear and tell where you have been!

The ship of your body is wrecked on that sea. O those who are poured into the sea of death like the fish, even if for one moment, come out of this water, show yourselves.

Or have you been pounded on the container of the days and became salt as pearls that were pounded on? But that salt is the salve to the eye of those seeking the truth.

To see well put that salve on your eyes, put it on. O those who come to this world by being born from the world of spirits! Don't be afraid when death comes! This is not death, it is a second birth, be born, be born to the beyond.[42]

Lovers of God who die being aware of truth melt like sugar in the presence of the Beloved.

Those who drank the Water of Life in the assembly of the Alast,[43] in the world of spirits, die in a different way.

Those who are aware of the beyond, those who gather themselves in the love of God do not die as the rest of the masses.

Lovers of God exceed even angels in clarity and purity. Therefore, dying in other than that rank is far away from them.

Do you think that lions die in front of the door just like dogs?

If the lovers of God die on the path of love they are welcomed by the king of spirits.

Lovers of God who become the spirit of each other and who know they carry the same spirit, the same gift, die with the love of each other.

Lovers fly to the heavens while the unbelievers die in the depths of hell.

When dying, the eyes of the hearts of lovers of God open and they see the unseen world.

Others die blind and deaf with the fear of death.

When the time of death comes those who spent the nights in worship and did not sleep for fear of God die without fear and in comfort.

Those who focus only on material things and concern themselves only with eating and drinking become like oxen and donkeys, and they die in the same way.

Those who do not want to fall from the sight of God while living today and seek that view die joyfully smiling in that view.

The king of spirit takes them to the lap of favor. They do not die in an ordinary and low way.

Those whose character and morals resemble that of Mustafa die like Abu Bakr and Umar.

In fact, death is far away from the lovers of God. They neither die nor annihilate. I am saying these words to describe how it would be if they had died.[44]

Finally, Rumi's tired body fell into the hands of his last illness. Fever never left Rumi. From among his dear friends, doctors Akmal al-Din and Gazanferi were at his bedside all the time. Yet they could never diagnose his illness. His body was burning with fever. He would put his hand in the cup filled with water next to his bed and put some water on his forehead. During the bedridden stage of his illness, earthquakes occurred for seven days and nights. The walls of many houses and gardens collapsed. There was chaos in the world. After the seventh earthquake, the public ran to Rumi and asked him to pray. Rumi smiled and said: "Don't be afraid, the poor soil is hungry. It wants a fat bite. It is necessary to give it to it." And he started saying his last words to those present: "I advise you to fear God in open and secret. I advise you to eat little and sleep little, abstain from sins, continue fasting and praying, refrain from lust, endure and be patient against all discomfort and mistreatment from others, avoid being with ignorant people and those who are preoccupied with satisfying their desires, be in the company of generous and good people because the best of people is one who benefits other people. The best of sayings is the one that is short but to the point." He was preparing for his migration. It was necessary to leave the house and go to the beyond. Rumi was preparing to leave the house of this world.

That day Shaykh Sadr al-Din Konavi came to visit Rumi with his most prominent dervishes. He showed great regard for Rumi. He was very sorry, expressing his wishes, "May God heal him very soon. May this illness be a reason for your level in the hereafter to rise. God willing, you will attain complete health shortly. Rumi is the spirit of the worlds. He deserves to be healthy." Rumi replied, "After this, may God give healing to you. Between the lover and the Beloved there remains only a shirt made of a very thin membrane. Don't you want holy light to be reunited with holy light?" And he began reciting this ode:

> How would you know what kind of a majestic company I have inside me? Don't look at my pale face, I have strong iron feet. I have turned my face completely to the king who created me and sent me to this world. Since He has created me I have thousands of thanks for Him.
>
> I sometimes resemble the sun and sometimes the sea full of pearls. Even if I seem to be a worthless being created of soil from outside, inside I am the most honorable, most noble creature.
>
> In this village of the world, I keep on buzzing like a bee. But don't just heed my buzzing. I have a hive full of honey. How frightening is the water that rotates the water-wheel, but I am the wheel of that water, I keep rotating on that water with pleasant sounds.
>
> All my particles are blooming, why should I perish, why should I decay? The Buraq that is under me has his saddle on and is waiting for me. Why should I be slave to the donkey?
>
> The scorpion didn't bite my foot. Why should I be far away from the moon? I have a strong rod. Why should I not climb out of the well?

To the dove of the spirit I became a dove. O bird of my spirit! Fly! I have hundreds of fortresses that are even stronger than this.

Even if I reach homes and fall on homes, I am the light of the sun of meaning (wisdom). I was born of soil and water. My mother is mud, but I am agate, gold, and ruby.

Whenever you see any pearl, inside that pearl, in its other face seek another pearl. For all the atoms are crying out, "I have hidden treasure inside me."

Every pearl is telling you, "Don't be content with my beauty. The light that is shining on my face is coming from the light burning inside me." I will be quiet, you don't seem to understand the truth. Don't shake your head saying, "I have a spiritual eye that sees and understands." Don't fool yourself

On Saturday, December 16, 1273, Rumi was somewhat better. He spoke to those who came to visit him until the evening. But his every word was like a last testament. Then the night came, and Konya was submerged in the darkness of the night. With Rumi were his friend of heart Husam al-Din Chelebi, his son Sultan Valad, and doctors. In those days, Sultan Valad was weak because of eating and sleeping very little. That night he was also very tired and exhausted. Shortly before morning, Rumi looked into the teary eyes of his son and quietly said, "Baha al-Din, I am fine, you go and sleep a little bit." Sultan Valad could not endure it. Barely holding back his tears he stood up. When he was leaving the room Rumi looked behind him with sorrowing eyes and recited this last ode:

Go put your head on the pillow. Leave me alone. Give up on the afflicted person who walks around at night and burns.

We keep on struggling between the waves of love all night alone till the morning. If you want, you come and forgive us. If you want, you can torment us with your separation.

You run away from me so that you may not have to face the same troubles as I do. You leave the path of troubles and choose the path of salvation. We are crawling and lamenting in the corner of sadness and shedding tears. If you want, come and build a hundred water mills with our tears.

We have a merciless Beloved whose heart is as hard as granite. He kills lovers but nobody can hold Him accountable.

For the king of beauty fulfilling one's agreements is not necessary. O lover whose face turned pale, you be patient and fulfill your agreement.

I have a sickness inside the only cure of which is death. How can I say, "Come and be the cure for this illness"?

Last night in my dream I saw an old man in the neighborhood of love. He waved at me implying, "Come over to our side."

If there is a dragon on the path of truth, there is also a love like emerald. Defeat the dragon with the light emitted from that emerald of love.

It is enough now, don't talk of things anymore, I am not conscious. If you have any talent talk of the history of Abu Ali Sina or mention the advice of Abu al-A'la al-Mu'arri.[45]

Rumi was on his deathbed. He had taken his first breath when he honored this mortal world in Balkh years ago, and now he was going to draw his last breath in Konya. His counted breaths, measured in blessings, love, and faith, were on the brink of being exhausted. He was still fully conscious and had a good memory. Most probably, Husam al-Din Chelebi must have written down on a piece of paper in his hand with the blood of his heart, shedding tears, this last ode that Rumi recited on his death bed. Sipehsalar narrates:

> After this, Rumi's health worsened. All notable people visited him day and night. Doctors Akmal al-Din and Gazanferi were both the best doctors of the time, and they were treating Rumi. Both would hold his blessed pulse, leave the house, refer to medical books, trying to make a diagnosis, and again return to his holy presence, hold his blessed pulse, and analyze. This time the pulse was beating differently. I asked them to see and understand the honorable state of Hadhrat Hudavendigar. They saw that the diagnosis was not possible and understood that the truth of the matter was something else. They understood that Rumi's will was toward another world. Those busy with treatment along with others present became very sad.

They could not help but lament. Everyone was anxious. The
people of Konya had stopped their work, and the people of the
surrounding villages came down to Konya. On Sunday, 17
December 1273, as the sun was setting, Rumi, the sun of the
realm of meanings, also set to the world of eternity. Rumi
closed his eyes to this mortal world in Konya, the city which he
had honored for forty-four years.[46]

That night Rumi's friends performed their final duties. All the
people of Konya, young or old, were present at the funeral. Since
Rumi was a tolerant, peace-loving, great saint who did good and
wished well to everyone, not only Muslims but also Jews and
Christians walked in his procession, shedding tears. Everyone was
crying and swarming in front of the coffin as well as behind. The
main street was completely full. In order to touch the coffin even
once, people flowed from the byways. The officers could barely stop
people with sticks and swords. The streets were so crowded that
the coffin taken out of the house in the morning could not be
brought to the place of prayer until evening. When the coffin was
put on the *musalla* stone, where the funeral prayer is performed,
the announcer Mu'arrif called out to Sadr al-Din Konavi, "O king
of shaykhs! Please come forward; you shall lead the funeral prayer.
That was Rumi's will." Unable to control himself, doctor Akmal al-
Din shouted out, "O Mu'arrif, follow good manners. The king of
shaykhs is but Rumi."

Sadr al-Din left the crowd and came in front of the coffin to
lead the prayers. As soon as he began the prayer with the phrase
Allahu Akbar, he became distraught, fainted in tears, and fell to the
ground. Qadi Siraj al-Din came forward and led the prayer. According
to Sipehsalar's account, when Shaykh Sadr al-Din was asked why
he fainted and fell, he responded by saying, "When I came in front
of the coffin to lead the prayer, I saw that the angels formed a line
in front of the coffin. From the awe of the moment, I lost my consciousness."[47]

After the prayers, the coffin was again carried above heads and buried in the place prepared in front of the graves of Rumi's father, Sultan al-Ulama, and Salah al-Din Zarqubi. The sun had begun to set. It was a sad evening in Konya. Rumi's material being had vanished from sight, but his spiritual being was present in hearts, and it was to remain there. Understanding this truth very well, Rumi said, "After our passing away, don't look for our grave on the face of the earth. Our grave is in the hearts of the gnostics."

Rumi's blessed corpse was buried next to the grave of his father, Sultan al-Ulama. But he is alive as Sultan al-Arifin (sultan of gnostics) and Sultan al-Ashiqin (sultan of lovers of God) in every home, in every assembly, in everyone's heart. Rumi had become hidden from the eyes and settled in the hearts. Everyone, rich or poor, arranged whirling ceremonies according to their means. One night, in the palace of Vizier Muin al-Din Pervane, the sultan of poets and literary men Badr al-Din Balkhi began to whirl. As he was whirling, he felt the presence of Rumi so strongly in his heart that he could not hold back his tears. Crying and whirling, he recited this quatrain:

> O our soul, O our sultan! There remained no eye that doesn't
> cry with your sorrow.
> There remained no collar that was not torn with your mourning.
> I swear by your luminous face that on the surface of the earth,
> No one better that you went under the soil.

Konya mourned for forty days. For forty days, there were visitors at Rumi's grave. It is amazing that even today people visit Rumi even though his grave has been converted into a museum and hence an entrance fee is charged. Not only Muslims, but also people of all creeds visit Rumi every day. One day Qadi Siraj al-Din came to visit Rumi's grave. He recited this quatrain standing next to the grave:

> O dear Rumi! The day when the thorn of death penetrated
> your foot,

I wish the heavens had hit my head with the sword of death so
that I didn't see the world without you.
Today I am here in front of your blessed soil. This is me, isn't it?
What a pity, what a pity. Soil to my head![48]

Again, in those days a dervish recited these lines on the death
of Rumi, causing those around him to weep:

O soil, because of the sorrow of my heart I cannot tell what
kind of a pearl today death has given to you and what kind of
a pearl you are hiding.
The trap that has been everyone's heart is trapped today.
The dear being who used to attract everyone's sympathy and
admiration is now asleep on your lap.

As Sipehsalar writes, after Rumi migrated from this mortal
world, wherever there is someone with a heart that is wounded,
burning, and sad, he will be shedding tears and reciting couplets
like these:

That sun of the hearts has set and hidden in the soil. Why
shouldn't I spill soil on my head all the time?
That bird of the spring of truth has flown from the mortal
plains. Why shouldn't I cry and lament like the clouds of spring?
The light that illuminated the universe burned out, melted, and
went out.
Why shouldn't my day turn into night suddenly?

Also in those days another event occurred that saddened Rumi's
family and friends and made them mourn a little more. Rumi's cat
did not eat or drink anything after his passing away and survived
for only seven days. Rumi's daughter Malika Khatun wrapped the
cat in cloth and buried it somewhere around the shrine shedding
tears. She cooked a dessert and distributed it to those who loved
Rumi. As Aflaki writes, shortly before Rumi's passing away, this cat
came to Rumi and mewed sadly. Rumi smiled and asked those
around him, "Do you know what this cat said?" They said, "No."

Rumi said, "Soon you will go to the heavens, to your homeland with safety. What will I do without you?"

Since Rumi was a mature saint completely on the Muhammadi path, he did not like ostentation and did not approve of magnificent shrines built over graves. The capital of the Seljuk Empire, Konya, has accepted many saints. But today when one talks of shrines in Konya, the first one that comes to mind is Rumi's shrine under a big green dome. Under this dome lie not only Rumi but also his father Sultan al-Ulama, his sons, his friends like Salah al-Din Zarqubi and Husam al-Din Chelebi, his grandchildren, and others among Rumi's relatives—more than fifty people. A few months after Rumi migrated to the world of eternity, Amir Alam al-Din Kayseri, a prominent official in Konya, began, with the approval of Sultan Valad, the construction of the shrine that fascinates visitors with its material and spiritual magnificence. The shrine was constructed under the supervision of an architect, Badr al-Din of Tabriz, with the monetary and moral support of Gurcu Khatun, the daughter of Ala al-Din Khosrau II and wife of Muin al-Din Pervane. Another architect, Abd al-Wahid, built the magnificent sarcophagus of walnut wood that is 2.65 meters in height and is considered one of the masterpieces of Seljuk wood carving. That sarcophagus was originally on Rumi's grave, but later it was transferred onto the grave of his father, Sultan al-Ulama, by order of Süleyman the Magnificent. A marble sarcophagus was built on the graves of Rumi and Sultan Valad. Although this master piece sarcophagus of wood covered with a golden-lace cloth originally was made for Rumi, why did Süleyman the Magnificent later replace it with a marble one? Süleyman the Magnificent, may his resting place be paradise,[49] was an admirer of Rumi like his father Sultan Yavuz Selim. He was a poet himself and lover of Rumi's poetry. With the intention of doing a service to the saint whom he loved, he had the sarcophagus of walnut wood removed and replaced with a marble sarcophagus made by the most famous craftsmen of his time. In this a manifestation of Rumi's spiritual power can also be seen.

Rumi was a saint who did not like to show off. He thought that the high and magnificent sarcophagus that was put on his grave would suit better the grave of his father, Sultan al-Ulama. The Sultan of the World, Süleyman the Magnificient, carried out Rumi's wish without knowing it. The sarcophagus seems to be standing up when one enters the shrine, and the public that observed it believed that Rumi's father had stood up to show respect for his son. In fact, all those buried there stood up when Rumi arrived.

CHAPTER II

Rumi's Personality and Views

A Peculiarity about Rumi's Life

The life of the great saint Rumi, who honored this mortal world in Balkh and in Konya migrated to the other world after exhausting his counted breaths, was very different from the lives of other great saints. Rumi's life was spent away from his homeland, both his real homeland, the world of eternity, as well as his worldly homeland. After leaving beautiful Balkh, the city of his childhood, Rumi traveled from land to land and decided to settle in Konya where he completed his life. Rumi's life does not resemble the lives of other great men. In my possession, I have many books about Rumi's life written in many different languages. Below I will mention the names of the authors to whose works I will refer. However, I could not see Rumi's name directly in any of these books. In these books, there are Rumi's father Sultan al-Ulama, his spiritual guide Sayyid Burhan al-Din Tirmidhi, Shams al-Din of Tabriz, Salah al-Din, the goldsmith, Husam al-Din Chelebi, but there is no Rumi, the sultan of our hearts.

My respected readers, pick a book from your library about the life of any great personality regardless of his or her area, someone who left a pleasant memory behind, and start flipping through pages. You will see that the person's life, what he went through, what he did, and the accomplishments he left behind from his birth to his death are all in that book. Yet in the books about Rumi, there is no Rumi. So, where is Rumi? In fact, Rumi concealed his life in his loved ones and their lives. Just as there is no poet called Jalal al-Din Rumi in the *Divan-i Kabir*, which contains thousands of laconic and meaningful poems that no other poet could write, and just as he concealed his name in the *Mesnevi Sharif*, which is actually a form of poetry honored by Rumi's use of this form, and just as *Husam-name* (the book of Husam) was not called *Jalalname* (the book of Jalal), he gave his life to his loved ones.

RUMI'S INNER AND OUTER CHARACTERISTICS

One can find plenty of images, portraits, and miniatures of Rumi. There is even mention of painters who painted pictures of Rumi in those days. There are also others like Aflaki who describe his physical characteristics. For example, someone told Muin al-Din Pervane that Rumi's face was pale due to continuous fasting while Sultan Valad had pink cheeks. Can we imagine Rumi's physical appearance based on these accounts and paintings?

Rumi had a thin and slender body and pale skin. It has been told that one day he went to a Turkish bath. When he looked at himself in the mirror, he noticed that he was very thin. He pitied himself and said, "In my whole life I was never ashamed of anybody; however, today after I saw my thin body in the mirror, I am ashamed of myself." Although Rumi had pale skin, he was very benevolent-looking and awe-inspiring. The eyes of the holy saint were very attractive. They were very sharp and filled with exuberance. The glances of his luminous eyes were so powerful that whenever somebody, unaware of the power of them, would look directly at Rumi's luminous eyes, he would come under their influence and would have to divert his glance away from Rumi.

All these accounts and descriptions are related to Rumi's physical characteristics. But what were his inner characteristics? In the *Mesnevi*, he says:

> How, I wonder, shall I behold my own face, so as to see what complexion I have and whether I am like day or like night?
> For a long while I was seeking the image of my soul, (but) my image was not displayed (reflected) by anyone.

"After all," I said, "what is a mirror for? That everyone may know what and who he is."

The mirror of iron is (only) for husks (external forms); the mirror that shows the aspect of the heart is of great price.

The soul's mirror is naught but the face of the friend, the face of that friend who is of yonder country (the spiritual land).[1]

Where can the Beloved that can reflect Rumi's inner world and character be found? Who can depict the inner characteristics of Sultan al-Ulama's son? How can Sultan al-Ashiqin, the King of Lovers, be described?

Nobody can completely understand or describe this great saint who was nourished with the wisdom, manners, and character of his father, the King of Scholars, and who was burned and melted in the pot of Divine Love. He was a superior being who was cleansed of grudge, hatred, evil, selfishness, and ostentation and of all human weaknesses through the experience of Divine Love. He was a man of goodness and perfection and a man of love and gnosis. When he dove into the ocean of love, he was freed from all contradicting views. He was detached from good and evil. In the *Mesnevi*, he says, "Since colorlessness (pure Unity) became the captive of color (manifestation in the phenomenal world), Moses came into peace with the Pharaoh."[2] Fluctuation, waves, foam, and the colors of blue and green all occur on the surface of the ocean, but in the depths of the ocean, there remains neither wave nor color.

This is why Rumi looked at all nations and sects from the same perspective. His approach to everyone and everything was from this point of view. He treated everybody in the same way. He looked at everyone with the same eye. In his view, Muslims, Christians, Jews, and fire-worshippers were all the same. Therefore, he reminded people that it was essential not to look down on non-Muslims and to respect others' religions and beliefs. In Islamic countries, it is common to see churches and synagogues next to mosques. Muslims respect all religions. This view of Rumi's, which is completely Islamic, should not be misunderstood. The Prophet of Islam is the Prophet of the Latter Day, and there came no prophet after him. Rumi's view of all religions as one should not bring to mind the thought that he saw Islam as the same as other religions. In terms of being a religion, all religions are equal. They differ in the practices they prescribe; however, their essence is the same.

Rumi regarded all religions, sects, and nations as waves of the ocean of Unity, as God sees all prophets as one, as stated in the Qur'an: ". . . We make no distinction between one or another of His messengers."[3]   In the same chapter He states that He sees some of the prophets as superior to others: "Those messengers we endowed with gifts and made superior some above others."[4] This way while all religions and sects are one, they have differed in the practices they brought. Rumi touches this issue in another part of the *Mesnevi* when he says, "In this world, there are stairs that stretch to the heavens step by step. For every group there is a separate stair. For every walk (of life) there is a different sky to which to ascend. Each of them is unaware of the others. The destination is an infinite land. It has neither a beginning nor an end."[5] These couplets illustrate this beautiful Prophetic Tradition: "The paths that lead to God are as many as the souls of the creatures." The way to see everyone and everything as one (*wahdat al-wujud*) and leniency were at their peak in Rumi. It is related that one day during a whirling ceremony while Rumi was whirling in ecstasy, a drunk entered among the whirling dervishes. He could not control himself. During whirling he would lurch and from time to time hit Rumi. Rumi's friends scolded him. Upon seeing this Rumi said, "O friends, he is the one to drink the wine, but you are the ones to get drunk. Why are you scolding him?" Everyone was amazed at Rumi's patience, tolerance, and tenderness. He never replied negatively to the slanders and gossip produced by his adversaries, whose spiritual eyes were blind. His good manners, gentle ways, and tolerant views helped him to bring these people around to the right views.

It also is related that one day Rumi said: "I am with seventy-two different sects and creeds." Siraj al-Din of Konya was a man of grudge. To hurt Rumi and to discredit him in the eyes of the public, he sent one of his religious friends to ask Rumi in public whether or not he actually said that he was with seventy-two sects and creeds. He advised him to insult, curse, and swear at him if Rumi admitted to saying those words. That man came and asked Rumi, "It has been claimed that you said, 'I am with seventy-two sects and creeds.' Is that true?" Rumi did not deny what he had said. He replied, "Yes, that is what I said." That man immediately started to swear and curse at Rumi. Rumi just smiled at him and said, "In spite of all that you are saying, I am also with you."

While a great scholar and a great saint, Rumi was very modest. He treated all with modesty—young or old, of high position or of common folk. One never found traces of arrogance, pride, or haughtiness in Rumi's life. He did not consider any difference between old and young, believer and unbeliever.

It is narrated that in those days a famous and learned priest in Constantinople (Istanbul) had heard about the greatness of Rumi and traveled to Konya to see him. The Roman priests of Konya welcomed and honored this priest from Istanbul. The visiting priest desired to visit Rumi. Coincidentally, they met Rumi on their way. The priest bowed down with reverence and put his head on the ground. He put his head on the ground thirty times in front of Rumi. When he raised his head he was surprised to see that Rumi also put his head to the ground in front of him. It is said that Rumi put his head to the ground thirty-three times. The priest started wailing and tearing off his clothes. Then he said, "O King of Religion, such modesty, such humility! Is a poor priest like me worthy of such respect?" Rumi replied, "Prophet Muhammad who said, 'Blessed is the person upon whom God bestowed wealth, beauty, honor, and the respect of other people and who was generous with his wealth, protected his dignity, and kept his humility in spite of having honor and respect,' is our Master and our Sultan. When I am among the followers of such a prophet how could I not show humility to the slaves of God? Why should I not display my humility? And if I do not do that, for what and for whom would I be good?" Upon hearing these words, that priest and his friends with him immediately embraced the faith and became disciples of Rumi. They exchanged their priestly garments for Muslim clothes. When Rumi came back to the school where he was teaching and also living, he told Sultan Valad, "Baha al-Din, today a poor priest tried to take our humility from our hands. But, thanks to God, with his favor and with our Prophet's help, we have not let go of our humility." This is because the believers inherited humility and modesty from Prophet Muhammad. Since Rumi was entirely on the Muhammadi path and of Muhammadi character, he always saw himself as insignificant and always abstained from arrogance and pride. We should read this quatrain of Rumi and take lessons: "They have valued my turban, my robe, and my head, all three of them, at one dirham (a small currency unit) or somewhat less. Haven't you ever heard my name in this world? I am nothing, nothing, nothing."

The fact is we are all in love with ourselves, but we cannot admit it openly.[6] In another quatrain, Rumi says, "As long as you remain with yourself and as long as you worship yourself, they won't give you a way from the obstacle of yourself. As long as your existence, the misconception that you are something, is with you don't think that you will ever find peace because you are still worshipping the idol of 'self'." Some people take pride in their wealth or position, while others boast of their skills and professions. The unmindful who think that they are walking on the path of Truth see themselves above the common folk due to their prayers, rosaries, and pilgrimages. This quatrain, which shows the immensity of Rumi's humility, as well as many of his other virtues and qualities, is very intriguing. How much value does Rumi attribute to his head, which is a sun of inspiration, to the turban circling that head like a halo and a symbol of knowledge and gnosis, and to his robe that is a cover for God's jewel of beauty? Just as we are fascinated with the humility and modesty displayed by Rumi, the respect shown by Rumi toward non-Muslims during that time is also astonishing.[7] The tolerance shown by Rumi to Christians, who had shed the blood of countless Muslims and ruined their cities during the Crusades, and to their priests, is remarkable evidence of Rumi's greatness and his humane side. During those ages when the mosques burned by extremist Christians were still smoking, Rumi saw everything as a manifestation and predestination of God and did not treat the Christians in a negative way. According to the account of Aflaki, one day an Armenian butcher living in Konya met Rumi. He put his head on the ground with respect. Rumi, too, put his head on the ground and showed the butcher respect.

Rumi showed love, respect, and affection to everybody—women, children, and men. One day Rumi was passing through a neighborhood where children were playing in the street. When they saw Rumi passing by, they came running and bowed in front of him with reverence. Rumi greeted them with love and affection. Meanwhile one of the children was still trying to come. He shouted, "Wait, wait, I am coming, too." Rumi waited till the child came and greeted him; then he caressed the child and made him happy.

One day Vizier Pervane had arranged a whirling ceremony at his palace for Rumi. When Rumi arrived at Pervane's palace, he waited a long time at the door until all the dervishes and friends entered the palace. After all his disciples had entered the palace, he entered as well. After the whirling ceremony was over, all the guests left. Only Rumi stayed there that night. Vizier Pervane showed Rumi a great deal of respect and thanked God that such a great saint was his guest. Once, Husam al-Din Chelebi asked Rumi why he had waited a long time at the door of the palace before entering. Rumi replied, "If we had entered the palace first, maybe the doormen would not have let in some of our friends who arrived after us. So they would not have been able to join our company. If we cannot let our friends in a vizier's palace in this world, in the afterlife, how can we let them in the Palace of Hereafter, the Highest Paradise?"

Like his father Sultan al-Ulama, Rumi gained much love and respect from the sultans, viziers, and kings. These men of high positions were very eager to see him. However, as seen above, Rumi seldom accepted their invitations. He spent most of his time with the poor and needy. He had disciples who were sultans and viziers but also many disciples from among the poor and common folk. He had closed his door to the sultans. While staying away from the ministers of Sultan Izz al-Din Keykavus, he showed sympathy toward the common people and the poor and spent much effort in helping them find the true path and in guiding them. Those who could not appreciate Rumi's treatment of the poor and people in difficulty and who only looked at the appearance of things would criticize him and say, "Rumi's disciples are strange people. Most of them are the workers and small business people of the town. Rich and learned men are rarely seen with him. Wherever there is a tailor, grocer, or a draper, Rumi accepts him as his disciple." Such was the gossip. Rumi ignored the gossip, some of which he actually heard, and he was not offended by it. He did not stint his help to those in need. He did not become angry with those who would object to him, and he would always reply to them with tender and comforting answers. He used to say, "If my disciples were people who didn't need me, I would be their disciple. Since they needed me, I accepted them to discipleship. In doing so, I wanted them to change, to attain the Divine Presence and to be good people."

Rumi always tried to be of service to everyone, good or bad, and he used to do every favor in his power for people. There was a prostitute at an inn in Konya, and she was very beautiful. She had with her several other young women who had been forced into this way of life. One day Rumi was passing in front of this inn. This woman came running out of the inn. She approached Rumi, fell at his feet, and started to entreat him in tears and to give him respect. Rumi called out to this poor woman three times, "Rabia! Rabia! Rabia!" Upon seeing this situation, others working for this woman came out of the inn and fell at Rumi's feet. He said: "Such strong people! Such strong people! If you had not borne the heavy burdens of this difficult life, who would calm down the furious men who are taken away by their desires and lost their way? If it were not for you, how would the dignities of the women of dignity be apparent?" Someone from the elite who heard these words of Rumi said, "It is meaningless for a great saint like Rumi to show sympathy to street women and compliment them like this." Rumi replied to this criticism by saying, "This woman is behaving just the way she is without any hypocrisy. If you are a true man, be like her. Leave two-facedness and two-coloredness so that your inside and outside will be the same. If your inside and outside are not the same, your everything will be in vain." Finally this pretty woman repented and became a woman like Rabia al-Adawiyya and freed the women who used to work for her. She gave away everything in her house to the poor. Joining the ranks of the women saints, she became a disciple of Rumi.[8]

One day while Rumi was praying in solitude, he was concentrating so hard that he did not even notice when a man walked in and said, "I am very poor, I have nothing." When he saw Rumi totally entranced in prayer, he took his prayer rug and left. When Hodja Majd al-Din Maraghi learned about this, he immediately jumped up and started searching for this man. He caught the man trying to sell the rug in the Tiz Bazaar. He dragged him to the presence of Rumi, but Rumi replied, "He must have taken this rug due to his need. Forgive him. We must purchase back this rug from him."[9]

According to Aflaki's account, one day Rumi was talking to his esteemed disciples: "All saints have opened the door of begging in order to crush the pride of their disciples and to repress their egos (*nafs*). Oil lamps in their hands and baskets on their backs, they set out to receive alms-giving and charity from the rich. We, on the other hand, have closed the door of begging on our friends. We have been carrying out the Prophetic Tradition 'Abstain from asking as much as you can, so that our friends can earn their living by their own income through trade, civil service, manufacturing, or any business where they will earn their living with the labor of their hands and the sweat of their brows. Whoever does not follow this way from our disciples, in our view, he does not have a value of even a penny."[10]

Rumi distributed to the poor and needy all the money sent to him from sultans and viziers as their alms-giving and charity. He used to get by with the money he earned from legal consulting and teaching at the seminary without having to rely on anybody or having to put himself under an obligation for any favor. In one quatrain, he said, "As long as my bowl of buttermilk is in front of me, by God, I have no leaning on anybody's honey. Even if poverty threatens me with death, I cannot sell freedom for slavery." Rumi had turned away from the world and worldly things. He led a dervish life. Whenever there was nothing at his home, he would be glad and say, "Thanks to God, today our home resembles to the home of the Prophet." Although he was not rich, he helped the poor, concealing his charity to the needy.

He also used to disguise his financial help to the students at the seminary in the following way: He would put the money under each student's mat as much as he deserved and needed without letting anybody see it and without telling anybody about it. When the students lifted the mats to shake off the dust, they would be surprised to find money under them.

Rumi's respect toward people is also indescribable. When he entered an assembly, the people there would stand up to honor and welcome him. When they forced someone to leave his place so that Rumi could sit, Rumi would be very sad. Aflaki writes that one day Rumi went to a Turkish bath. He entered the bath and immediately came out, put his clothes back on, and prepared to leave. His friends asked him, "O our Master, why did you come out so quickly?" Rumi answered, "When the bath attendant saw me entering the bath, he moved aside someone at the edge of the pool to make room for me. I was so ashamed to have caused this displaced person to be discomforted because of me, and I became very sad."

Rumi's good manners, mercy, politeness, in short, his humane character cannot be described adequately within the limited scope of this work. Even though he lived in an age where slaves were bought and sold as animals and employed in houses, gardens, fields, and in every line of work, not just in Islamic countries but also all over the world, he said, "I have faith in a God that has not created any slaves," and he viewed all human beings as one and equal in accordance with the following Qur'anic verse: "Your creation and your resurrection is but as that of a single soul."[11] In his view there are no conceptions such as slavery or mastery.

One day Rumi entered a room in his house where his daughter Malika Khatun was scolding her female slave and said, "Why are you hitting this slave? Where do you get the right to hurt her? What would you do if you were the slave and she the master? Would you like me to issue a religious ruling that in this world nobody has slaves except God? In fact, all the slaves are our brothers and sisters." His daughter understood her mistake, apologized, and freed the slave. What she was wearing she gave to her slave, and as long as she lived, she never hurt any slave again and abided by the Prophetic Tradition.[12]

Rumi showed mercy to and helped not only the poor and needy human beings, but also animals. According to the account of Shaykh Nafis al-Din of Sivas, "One day Rumi asked me to buy some pastries for two dirhams (penny). Those days the price of a plate of pastries was one dirham. I immediately bought the pastries. After taking the pastries from me, Rumi wrapped them in a piece of cloth and started walking. I walked slowly behind him. Finally, he arrived at a ruin. There I saw a dog that recently had given birth. Rumi gave all the pastries to the dog. I was perplexed by the compassion and mercy of this great saint. Rumi told me, 'For the last seven days this poor dog has not eaten anything. She could not leave this place because of her puppies.'"

It is also narrated that one day Shihab al-Din Guyanda was riding a donkey when the donkey suddenly started to bray. Shihab al-Din got angry at the braying of the donkey and hit its head a few times. Upon seeing this, Rumi said, "This donkey is carrying you. Instead of loving and petting the donkey because you are the rider and it is the carrier, you are hitting the poor animal. For God's sake, if it was just opposite, what would you have done?"

It is narrated that a Christian craftsman was building a fireplace in Rumi's house. Rumi's friends wanted to tease the craftsman, and they said, "Why don't you become Muslim? Islam is the best of religions." He replied, "For fifty years I have been in Jesus' religion. If I abandon my religion now I am fearful, and I would be ashamed in front of him." Upon hearing this Rumi said, "The essence of faith is fear. Whoever fears God, even if that person is a Christian, he is a man of God." That Christian craftsman was moved by these words of Rumi and embraced Islam.[13]

One day Rumi said, "It has been forty years that I have been struggling day and night to be rid of this sickness of 'scholarship,' and unveil this curtain. But I still see that there is a trace of it in me. The purer the mirror of the heart, the easier it is to be closer to Truth." Again he said, "My father Baha al-Din Valad who was the king of the scholars in the world always used to say, 'If I didn't have the knowledge obtained by studying, my gnosis would be stronger than the knowledge.'"

> When I cleansed my heart from knowledge and worldly learning, I attained greater awareness of and closeness to the Truth. I escaped the darkness of the existence and reached the light.[14]

Knowledge that does not bring us closer to the Truth and that does not teach us more about the Truth is not genuine knowledge. Yunus Emre says, "Wisdom is to know; it is to know about the Truth." Moreover, as pointed out above, when knowledge leads its possessor to selfishness and pride, it drives that person away from the Truth and leads to suspicion and skepticism. It is for this reason one of our poets writes, "Is it not better to remain illiterate along with an attraction to the religion than being learned and suffering chastisement?" In other words, an illiterate person who is captured by the attraction of the faith and this way finds the Truth in his heart is more valuable than a learned man who is tormented by suspicions and skepticism.

One day Rumi was offering pearls of wisdom to a person in a high position: "In this state of yours, you are like gold. But you need to be more gold than gold. For some time you will go into a pot, boil many times, suffer hammer strokes on the anvil of asceticism so that you may become the ring of Solomon or the earring on a sultan's cheek. Now all these people are human beings and seem to be Muslims. Only after they have entered the pot of love, suffered powerful strokes on the anvil of patience, endured impossible things, and withstood the pain and discomfort of the lay can they cleanse and become people of truth."

One day while walking, Rumi stopped in front of a tannery next to the river that ran through the city. The water first passed through the city, and then reaching the tannery, it flowed onward and away. Rumi saw that this water was very dirty and cloudy. After staring at the water for a long time he said, "O poor water, be grateful that you are not passing through the hearts of the town's people. If you had passed through their hearts, you would have seen how dirty and contaminated you would be. Nevertheless, it is hoped that the Truth that is most pure will liberate you from this dirtiness with His pure clarity." Rumi also says water that is contaminated by different sources, runs in the gardens, goes underground, and does many things. It nourishes the plants, rises in the air with the sun, becomes a cloud, and finally, in the form of clean and clear rain, falls back to the earth as God's mercy. "When that contaminated water returns next year dragging her skirt, they ask her, 'O that which is in the sea of the pleasant, where have you been?' 'I was contaminated here, but by dressing in beautiful clothes I came to the earth. O you who are dirty! Come to me. My habit has been accorded with the habit of God. I take away all your ugliness, make the devil as pure as an angel. When I get dirty here, I again go there. I return to my essence, the essence of all cleanliness. It takes off my dirty clothes and gives me new and clean clothes. That is what it does, and this is what I do. The Lord of the Worlds decorates and beautifies the world.'"[15]

One day one of the prominent *hafiz*s (someone who knows the whole Qur'an by heart) of Konya requested Rumi to explain the Prophetic Tradition: "There are many reciters of the Qur'an who are damned by the Qur'an." Rumi said, "Most of the verses in the Qur'an include commandments and prohibitions, inner and outer manners. One person reads the verse: 'Perform the prayers and give the compulsory alms'[16] and does not pray and does not give the compulsory alms. Someone else reads the verse: 'God commands justice and goodness' but does not refrain from oppression. That person is miserly, stingy, and deceiving. Of course, the Qur'an curses these people with its language of disposition (*lisan al-hal*), counts them as cursed people, and becomes their worst enemy on the Judgment Day."[17]

> Ask the meanings of the Qur'an only from the Qur'an and from a person who has mortified all his corporeal desires and has crushed all his bad habits under his feet.

Again one day, the scholars of Konya asked Rumi the meaning behind the Prophetic Tradition: "Deeds, worship, and actions are judged with respect to their endings." Rumi explained the reason behind this Prophetic Tradition as follows: "At the time of the Prophet, there used to be a young man notorious for his bad deeds. This young man known for his sins suddenly died. Since his relatives were very much ashamed of all this young man had done, they buried him at night without letting anybody know. The next morning the archangel Gabriel, the Trustworthy, came to the Prophet and told him to go and pray for this young man. The Prophet asked the wisdom behind this. Gabriel gave him this answer: 'God said that this young man declared his faith with his last breath by saying: "I bear witness that there is no deity but God, and I bear witness that Muhammad is His servant and His messenger" and asked for forgiveness for his sins. At that time I pitied him and forgave all his sins.' Hearing this made our Prophet glad, and he said "Deeds, worship, and actions are judged with respect to their endings."

> Do not look down on a unbeliever as he may die as a believer.
> God said: "Even if you are a unbeliever or an idol-worshipper,
> when you pray to me I will answer."

After declaring "there is nobody other than God that does good to the people who commit vice and evil," Rumi continued with this story: "One day while Asma'i was traveling to Makka for the pilgrimage, he threw two punches at a poor Arab because of a pond. Soon afterward he regretted it, repented for it, and with the intention to apologize he started looking for that man. Despite all his efforts, he could not find the man. When he climbed Mount Arafat during the pilgrimage, he found the Arab there and praying for him (i.e., for Asma'i), 'O Lord, don't scold him because of me. It was because he didn't know.' Asma'i immediately fell to that Arab's feet and said: 'I am the one who should be praying for you.' But the Arab replied: 'No, I am aware of my humanity. Therefore, I take great joy in doing good. I have the desire to live as a good person. So it is my job to ask for your forgiveness.'"[18] Now you think what our Lord of Absolute Beauty and Absolute Goodness will do on the Day of Judgment and compare.

Again one day the notables of Konya came to visit Rumi. He was explicating the Qur'anic verse, "one whose heart God has opened to Islam."[19] He said, "When this verse descended from the heavens, they asked the Prophet as to whether there were any signs of this kind of an opened heart and chest. The Prophet said, 'When the holy light of Truth comes to one's heart, that heart opens up and expands. Whenever God wants to beautify and expand one's heart and make him a "possessor of vision," He opens up that heart with His holy light. The sign of this is that the holder of such a heart distances himself from the world, inclines toward the hereafter, and divorces this world before this world divorces him.'"

The day our Prophet migrated from this world, 'Aisha, the mother of believers,[20] was crying, but that crying was nothing like yours and mine. She was not crying like us for the loss of a worldly possession or wealth or things that she loved. She was rather weeping, "O he who never slept comfortably on the bed! O he who never wore silk in his life! O he who never ate barley bread until he was full! O he who used to sleep on a rush mat." The day the Prophet gave back his coveted soul to his beloved God, he was lying on a bed that was filled with fiber from a date tree. The fibers had left traces on the holy skin of the Prophet. Next to the bed there was a wooden bowl with water in it. He was dipping his hand into the bowl, putting some of that water to his burning chest and saying, "O God! Protect me against the terror of death and its unpleasant things." This is how the Great Prophet reunited with his God.

Also in this worldly life, anyone who wants to achieve a goal endures certain difficulties and inconveniences. Someone who does not sacrifice his sleep is scared away from the path, and one who does not endure the difficulties of this path cannot reach anywhere. Now how can a person who loves the Truth and wants to walk on the path of Truth attain Truth while sleeping a lot, eating to fill his stomach, and living a comfortable life?

> It is amazing how a lover sleeps! For sleep is forbidden completely for the lover. O David! If someone who sleeps and does not think of me claims to love me, he would be lying. When it gets dark the lover goes crazy.

> O lover! Wake up and jump from sleep. Be a little uncomfortable and endure difficulty. While there is the noise of the water on one side, how can the thirsty sleep?[21]

The sultan of the literary men Salah al-Din of Malatya has related, "I was in the town of Eregli in the house of Nur al-Din Vefadar with the assembly of the high dome and great shaykhs. Shaykh Janadi arrived with a number of Sufis from Konya. They welcomed and honored him. After greetings, the meal, and various conversations, I asked Shaykh Mu'y al-Din what Shaykh Sadr al-Din Konavi (d. 1273) was saying about Rumi and how he described Rumi in his absence. Shaykh Janadi said, "'By God, one day we were sitting in Shaykh Sadr al-Din's presence with his closest friends. Fahr al-Din Iraqi, Sharaf al-Din Mavsili, and Shaykh Said Fargani were also present. The topic of the conversation became Rumi's states and character. Konavi was inspired with complete honesty and deep understanding and said, "'If Bayazid and Junayd lived today, they would show respect and love for Rumi, the man of God. He is also the servant of the poverty table of the religion of Muhammad. We have been benefiting from him as dependents. All our joys and ecstasy are from his holy feet's fertility.'" All the dervishes present were wise people and accepted and admired these words.'" After telling this, he went on to say, 'My poor self, too, is among the supplicants of this great sultan,' and he recited the following couplet, 'If there is a Divine manifestation in us, a Divine form, it is you. I do not hesitate saying this.'"[22]

One day Rumi was preaching about self-effacement, refraction, and humility. He said, "Fruitless trees like cypress and poplar raise their heads high in the sky, and their branches also stretch high. When fruit-bearing trees have fruits on them, their branches hang down from the tree. Mature people are modest just like this." The Prophet was very modest. Without any doubt the Prophet was more modest than all other prophets and saints. He said, "I am ordered to be nice to people and treat them well. No prophet has ever endured as much ill-treatment as I have." When they hurt his blessed head, when they broke his blessed tooth, because of his infinite mercy, he entreated God, "O God, guide my people to the right path, because they are ignorant and they do not know." When other prophets were subjected to insults, some of them cursed their people. They let stones fall from the sky; their people were targeted by many calamities whereas our Prophet has so much wanted the well-being of people.

> The nature of man is from soil. If a man is not as humble as soil, he is not man.[23]

One day a barber was trimming Rumi's beard. The barber asked, "What would our Master command, how much should I trim?" Rumi replied, "Just enough to differentiate a man from a woman." Another day he said, "I envy the Kalenders because they have no beards." And after relating the Prophetic Tradition: "Little beard is the way for man. That is because the beard is a man's accessory. Much of it leads one to boast and this kills one spiritually." He went on to say, "Sufis like much beard, but while the Sufi combs his beard, the gnostic attains God."

One of Rumi's close friends died. They came to Rumi and asked, "Should we bury him with a coffin or without a coffin?" Rumi answered, "Do as our friends see appropriate." Karam al-Din, son of Bektemur, who was a gnostic of holy light and among the people of vision and high levels, said, "It is better to put him in the grave without a coffin." The friends asked: "Why is this better?" Karam al-Din said, "A mother takes care of a child better than a sibling. Human nature is from the soil; wood of the coffin is like a child of the soil. Thus, the coffin is like man's sibling, and the soil is the mother. Therefore, it is better to leave the deceased to the lap of the affectionate mother." Rumi admired this statement a lot and said, "This point has never been mentioned in any book."

Sultan Valad reports from his father, "Baha al-Din, if you want to love your enemy and your enemy to love you, talk positively about him for forty days. That enemy becomes your friend, since there is a path from the tongue to the heart just as there is a path from the heart to the tongue. It is also possible to obtain God's love through His Glorious Names. God said, 'O slaves, to form purity in your hearts, do not abstain from mentioning me a lot. The more purity, the brighter the holy light of God in the heart.'"[24]

One day Shaykh Sadr al-Din was busy teaching a lesson in Prophetic Tradition at his dervish lodge. The most noble and famous people of Konya were present at that assembly, too. Suddenly, Rumi entered at the door. The shaykh asked Rumi to deliver that day's lecture. While explaining each Prophetic Tradition, Rumi referred to other related Prophetic Traditions and gave very remarkable explanations. He also mentioned in which context these Prophetic Traditions were said. He brought up such deep points that the attendees were amazed. Shaykh Sadr al-Din thought to himself, "I wonder whether the meaning of this Prophetic Tradition is as Rumi says or is it different because we have never heard such interpretations from any of our teachers and never listened to such a style." That very night Shaykh Sadr al-Din saw our Prophet in his dream. The Prophet was sitting at the end of the dervish lodge. Shaykh Sadr al-Din went up to the Prophet and kissed his blessed hand. The Prophet said, "The meaning of that Tradition and my purpose in saying that is exactly as Rumi put it. It is not that he added to it."

Out of joy Shaykh Sadr al-Din woke up. Before he could tell his dream to the dervishes, Rumi came to the dervish lodge and took a seat on the sofa and recited the verse: "O Messenger! We have sent you as a witness, a bearer of good news, and a warner."[25] And he then said: "That is, the testimony of such an honest witness about the slaves is credible since if God wants, it becomes trustworthy." This increased Shaykh Sadr al-Din's faith, love, and trust in Rumi.[26]

One day a *rebab* (a musical instrument) was being played in Rumi's presence. Rumi was listening with great pleasure. Suddenly a respected man came in and said, "The call to the afternoon prayer is being heard." Rumi stopped for a moment and then said, "No, no, that voice is calling to God; this voice is also calling to God. The call to prayer is inviting the outer aspect of human beings to duty, while that voice of the *rebab* is inviting the human spirit, his inner face and his invisible aspect to God's love and awareness."[27]

The Seljuk vizier Muin al-Din Pervane wanted to appoint some-one as a judge to Konya. This person was Vizier Taj al-Din's son. He had a lot of virtues, and he was well-informed, but because of his knowledge, he was arrogant and without manners. This person told Vizier Pervane, "I will accept the position of judge on three conditions: First condition, you will ban the instrument called the *rebab*. Second condition, you will fire the old court officials who are like executioners of the courts. Third condition, you will pay good salaries to the new court officials, so that they may not take anything from the people." Pervane said, "I accept and commit to two of your conditions. But I cannot ban the *rebab* because it is being played upon the command of a very great king." Due to this Vizier Taj al-Din's son did not agree to become the judge. When this story reached Rumi's ear, he said, "Well done, O holy *rebab*! Praise be to God that the *rebab* has held his hand and rescued him from the hand of fate."

Let us see what Sipehsalar, who was blessed with the fortune of living with Rumi for years, has to say about Rumi in his *Risale*:[28]

> O Rumi, the well of "Water of Infinite Life" is submerged com-pletely in shame from its envy of the beauty and grace of your words. It shows itself to no one.
> O Rumi, who accumulated all the good manners and morals of the Prophet who honored the world in order to complete good manners and morals! O unique explainer of the Qur'anic verses in a most correct and most beautiful way!
> What can I write to describe you? What can I say? Even if I use up all the words, your attributes still will remain to be told because your attributes are infinite. Your good manners and habits are innumerable; they cannot be described with words.

Tolerance and other good manners of Rumi, as they are asso-ciated with all saints, are actually Prophet Muhammad's tolerance and good behavior. Sipehsalar describes Rumi as the "unique explain-er of the Qur'anic verses in a most correct and most beautiful way." When commenting on some Qur'anic verses in the honorable *Mesnevi*, Rumi touched on some aspects of these verses with a divine inspiration that no other famous commentator up to his time had been able to touch upon. It is for this reason that Ismail Hakkı of Bursa (d. 1725), explained some Qur'anic verses in his *Ruh al-Bayan* commentary by quoting from the honorable *Mesnevi*. Sipehsalar, who expressed his admiration of Rumi because he knew him very closely, abstained from causing division among other dervish orders because he loved not only Rumi, the saint, to whom he was devoted, but also all other saints and set a good example to those who love God and the Truth.

The degree of Sipehsalar's admiration of Rumi can be understood through such statements as "I have washed my mouth with musk and rose water a thousand times, but I still didn't think my mouth was worthy of mentioning your name." Sipehsalar continues, "I have observed some of Rumi's innumerable extraordinary attributes with my own eye, some others I found in my heart and consciousness. How can I explain what I have seen with the eyes in my head and what I have sensed with the eye of my heart with my tongue as incapable and as inadequate as my pen cut short at one end? Not everything that is known is seen, not everything that is seen can be told, and not everything that is told can be written." The proof of this is as follows: Each of the saints has taken God's attributes by removing everything other than God from the mirror of their hearts, by being completely cured from envy, anger, and lust through their worship, good deeds, and patience in the face of whatever happens to them, their efforts and struggles against their bodily desires (*nafs*), and the weakening of their bodies. The Prophet says, "If one wants to find God in his heart and sit with Him, he should sit with the people of Sufism." My shaykh Rumi also said in his *Mesnevi*, "Whoever wants the company of God and to feel God in his heart, he should sit in the presence of the saints. Since they are saved completely from human attributes, these special servants of God have to be alive with God, to speak with God and to hear with God. Just as the Great Prophet, the Master of the Universe tells us in a *hadith qudsi*[29], 'God says: 'When I love a servant of mine, I become his ears with which he hears, the eyes with which he sees, and the tongue with which he speaks.'"

Those who at the "Assembly of *Alast*" gave their heart to God are still intoxicated with the covenant of *Alast*. Like slaves their feet are tied in this world, the place of suffering, but they are very generous in giving their lives. These special slaves of God have effaced their selves in God, and they are sustained in existence with the Friend. The amazing thing is that they really do not exist although they seem to be there at this moment. "These are the real people of Unity."[30]

Sipehsalar continues to describe Rumi as follows: "There are many compelling reasons for this poor Sipehsalar to tell of the levels Rumi attained. First, let me say that our Honorable Master was very proficient in the Arabic language. He knew all the intricacies of the Arabic language and vocabulary. He was among the most learned people of his time in Islamic Law, Qur'anic commentary, Prophetic Tradition, logical and narrative sciences, and had attained advanced degrees in all fields of knowledge. In Aleppo, when he was advancing his studies in the earlier part of his youth, his friends would ask him matters with which they had difficulty. Rumi would show them so many ways to resolve these matters that those who listened and those who understood these seemingly complex matters would fall in a state of excitement due to the joy of hearing and understanding. The blessed solutions he offered for the question at hand were not written in any books. Rumi's blessed glances were reading and answering the most difficult and complicated matters from the book of the heart." After writing these things about Rumi, Sipehsalar offers the following,[31] which expresses the manifestations within a lover of God:

> O heart who, as the zephyr, has felt the joy of the early morning and sensed the meaning of divine manifestations at those times!
>
> Are you enraptured with what you have seen or with what you have not seen?

Has what you have seen or what you have not seen taken you from yourself?

Sometimes you run to the outskirts of the mountain, you struggle and you see the ore of truth and amber of love there.

You have gone beyond the eye and beyond the heart.

For you hundreds of windows have opened up, you have gone out of the earth and the heavens, flown away and seen hundreds of skies.

Such rapture, such fog has fallen onto the sea that from the joy of watching it his whole head became an eye.

The tears that flow like a flood in waves from the eyes because of love have joined the sea.

How surprising! How amazing!

Tears and sea have become an ocean, or the sea has become an eye. In his sight both worlds are like a grain put in front of a chicken.

Indeed a clean eye, which has seen the truth and majesty, is like this. In the universe of unity one who sees the attributes of the seeker and sought as two different entities is neither the seeker nor the sought.

Who knows God?

One who escaped from *la* (unbelief).

Tell the one who asks, "Who is saved from *la*?" "The lover stricken with calamities."

The lover of God has understood the real meaning of Bayazid Bistami's saying: "There is none but God under my robe" and has seen that robe as a simple, invaluable piece of clothing and has wanted to remove that robe of himself to be seen with this real being.[32]

After citing this poem, Sipehsalar continues, "In order to attain the view expressed in the above poem and to feel that spiritual joy one should know that knowledge alone is not enough." Maintaining that scholarly knowledge and studying it can sometimes be an obstacle and a curtain on the spiritual path. Sipehsalar concludes the section by quoting this couplet from Rumi: "I wanted to wash away the knowledge from the heart, escape from myself, make myself unaware of myself because it is not right to go to the presence of the most coveted Beloved as a learned man."

ASCETICISM AND ECSTASY

Rumi, who was completely on the Muhammadi path and took Muhammad as an example in everything, was very much attached to asceticism and self-mortification due to the abundance of divine love in him. At this point, let us listen to Sipehsalar once again:

> This poor slave of God had been in Rumi's service for forty years. He continued his worship from his youth to his death without decreasing. I have never seen him put his head on a pillow and comfortably rest on the bed. It is a fact that God always brought to motion the body of his holiness who was subjected to self-mortification, and He gave strength to it. How can one describe his sleeplessness and discontent? Once during a night of whirling ceremonies when sleep had overtaken those present, his holiness leaned his back against the wall and put his blessed head on his knees. Shaykh Muhammad Khadim came and brought a big blanket and put it on his blessed shoulders and covered his whole body with it. When the friends fell asleep his holiness stood up. He started praying. Then he walked around a little bit. He never rested and stopped.

Sipehsalar tries to explain Rumi's state of ecstasy and discontent with this poem from the *Divan-i Kabir*:

> I have lost my mind for love because there is no strength in my heart that has lost its hand and feet to resist His love.
>
> Day and night I keep on chewing on one end of the chain of love that ties me.
>
> I am covered in blood all over my body.
>
> I am afraid if the vision of the Beloved comes, I might spill the blood of my heart over Him.
>
> Ask the fairies of the night of this lover who burns with the fire of love and cries and weeps.
>
> When I come and go in the darkness, my feet touch fairies.

My heart, which is shattered in pieces, is traveling all night by burning like a star.

By the spell of the unfair and cruel Beloved all my sleep has gone.

O my Beloved, let me wear a dress of fire like the sun and with that fire let me beautify and enlighten the world like the sun.

My love is a moment of Your love.

Even if I escape and rest, my spirit never relaxes and rests.

I attain peace and comfort that very moment when I do not separate from Your love, never rest but continuously burn and be burned.[33]

In another poem, Rumi points to the same state and says, "Everybody went to sleep. I, the lover who gave away his heart, did not sleep. All night my eyes are counting stars in the sky. Your love drew sleep away from my eyes such that it never returns. My sleep has drunk the poison of Your separation and died."

Rumi's patience and endurance in terms of fasting were at an amazing level. He had attained the essence of the meaning of the Prophetic Traditions: "Hunger is the food of God on earth. He keeps the bodies of those He loves alive with it," and he was practicing it. According to Islamic principles, there is only one month of compulsory fasting. People of piety, those who fear God very much and those who follow his orders, fast also some days during the other holy months. There are also others who fast three days a week or more. But all who fast break their fast at sundown for the night. It is narrated from the Masters that even those in the forty-day Sufi seclusion break their fast in this way. But Rumi had taken hunger to its highest level. For years, he never ate to fill his stomach and said, "For forty years there was never food in my stomach at night."

Now that I have spent the night in the presence of my Lord, now that I have attained that happiness, the nourishment of my Lord has reached my spirit and made me spiritually full.

When he first met with Shams of Tabriz, they sat down for six months and stayed away from human desires such as eating and drinking. Whenever they broke their fast, they ate one kind of food. The most food Rumi ate was not more than ten bites. He said, "There is such a dragon in me that cannot stand eating." On the matter of hunger, he said, "The bird of your heart cannot crack the egg due to eating in excess and being sick. It remains in this prison of an egg. You come out of the egg of imprisonment of the lower self (*nafs*) so that your wings can open up and you can soar in the spiritual heavens."

The above descriptions are related to the physical fasting of Rumi. The one who best observed the spiritual fasting, the fasting of heart, which means to leave everything other than God, is again Rumi. In fact, people of gnosis have said, "There are three kinds of fasting: fasting of the lay, fasting of the elite, and fasting of the elite of the elite. The fasting of the lay merely consists of giving up eating and drinking. The fasting of the elite is the fasting of the hands, feet, eyes, tongue, and other limbs by protecting them from doing evil. The fasting of the elite of the elite is leaving everything other than God." Rumi's fasting was this third kind.

He became upset whenever his family made major plans for cooking; whenever there was little burden and trouble for cooking, he would seem very happy and compliment his family saying, "Today the light of poverty is shining on the foreheads of my family." In one of his odes he says, "The one killed by lust is contaminated, but the martyr of love is pure and clean. Poverty has set its tent at a place far away from that clean one and that dirty one. The hearts of all lovers formed a circle around poverty. It was as if the poverty was the shaykh of shaykhs and the hearts of all his disciples."[34] Elsewhere in the *Divan-i Kabir*, Rumi says, "Every person who saves his heart from the desires of both worlds and cleans it and never seeks pleasure in this world or the other, understands that it is poverty and nothingness to reply 'Yes' to the voice of 'Alast' (Am I not your Lord?)."[35]

As Sipehsalar writes, whenever the time for prayer came, Rumi would face the *qibla* (the direction of holy shrine in Makka) and the color of his blessed face would change. Rumi's preparation for daily prayer would remind one of Ali's prayers. As commonly known, the Commander of the Faithful, Ali's face would change color, and he would start shaking out of fear when the time for prayer came. When he was asked, "O Commander of the Faithful, what is happening to you," he would answer, "It is time to turn to God and perform the duty of the Divine Entrustment God offered to the heavens, earth, and mountains, and they were afraid and declined the responsibility. I am afraid that I don't know whether I will be able to perform the duty that I have assumed."

Rumi's prayer was performed with an open heart and a forgetting of self. In his prayer he would find himself completely in God and reunited with God. In fact, the purpose of prayer is to find God spiritually, to reunite with God by forgetting about one's self and escaping one's imaginary existence. It is for this reason that the Prophet says, "Prayer is reunification with God." But those who look at only the appearance of things cannot see and understand how this reunification will happen. It is also for this reason that prayer is viewed as the pillar of the religion and ascension of a believer to heaven. It frequently observed was that the great Prophet started a prayer after the night prayers and continued praying until the next morning, praying the two-*rakat* prayer, forgetting himself in the presence of God. It was also observed that he remained in prostration and bowing for a day or for a night.

Rumi's prayers were not like the prayer of any other believer, performed only as a duty to attain God's pleasure. Rumi's prayers were not only a prayer for God's pleasure but also a prayer of heart and a prayer of love. The following passage from the *Divan-i Kabir* illustrates Rumi's state in prayer:

When it is time for the evening prayer, everyone lights up his house and prepares the table, but I find the spirit of the Beloved in my heart and start to cry out and lament.

Since I make ablution with my tears, my prayers are fiery.

When the sound of *adhan* (call for prayers) reaches the door of my mosque, it burns it down.

Which way is the *qibla*?

I missed my prayers; I need to make them up.

You and I receive a lot of challenges because of these missing prayers.

I wonder if the prayers of those who are enraptured with God's love are right.

You tell me because the ecstatic never knows time and place.

Is this the second *rakat* that I am praying? Or is it the fourth? Which chapter did I recite?

I cannot speak because of excitement.

How can I knock on God's door when neither hands nor heart remained in me? I am not in me.

You took my hand and heart. O my God! Nothing remained of me. At least you give me assurance and trust.

By God, I do not know how I pray.

Did I complete the bowing? Who is the imam? I have no idea.

From now on let me be like a shadow in front and behind every imam so that sometimes I may shrink and prostrate with the fear of the One who created me . . .[36]

Since we love this world and focus too much of our attention on our daily business, we do not realize that we are in God's presence in prayer, and we think of the things we have done or we are going to do. No matter how much we try, we cannot escape these random thoughts. We concentrate on the matters of the world that randomly pop up in our minds and confuse prayers. Unlike Rumi, who confused his prayers because he was enraptured with the love of God, we confuse our prayers because of our intoxication with the love of this world.

Sipehsalar writes, "If I were to describe one tenth of Rumi's ecstasy, love, and divine attraction, I could not fit it into this book."[37]

O reader, may God give you success. Know that rapture of attraction is a state of fascination and ecstasy induced by God attracting his servant to Himself. It is being overwhelmed so that one forgets one's self; it is being fascinated by God's greatness, power, and attributes. Attraction is reunion with God, dying before death, and attaining God while living. If there is no spiritual talent in a person to walk on the path of God, no matter how much that person strives or how much he performs self-mortification, he never attains union with God. Attraction is a favor of God, the Most Glorious, in the eternal past. It is a spiritual bestowal that God has granted in the souls of some people in the world of the spirits before coming to this world.

Our Prophet says, "There is an attraction among the attractions of God that is better than the worship of the whole of humankind and *jinn*." If there occurs a pause, a joylessness, a hopelessness to the person who walks in the path of God when he reaches a level, God, the Most Dominant, the Most Glorious, takes the traveler on His path to safety with His attraction due to the abundance of His mercy and favors and makes him attain his destination. The eternal attraction bestowed by God was clearly visible in Rumi. Therefore, of every level and stage he attained with continuously overflowing divine attraction, he related:

> The love Buraq of meanings has taken away my mind and my heart.
> Ask me, "Where did it take them?"
> It took my mind and heart to that side which you do not know, to the
> beyond. I reached a pavilion from where I saw no moon, no sky.
> I arrived in such a world that even the world ceases to be the world. For one
> moment, excuse me, spare me, so that my mind returns to me and I can tell
> you what the spirit is and talk about its beauties.
> Do not disregard my words. Listen to me, you, too, have a spirit.
> Try to understand the spirit. There are favors of the Beloved upon
> us—bestowals, grants, and gifts.
> These are amazing, never before seen favors and bestowals.
> These are unique gifts.
> From the path of the senses come clear lights, and hearts are enlightened.

When the spirit, which resembles the star of Canopus, appears from the
direction of the Yemeni corner of the Ka'ba, the moon ceases to be
visible as well as the sun and the seven poles of the skies.
The light of the spirit overpowers them all. For a moment take the religion
which resembles a piece of gold and put it under your tongue so that you
may realize how valuable an ore resides in your heart, inside yourself.
Enlighten the lights of the five senses that are in you.
See them as the five daily prayers.
Your heart is like the *fatiha*, which consists of seven verses.
Every morning there comes a voice from the heavens.
If you can remove the love of this world from your heart, you can hear it
and find the trace of the path of truth and begin to walk on it.[38]

In another poem, Rumi describes the same state:

Once again happiness came and pulled our gown.
Once again we set up our tent on the heavens.
Yesterday the Beloved asked me, "How are you at the mercy
of this disloyal world?"
How is one who sees his smiling fortune and luck?
Praises to God, I found that candy that Egypt could not even
dream of next to my tooth.
We are a great person even though we are not rich or do not
hold a high position. We are a king without subjects or army.
We are eating sugar from our sugar cane field.
Though the revolving of the moon wears out life and short-
ens it, our Beloved has granted a lot of long lives in His revo-
lution.[39]

Each word that Rumi said when losing his consciousness under
the influence of God's love is the key to thousands of spiritual treas-
ures. If one attempts to explain all this, the matter lengthens and the
purpose gets lost. My dear readers, most of the books written about
Rumi's life and views try to explain his *wahdat al-wujud* by comparing him to others. However, Sipehsalar explained Rumi with Rumi.
That is, he explained his ideas, feelings, and views by taking exam-

ples from his work. In this regard, to explain the spiritual joy in the world of spirits, Rumi says:

> O my God, my love was at the level of perfection when You created me in the eternal past.
>
> At that time there was no earth, no world. Neither the sun existed nor head of a man, nor his hat.
>
> There was nothing when you selected me for your love. I was with You in the eternal past, I was Your companion and friend.
>
> Now that I have been with You and You have been with me, why are You hiding now? Why are You not revealing Yourself?
>
> The eye that sees is You, the one that says is You, the one that hears is You.
>
> You are the One who puts up curtains before our eyes to prevent them from seeing the truth and who tears up those curtains.[40]

Most of Rumi's beautiful and influential poems were recited when he was in a state submerged in rapture (*istighraq*) with divine love. What is this state of being submerged in rapture? When the special servants of God attain the level of closeness and union with God, they are fascinated by His Beauty, Power, Majesty, and Generosity. Coming under the influence of the Creator, the Absolute Beauty, they become ecstatic and intoxicated as if they had drunk a spiritual wine, the wine of love. The Prophet tells us of their state: "God has prepared a wine for his saints that when they drink it, they become intoxicated; when they become intoxicated, they become enraptured; when they are enraptured, they become silent." Our Prophet was honored by vicinity to God, as indicated by the Qur'anic verse: "At a distance of two bow lengths or (even) nearer."[41] When he was bestowed with that favor, when he saw God, Possessor of Absolute Majesty and Absolute Beauty, with his spiritual eye, when he discovered the Divine Entrustments and secrets, he went into a state of indescribable joy. This spiritual wine that enraptured our Great Prophet was the wine of love, the wine of truth.

Rumi recited many poems that describe this spiritual wine that enraptures the saints and special servants of God. I could not proceed without sharing one of them here. If we read these poems carefully and reflect on them, with the grace and help of God, we can understand at least somewhat this spiritual state, which is very difficult to explain and to understand:

> It is such a wine that if a drop of it falls on the ground, rose gardens grow from the barren soil.
>
> It is such a ruby wine that if it foams and becomes exuberant at midnight the earth and heaven fill up with light and every place becomes illuminated.
>
> Come, come, I have secrets in my heart. Serve that ruby wine, serve it so that the curtain of the heart opens up and the secrets reveal themselves.
>
> O my Beloved, watch me when you exhilarate me with Your Beauty. See how spirited lions are in the vicinity of prey.
>
> Observe the youths of the People of the Cave. They drank this wine and they were intoxicated and slept in the cave for three hundred and nine years.
>
> What kind of wine was it that when Moses gave it to the magicians they were intoxicated and had their hands and feet cut?
>
> The women of Egypt were intoxicated with the beauty of Joseph and cut their fingers in pieces.
>
> The Companions who threw themselves in front of swords without any armor or shields were intoxicated with the wine of faith served by Prophet Muhammad.
>
> No, I said it wrong. Muhammad was not the cupbearer, so he could not serve the wine. He was a glass full of God's wine.
>
> It was God Almighty who served wine to the good people.
>
> What kind of wine did Ibrahim Adham drink that he left his throne and crown and ran away from his country? What kind of a rapture was that?
>
> When Bayazid drank from this wine, he said, "I dissociate myself from imperfect attributes."
>
> When al-Hallaj drank the same wine, he yelled, "I am the Truth," and went to the gallows.

When water received the smell of that wine, it became crystal clear. The drunks prostrated and started running to the ocean like floodwaters.

What kind of wine does this dark night have that makes people sleep with one glass and keep them from everything?

Which one can I mention of the favors and graces of the Great and Unique Artist?

The shores of the ocean of His Power cannot be seen ... Let us drink the wine of love; like drunken camels let us join the caravan and pull the burden of love.

Where is the pure and clean wine of God?

Where is the wine of grapes? That pure and clean wine grants infinite life. The other is dirt.

The wine of grapes make one who drinks it sometimes a pig, sometimes a monkey.

That red wine makes your face eventually black.

The pitcher of the wine of God is the heart. Open up the lid of the pitcher because the human desires that do nothing but evil have covered the pitcher's lid with mud. Remove that dirty mud from the lid and throw it away.[42]

In another poem, Rumi explains the secrets of the heart in divine love:

O heart, there is something different about you since the morning. You are so exuberant, so enraptured that you cannot see me who is enraptured and scattered like you.

O heart, what kind of a fire are you that every wind no matter from where it comes exhilarates you and increases your flames? No, no, you are above fire and above wind.

O heart, I cannot explain you, you are what you are. But I know this much that now you are tearing apart the curtain of the heavens like the sun.

O heart, what kind of a pearl are you? Neither heaven nor the planet of Jupiter can appreciate you fully. May my life be sacrificed to You since You created the heart.

O my God! For thirty years I have been running after You like a crazy lover. In fact, I have been running after You in an uninhabited and wild island where there was no wet or dry thing. Those times I was not aware that everything, every being was Your creation.

My mind was stuck with the thoughts of faith and unbelief. However, faith is the gift of Your holy light that comes from You.

Unbelief, suspicion, and belief that You are Omnipotent are all Your Predestination. You are both the paradise and the hell and the pool of Kawthar.

O heart, you are out of these two worlds, you are a universe, everything is in you and you are above and beyond everything.[43]

If we attempt to explain the secrets of heart and love that Rumi touches upon, books fill up and the subject is not exhausted. O friend who seeks God and truth, know well that our Master Hudavendigar had limitless majesty, magnificence, and glory in love. From the day he came of age to the day he passed away, his love and enthusiasm kept on increasing. He was never content with his love and enthusiasm; he always wanted them to increase even more. In one of his poems about his ecstasy and self-effacement, he implicitly points to his valuable being and says:

The phenomena of our physical being, of our body are limited, but our spiritual being beyond our physical being is complete.

The matter was completed with the first glass of wine drunk in the eternal past. I have a heart devastated on the path of love.

Its strong attachment to the tavern of love has devastated it, ruined it.

Tell the love: 'If you are looking for someone who gave his heart to you and is overcome with your love, the lover you seek has fallen on the ground and is lying there.

Come, hold his hand and lift him up. Don't come too close to this poor person overcome with your love, watch him from a distance because I am afraid that the flames of the fire inside me may burn you, too.

If its flames set you on fire then come to the front of my eyes, tears are flowing like floodwaters from my eyes that are scattering pearls. My tears can put out your fire.

Cry out, "His ailing eyes heal." Call out, "Wherever there is an ill person, may he come because the time of healing has come."

Go to the mountains, wherever you see a person whose heart is sleeping, let them know that the awake fortune of love will grant vision and knowledge to everyone whose heart is asleep. Call out to them, "Come, come!"[44]

"The light of the verse . . . one whose chest God has opened for Islam so that he has received a light from his Lord" comes from such a candle whose flame does not fit into the two worlds.[45] This couplet of Rumi reminds one of the following couplet by Shaykh Ghalib: "The candle of spirit has such a flame that it does not fit into the lantern of the heavens." In another poem, Rumi tells of the joys of a magnificent spiritual level to which love has elevated him:

> Who is this that is coming in the middle of the night
> shining like the moon?
> I know, I know, this is the messenger of love,
> coming from the mihrab.[46]

The messenger of love has brought a torch and set sleep on fire and burned it down. Where did he come from? Who sent him?

He came from the side of the King of Kings who never sleeps.

Who makes his noise, this cry in the city? Who came to the dervish's harvest like the flood, which is unique and peerless, the person that none exists other than him in the universe of existence?

Tell me! A king stood up in the middle of the night and came to one of his invaluable slaves.

Who is he? He is the one who opened up a table of generosity to his creatures and is letting everybody eat from it.

He came smiling to invite the friends. In front of his Greatness and Power all hearts are shivering and all spirits are impatient.

The smallest particle of that shivering and fear has fallen onto the quicksilver and that's why it is shivering continuously.

The softness, the gentleness that he shows to his slaves, a small piece of it is manifested on the skin of a squirrel.

A wet melody from the sorrows, cries, and laments brought by love has been given to the water mill and therefore it turns, crying and lamenting.

Love carries a set of keys under his arm. It came to open all doors that were closed.[47]

Love is such a tree of holy light that its branches are in eternity and its roots are in the eternal past.

This tree neither rests on the Throne nor on earth, this tree has no trunk. We have freed the mind from all work and beaten desires thoroughly.

Because this greatness is not suitable for this mind and these habits, you have a desire and longing for the mortal beauties.

Know that this desire is an idol for you.

When you find yourself in yourself and become your beloved there remains no longing in you.[48]

May lives be sacrificed for the sake of lovers, love is a pleasant devotion. O son, attach yourself to love, all other things are useless and meaningless.

There is a fiery chain of love hanging from the heavens to the earth. If you love God and the truth, grab that chain and ascend to the heights.

Don't ask, "What kind of thing is love?" Love is a kind of insanity and craze. It makes one chained, but this is not the chain used to restrain the ignorant.

Who would be your enemy once you set out on the path of love and reach nothingness?

Who would have your power? You are a real fire that burns and roasts.[49]

Be a lover, be a lover so that you may be saved from sorrow. You are a prince, son of the sultan, until when are you going to stay as a slave of the world?

Let nobody know you in this mortal world, let nobody recognize you. But you are peerless and unique in that world where there is no direction.

In this world everything is transient, this world is the mortal world. So what if you are not a rich man in this world?

You are not dead, you are living. Isn't this enough? You are a lion of God in the form of a man. This is clearly seen from your virtues, endeavors, and courage.

Life has come and gone. But now that you exist and you exist in the holy light of God, it doesn't matter whether it is later or sooner.

The value of the beloved depends on the nobility of the lover. O helpless lover! Look to see what is your power and value.[50]

Don't count the lifetime that has passed without love, don't think you lived.

Love is the Water of Eternal Life. Accept it wholeheartedly.

Consider others as fish out of water. Even if he is a vizier, think of him as dead and decayed.

When love opens its bag to unpack, all trees become green. New leaves appear from an old tree, and it gives fruits every moment.[51]

It is better for a soul that has never fallen in love and has never made that love his main concern to cease to exist because its existence is nothing but mistake and shame.

Be ecstatic with real life and be unconscious because everything that is in this world is all but love. There is no appropriate thing to do for the Friend other than being occupied with love.

When they ask, "What is love?" tell them, "Love is leaving the will, the discretion of whether to do something or not."

There is no goodness in one who does not abandon the choice; he is not a good person. The one thing that is eternal is love.

Do not devote yourself to anything other than this; all other things are imperfect. Until when are you going to embrace the mortal beloved who can be considered dead?

Embrace such a spirit that there is no end to it. Whatever is born in the spring dies in the fall. In the rose garden of love there is no help from the spring.

Would the flowers of love ever need the assistance of spring? Do not shake on the horse of your body, come down.

Be a barefooted wanderer that goes faster than that. God grants wings to a person who does not let himself be overcome by bodily desires and feelings and saves himself from their influence.

Leave thoughts and worries. May your heart be as pure as the face of the mirror on which there is no image.[52]

TAWHID (UNITY OF GOD) AND ITTIHAD (UNION WITH GOD)

O reader who seeks the truth! May God make you attain the highest point of the truth and the intrinsic knowledge that you are seeking. Know that it is very difficult both to understand these spiritual states and to describe them. These spiritual levels and stages that God's beloved servants attain are not physical levels or visible ranks or states that may be described and explained. Even though this is the case, let us at least try to understand a little.

Tawhid, the belief in unity, means to know and consider something as being one. That is to know and believe that God is One, Unique, and Peerless. God says in the Noble Qur'an, "Do not set up besides God any other deity."[53] *Ittihad* means to be one. The level of *ittihad* is superior to the level of *tawhid* because in the former there is only the notion of knowing God as one, while in the latter there is the notion of being one with God. How is that possible? How can a human, a powerless and mortal being, be one with God? God is indeed not a physical being; we cannot go and be one with Him and stay together with Him.

Some people with limited understanding think of man as being one with God as *hulul* (God's incarnation), and thus are mistaken. The concept of *hulul* carries the meaning of taking on a body and as such is not an Islamic belief, bringing a believer to unbelief. In this matter, Rumi says the following: "*Ittihad* is not *hulul*, it is your effacement." The main point of being one with God, of *ittihad*, is this: If the person who enters the path of God, cleanses his lower self (*nafs*) by properly and thoroughly performing asceticism, self-mortification, good deeds, and worshipful duties, that person has found a way to *ittihad*. That person's being one with God means that he is obeying God's commandments completely, and that he is dissolving his personal choice and will into God's choice and will. Awhad al-Din Kirmani, a great saint, said the following concerning this issue: "Walk on this path until duality disappears. If there is duality, it can be removed by a friend of truth. You do not become Him, but if you struggle and endure, you come to a point where "you-ness" is removed from you."

If a person's will is effaced in God's will, that person has attained God. If a person who does not know how to swim falls into the sea and moves his arms and legs in an attempt to get out, yet does this in an incorrect way, then he will sink deeper into the sea. If that person dies and remains motionless on the sea, then any motion made by the body is dependent on the sea. In this regard, Rumi says in the *Mesnevi*, "The water of the sea takes a dead man on its head and carries him on the surface of the water. How can a living person escape the sea? If you kill your desires and do away with your human attributes, the sea of secrets carries you over its head."[54] In this case, when a person becomes *insan al-kamil*, or an ideal human, any word related to this intrinsic meaning which comes from him will originate from God; as stated in the Noble Qur'an, such a word came from a tree: "When Moses reached there, he was addressed by a tree from the right side of that holy valley: 'O Moses, verily I am God, Lord of the Worlds.'" Inspired by this event Rumi says the following in one of his poems:

> I saw a tree of fire. It called out to me, "O my beloved!" That fire was calling me.
>
> Or am I Moses, the son of Imran? Stricken with calamity, I wound up in deserts;
>
> I ate dessert of power and quail.
>
> I have been traveling in the desert for forty years like Moses. O my beloved, come, you, too, are a Moses.
>
> This body is your staff. If you grasp your body and hold on to it, I will turn it into a stick of wood.

But if you throw it away, if you throw it on the ground, I will make of it a dragon with many powers.

You are a Jesus, and I am your bird. You made a bird of clay, and when you breathed on it, I gained life, spread my wings, and soared in the skies.

I am the pillar of the mosque in Madina, the Prophet gave his sermons leaning against me; if he leans against anything else it starts to lament and cry with the sorrow of separation.

O Master of the Masters! O King of Kings! O God who creates figures and shapes while Himself remaining pure of them.

What shape are You going to put me in? I cannot know this. Only You can know.[55]

Our Hudavendigar (another title of Rumi) says this in one of his poems:

I do not know how I have become effaced; is it due to that wine of divine love,

Or where I am due to that Beauty of Nowhere? I arrived at such a place that I do not fit into the world.

Now I do not suit anyone other than that Unique Beloved who is not associated with a place.

You are telling me, "Why aren't you coming to yourself (to your senses)? You show to me myself and who I am, and I shall come to myself. You are the light, you called out to Moses, 'I am God, I am God!'"[56]

If a voice saying "I am God!" can emanate from a tree, then why cannot such a voice come from man, the most honorable of the creatures and one who carries the Divine Entrustment? Rumi says, "God called out from a tree, 'I am God!' Everybody heeded and was pleased by this call. If a man says the same thing, do not say that this word cannot be uttered due to your spiritual blindness." The sultan of the gnostics, Bayazid Bistami, in a state of ecstasy, said: "I dissociate myself from all imperfect attributes. Great is my Glory!" And he saw the divine manifestation in himself. The *qutb*[57] of his time, Junayd of Baghdad (d. 910 CE) said, "There is none but God in my robe." Mansur al-Hallaj (d. 922 CE), who pleases the hearts of the lovers of God with his spiritual states and who was hung for the love of God, said, "I am the Truth (God)" and was taken to the gallows.

Rumi was also subject to these manifestations and attained the highest point of this spiritual level; he, too, said many similar things in states of ecstasy. For example, in this couplet, he says, "Everybody drank from a glass of the divine sherbet, the sherbet of "I am the Truth." I, on the other hand, drank a glass full of it." And in another poem, he expresses the same idea:

> We are alive with the holy light of God, that light is keeping us alive.
>
> We are both very close to Him, very familiar with Him and very far away from Him, very foreign to Him.
>
> Were we to show our real face, the moon would repent seeing itself and showing its face.
>
> Were we to spread our wings, we would burn even the wings of the sun. This pure body of ours, our physical being that appears in form of a human, is the veil of real existence.
>
> In fact, we are the *qiblah* of all those who prostrate.
>
> Do not look at Adam, created of clay, but rather see the breath that was breathed into him and be fascinated by it.
>
> Satan saw only our outer appearance and not what was in us and therefore thought that we were separate from God.[58]

Elsewhere Rumi says, "Mansur was hung by people since he implied secrets of *tawhid*. If he were alive today, he himself would hang me because of the abundance and exuberance of my secrets."[59]

Rumi has explained the secrets of *tawhid* with many other meaningful poems like the ones above. I do not want to lengthen this section more by considering other poems. But I could not proceed without citing the two couplets that Sipehsalar attributes to Rumi, which I could not find in the *Divan-i Kabir*:

> O my God, this thorn stuck in my foot which prevents me from reuniting with You and walking on Your path comfortably is my own existence.

Therefore, I would like to get away from myself, save myself from myself. This way when I escape from myself, my ego, duality disappears. I become You, You become I.

I cannot sit with You as much as I want as long as Your love does not empty myself from myself and as long as I do not give up on myself, my anachronism.[60]

As the gnostics state, this spiritual state of *ittihad* is such a spiritual level, such a spiritual state that a person who attains the fortune of reaching it cannot stay in this state indefinitely. He cannot carry this heavy burden.

"THERE IS NOTHING ON EARTH OR IN THE HEAVENS THAT DOES NOT PRAISE GOD."

If someone were to come up to you and say that the things that we see on earth and distinguish from plants and animals because we consider them to be lifeless actually were alive, would you believe that person? What does lifeless mean? Lifeless means that it is an object with no soul or spirit; for example, stones or soil. A plant or an animal is alive because the animal moves, eats, drinks, and breeds, and the plant grows, blooms, and bears fruit. We can observe and understand that these are living but we cannot make much sense of the claim that a rock, the soil, cut and dried trees, the water we drink, the dresses we wear, and the personal items we use are all living. However, the Noble Qur'an tells us, for example, "The seven heavens and the earth, and all beings therein, declare His glory. There is not a thing but celebrates His praise; And yet you do not understand how they declare His glory."[61] "We subdued the hills to hymn the praises (of their Lord) with him at nightfall and sunrise."[62] For objects to praise God, they have to be living in some way. In some of his Prophetic Traditions, the beloved Prophet stated that objects also have a form of life. For example, he reminds us, "Do not disturb objects unnecessarily because they are in a state of praise." In a Prophetic Tradition recorded in one of the most trustworthy books, he said, "Before I was charged with the duty of prophethood, I knew a stone that would greet me in Makka. Still at this moment I know which stone that is."[63] Ibn al-Mas'ud (one of the Companions of the Prophet) relates, "While eating with our Prophet we used to hear praises from the food in front of him." Abu Zar said, "When the Messenger of God took some stones in his hand, we used to hear those stones praising like the buzz of a bee, and we would also hear the stones praising the same way in Abu Bakr's and 'Umar's hands." Also the Prophet said: "Do not leave animals with a burden tied on their back. Ride the animals, but do not use them as a stand for your conversation on the street" because they too are in a state of praise. How many animals are more valuable than the people riding on them?

In both the *Mesnevi* and the *Divan-i Kabir* Rumi elaborates on this issue. For example, he says, "(They all say), 'we have hearing and seeing and are happy, (although) with you, the uninitiated, we are mute.'"[64] Since our old scholars took their faith from the Qur'an and the Prophetic Tradition, they conceived that objects like rocks and soil, collectively *jamad*, or lifeless, are alive. They believed that animals have an animal (zoological) spirit, plants a vegetal (botanical) spirit, objects like rocks and soil an inorganic spirit, but that humans have both an animal spirit and a human spirit. The fact that all creatures and things praise God and hence they are alive, which was first made known to us by the Noble Qur'an fifteen centuries ago, is recognized today by science as well.

Today's science and technology has shown clearly that in everything around us that we take to be inanimate there is a kind of life and consciousness that we cannot perceive; all objects that we see around us, all creatures, are made up of atoms. In the center of every atom there is a nucleus composed of protons and neutrons. The electrons around this nucleus revolve at a mind-boggling speed. For example, an electron in a hydrogen atom revolves around the nucleus at 50,000 km/per second. In every object, animate or not, there is constant movement, that is, there is "life." Be they of stone, soil, water, iron or copper, the same events are taking place in all atoms. In the atoms of all these substances, the electrons that travel at mind-boggling speeds are revolving millions of times in a second around their orbits. Thus, it becomes clear that the objects that are in motion are not inanimate; they are alive. This order in the atom, the smallest particle of matter, this mind-boggling design, makes one fascinated with the Creator's Power, Strength, Art of Creation, Uniqueness, and Greatness. With this motion of all the objects around us, it becomes clear that they are alive, praising God, and telling the Highness of His Glory. It is as if the smallest particle, the atom, is a most perfect model of the unique order of a giant solar system.

A true Muslim does not need science and technology to uncover this truth. A believer believes in the amazing things that are relayed by the Qur'an and the Prophet without seeking a scientific explanation. He or she believes in them, but he or she also likes it when science and technology confirm his or her faith with new discoveries. The confirmation of the truths transmitted in the Qur'an centuries ago by today's science and technology acts as an invitation for the non-Muslim scientist to Islam.

The atom is a model of the solar system in which we live. It is possible to think of the atom's nucleus as being the Sun and its electrons as the planets. When one ventures into the depths of the atoms and magnifies a particle billions of times, one can create a giant universe—a universe too amazing and too strange for the mind to perceive. The diameter of an atom is about ten millionths of a millimeter. Yet in every atom there is embedded a solar system. Sensing this truth, the author of the *Gulshan-i Raz* wrote, "If you split the heart of a drop, hundreds of clear seas will be formed from it." The atomic bomb lends us an illustration of the power of the atom. According to the calculations of the scientists, if the energy stored in the atoms of a teaspoonful of coal dust were liberated, it would be enough to heat a city of one million residents.

Seven centuries ago Rumi explained, through analogies, how some objects that are thought to be inanimate have been able to speak. For example, let us read the following couplets:

> Since He (God) made your piece of earth a man, you should recognize (the real nature of) the entire sum of the particles of earth:
>
> (That) from this standpoint they are dead and from that standpoint they are living; (that they are) silent here and speaking yonder.
>
> When He sends them from that quarter toward us, the rod becomes a dragon in relation to us.
>
> The mountains too sing a song like that of David, and the substance of iron is (as) wax in the hand.
>
> The wind becomes a bearer for Solomon, the sea becomes capable of understanding words in regard to Moses.
>
> The moon becomes able to see the sign in obedience to Ahmad (Muhammad), the fire becomes wild-roses for Abraham.[65]

In another volume of the *Mesnevi*, Rumi mentions that the pebbles in Abu Jahl's palm began to speak as a result of a miracle of our Prophet:

> There were some pebbles in the hand of Abu Jahl: "O Ahmad," said he, "tell quickly what this is,
>
> If you are the Messenger (of God), what is hidden in my fist? (Speak), since you have knowledge of the mysteries of Heaven."
>
> He said, "How do you wish (me to do this)?
>
> Shall I say what those (hidden) things are, or shall they declare that I am truthful and right?"
>
> Abu Jahl said, "This second (thing) is more extraordinary."
> "Yes," said the Prophet, "(but) God has greater power than that."
>
> Without delay, from the middle of his (closed) fist every pebble began to pronounce the (Muslim's) profession of faith.
>
> Each said, "There is no deity," and (each) said, "except God"; (each) threaded the pearl of "Ahmad is the Messenger of God."
>
> When Abu Jahl heard this from the pebbles, in his anger he dashed the pebbles to the ground.[66]

Rumi also touches on this issue in other volumes of the *Mesnevi*. For example, "The obedience of the stone to the Prophet and the rod to Moses are made manifest and give information concerning the other lifeless things; (they say), 'we are cognizant of God and obedient (to Him): we all are (bearing witness to His wisdom) not created by chance or in vain.'"[67] Rumi mentions the stones: "We are not unnecessary things that are created in vain"; this reminds me of the following couplet in the Word of Isaac section of the *Fusus al-Hikam* by Muhy al-Din Ibn al-'Arabi: "O You who created all the beings in His Self! You are all that You created." From this, one should not arrive at the understanding that everything created is God Himself. This belief is the belief of the pantheists. The Islamic understanding of this doctrine is called the "Unity of Existence." Muhy al-Din Ibn al-'Arabi, who is the greatest representative of this belief, wants to say, "O my God! In all the things that You have created, in the smallest particles as well as the stars, Your Greatness, Infinity, and Power are manifested. They are like the galaxies that revolve around the stars at an incredible speed, without colliding with one another in the heavens, in space, that symbol for vastness, depth, and infinity. All particles and atoms in all beings revolve around their nucleus at an amazing speed. It is as if a galaxy has been fitted into the heart of an atom. O my God! The Light of Your Power that shines on all the creatures that You have created is enlivening them, and they whirl with Your love and praise You."

In another couplet from the *Mesnevi* Rumi says, "If the mountain and rock had not been endowed with sight, then how should it (the mountain) have become a friend (accompanist) to David?"

Elsewhere in the *Mesnevi*, Rumi mentions the weeping and crying of a date tree, the pillar of *hannane*, because it had become separated from the Prophet:[68]

> The moaning pillar was complaining of (its) separation from the Prophet, just as rational beings (might do).
> The Prophet said, "O pillar, what do you want?" It said, "My soul is turned to blood because of my parting from you.

I was your support: (now) you have run away from me: you have devised a place to lean against upon the pulpit."

"Do you desire," he said, "to be made a date-palm, (so that) the people of the East and the West shall gather fruit from you?

Or that He (God) should make you a cypress in yonder world, so that you will remain everlastingly fresh and flourishing?"

It replied, "I desire that whereof life is enduring forever." Hearken, O heedless one! Do not be less than a piece of wood!

He (the Prophet) buried that pillar in the Earth, that it may be raised from the dead, like humankind, on the day of Resurrection,

So that (hence) you may know that everyone whom God has called (to Himself) remains disengaged from all the work of this world.

Whosoever has work and business from God gains admission there and abandons worldly work.

He that has no portion of spiritual mysteries, how should he believe in the complaining of inanimate objects?

He says, "Yes," not from his heart, but for the sake of agreement, lest people should say that he is a hypocrite (in his religion).

Without those who know of the (Divine) command "Be!" this doctrine (that inanimate things are capable of speech) would be rejected in the world.[69]

As can be seen in the above couplets from the *Mesnevi*, Rumi wants to awaken our insight and consciousness by descending into the depths of our spirit. "O those who have disillusioned themselves in the material world, and have a high opinion of themselves by relying on their mind," he says, "you cannot make sense of the fact that the objects that are thought to be inanimate have life and emotions, can you?" During the life of our Prophet there used to be people like Abu Jahl who did not believe even though they heard the pebbles in their hand declare faith. There were even those who had objected to the Qur'anic verses that talk about the resurrection after death. God has responded to them with verses like these: "Would the One who is powerful enough to nurture a clot of blood into a human being not be able to resurrect the dead?"[70] And: "When God wills something to be, He says 'Be' and it is done at once."[71]

Can we comprehend everything with our mind? Ziya Pasha (d. 1880), an Ottoman intellectual, sensed this truth and expressed it by saying, "Our small minds cannot comprehend these higher truths because this scale of mind cannot weigh those deeply meaningful thoughts." Indeed, can our minds comprehend the depth and extent of outer space, or rather its infinity? The Galileo satellite that was launched into space in 1995 traveled a distance of 3,700,000,000 kilometers, going at the speed of a bullet and reached the orbit of Jupiter. There are countless more suns and stars in the Milky Way Galaxy. According to the latest discoveries, there are 50 billion galaxies in the universe. Stars that are fifteen billion light years away are being discovered. Can the human mind ever grasp the infinity of space? "Think of a plane that can travel at a speed of 186,000 miles an hour (speed of light)," scientists say. "This plane can travel around the universe in one billion years." They came to this conclusion after precise calculations. This is not a product of our imagination. In order to have an idea about God's Greatness, Might, and Power of Creation, we need to think about the infinite skies, be amazed, and plead to God, as our Prophet did, saying, "O God, increase my amazement!" And when we say, "God is Great," we should not say it merely with our lips, without feeling any excitement. Our heart, our intuitive faculties, and consciousness should also be aware of this greatness and this infinity.

Muhy al-Din Ibn al-'Arabi writes in his *Futuhat al-Makkiyyah*, "I hear the praises of things with my own ears. Among the existing objects, the ones that praise God the most are things like the stones and soil that we call inanimate. Then come the plants, the animals, and finally, humankind. It is amazing that man, whom God has created lovingly and who is the 'most honorable of all creatures', is the creature that praises God the least when compared to other creatures, because he is more attached to other creatures." As the Qur'an, our Prophet, and the saints relate, everything that exists on Earth praises God. Our Prophet banned us from killing frogs, saying that their croaking is praise. The frogs praise, the trees praise, the noise of running water praises, the creaking of a door praises God because there is nothing that does not praise God. I could not end this section without including the following poem of a gnostic poet:

> All the sounds of creation, high or low, are all sounds of wisdom, listen to them and hear, O heart, they are all signs from God.
>
> The sea, land, and the skies are like a school, creatures with spirits study there secretly or openly with their teacher, the intellect.
>
> The roaring of the lions comes from Majesty and gives fear to the creatures. The melody of the bird comes from Beauty and is composed of good news.
>
> Don't think that they say "quack, quack"; the goose and the duck in the lake say, "Ya Haqq." The "coo, coos" of the turtle doves in the tree are an act of worship toward God.
>
> The nightingale sings in the rose garden; rumors are being spread about it. The beloved of that bird is the rose. To think that it is the hyacinth is ignorance.
>
> The canary sings and strikes its wings with the wave of unity. To think that it is because of the sound of sweet smell is folly.
>
> The cries of the *nay* (reed flute) are always "Forgive us, You are our Master."[72]
>
> The violin undoubtedly says nothing but "God is Great."
>
> If a lover of God listens to the sound of music, he is enraptured spiritually. Everything that he hears from the strings of the *saz* (lute) is the chant of unity.
>
> "O God, You are my ultimate aim" is the aim in all sounds. The pleasure of God is the desire of all. The rest is but tales.

LOVE

After Rumi had discovered his self and sensed what was in him, he began to see in others, too, what was in him. This way he unified the Love of God with the Love of Humanity. He came to the conclusion that to love humans is to love God. When read carefully, the following couplet makes it quite clear to whom Rumi's infinite love of Shams really was addressed: "Shams of Tabriz is a pretext. We are the one praised in beauty, we are the one praised in grace."[73] In another poem, Rumi advises us to appreciate the value of each other and to love each other because we love our loved ones not because of their physical beings but because of God.

> Come, come, let us appreciate each other, be aware of the value of each other. Because you never know, we might be suddenly separated.
>
> Now that our Prophet has said, "The believer is the mirror of the believer," why are we turning our face from the mirror?
>
> Grudges and hate darken friendship and injure the heart. Why don't we tear out and throw away grudges from the heart?[74]

> Come, join us. We are Lovers of God; join us so we open for you the doors of the garden of love.
>
> Sit in our house as a shadow; we are the neighbors of God's sun. We are invisible to the eye, just as is the soul.
>
> We have no trace or mark, just as the love of the lovers. But our signs are in you and in front of you because we are both hidden as well as apparent, just as the soul.
>
> Whatever you may be speaking of, look further and higher and even beyond that because we are beyond the beyond.
>
> You are like water, but you remain in a hole; you are imprisoned. Open up a way for yourself so you may join us, because we are a flood flowing toward God.[75]

> Come so we may speak to each other from spirit to spirit, talk to each other in a way hidden from eyes and ears.
>
> Let us laugh without lips and teeth just as the rose garden. Let us discourse without lips and mouth just as the thought.
>
> Let us tell the secret of the world completely with our mouth closed at the level of *'Aql al-Awwal* (the First Intellect) and in the awareness of God's existence.
>
> Nobody talks to himself in a loud voice. Since we are all one, let us call out to each other from our hearts without mouths or lips.
>
> How can you say to your hand, "Hold!" Is that hand yours? Since our hands are one, let us talk about this issue.

Hands and feet are aware of the state of the heart. Let us give up conversation made with our tongues and vibrate our hearts.[76]

Rumi's love of humanity is infinite. Beginning with the ancient Greek and Latin poets, including all the classical poets, dramatic writers, philosophers, and sociologists of the West, none had the love of humanity that Rumi felt and made his readers feel.

Come, come, get closer. Till when is this banditry going to continue? Since you are I and I am you, what is this "us and them"? We are God's holy light; we are God's mirror.

So why are we struggling with each other? Why is one light running away from another light so much?

We, all humans, are gathered like a body in the being of a mature person.

But why are we squint-eyed? Although we are limbs of the same body, why do the rich look down on the poor?

Why does the right hand look down on the left hand of the same body? Since both of them are hands of your body, what is the meaning of lucky and unlucky on the same body?

We, all humans, are in reality all one essence. Our minds are one, and our heads are one.

But we have seen one as two because of the curvature of the heavens. Come, liberate yourself from this selfishness and reconcile with everybody and be nice to people.

As long as you are in you, you are a grain, a particle. But when you mix and unite with others, then you become an ocean, a mine.

Every human carries the same soul, but the bodies are in hundreds of thousands.

Similarly, there are countless almonds in the world, but there is the same oil in each of them.

There are many tongues and dialects in this world, but the meaning of all of them is the same.

Waters put in different containers unite when the containers are broken and start to flow together as one stream.

If you understand what unity, *tawhid*, means, if you attain unity and if you rip and throw away meaningless words and thoughts, the spirit sends news to those whose hearts' eyes are open and tells them the truth.[77]

In the above examples, Rumi's thoughts on the love of humanity are illustrated. Rumi will whisper many secrets in the ears of those who carefully read these and reflect on them thoroughly.

Every saint has his own way of feeling. As a saint, Rumi, always speaks of love and lovers. For this reason, Rumi has been titled, "The Sultan of Lovers." In one of his poems, Rumi says:

> Our prophet's way is the way of love.
> We are the children of love, and our mother is love.

There is no doubt that Rumi, throughout his works, emphasizes the concept of love over all else. In the many stories narrated in his book *Mesnevi* and in flowing poems that compose his book *Divan-i Kabir*, the focus is on love. The love of which Rumi speaks is not a transient love. It is not a metaphorical love (*Ishq Majazi*), it is real. The love of which he speaks is love toward the True, which is also called divine love, the love felt for God. Stating that love is an attribute of God, Rumi says:

> Love is the attribute of God, who has no need of anyone. To be in love with other than Him is metaphorical love.[78]

In order to understand the concept of love, we have to elaborate the concepts of *Ishq Majazi* and *Ishq Ilahi*, which are also known as real love. These two kinds of love are known in the teaching of Rumi. The first one, *Ishq Majazi*, is related to the material world and bodily love, like the love between male and female. As real love, *Ishq Haqiqi*, is the love which is felt toward God. In other words, the metaphorical love is transient and, therefore, fleeting. However, real love is eternal and infinite.

Some saints think that what is known as metaphorical love is not an empty one as long as it is not stained and contaminated with bodily desires. It is believed that this type of love can be a bridge to real love. According to this group of saints, love for the beautiful is not love for a person, but it is love for the beauty that the person has. The amazing beauty of the beautiful is a reflection of the beauty of the Creator, His art, His power, and His majesty. To be amazed by such beauty opens the way to the real love. Rumi says:

> Love, be it real or metaphorical,
> Ultimately takes humans to God.[79]

A question needs to be answered here. Why has this metaphorical love, *Ishq Majazi*, been given to humans? Centuries before Freud, the psychoanalyst of modern times, Rumi mentioned the concept in the following poem:

> God has created a desire between man and woman.
> As a result of their union, life in the world continues.[80]

Ibn al-ʿArabi (d. 1240), a prominent Muslim mystic, thinks of this desire mentioned above as complementary. He says the following: "Humans, male or female, are complete after marriage. Alone, woman is a half and man is a half. The man completes himself with the woman. The woman completes herself with man. This union is not a material one, but a spiritually complementary one."[81] Therefore, this desire or romantic love, in fact, is a reflection of the Qur'anic verse, which says, "I have breathed my spirit into Adam and the children of Adam." Therefore, a union of man and woman is, in fact, not a worldly or false desire; rather, it has a relationship with the world beyond material life. It is a relationship between acquainted spirits, and it is an expression of love to one another. However, this love should not be undervalued down to the mere biological level, like that of animals. As the most honorable creatures of God, we have to have different levels of this love through marriage and through the principles of the Law of Islam. Therefore, the religion of Islam does not prohibit romantic love and also does not prohibit marriage. As Rumi says, "This romantic love or desire has been given to people for the continuation of humanity. At the same time, human beings are expected to struggle against their biological desires."

There is no institutionalized celibacy in Islam for males or females, but there is chastity and a pure life and control over desires.

The relationship between males and females is limited to the concept of marriage. Rumi believes that marriage satisfies, allowing a person to control his or her desires. Immoral relationships stain one's conscience. Therefore, this type of relationship is prohibited in Islam. Love is not prohibited, but adultery or fornication is. The following prophetic tradition explains the dimension of this love. The Prophet says,

> The one who falls in love and keeps it to himself and stays chaste and dies, is a martyr.[82]

This tradition suggests that those who avoid adultery and fornication, struggling against their desires, when they die in chastity, are considered martyrs because biological desires are among the most dangerous enemies of human perfection. To defeat these desires is considered to be one of the most heroic acts. In another poem, Rumi says,

> Anger and desire make humans blind.
> Therefore, they change the direction of the spirit.[83]

If romantic love is not kept under control, it may deviate believers from worshipping God and may ruin their happiness and even may take them away from the real sense of humanity. All bodily desires, since they are fleeting, if they are satisfied in an immoral way will be replaced by a pained and guilty conscience after the desires leave. As a Turkish poet says,

> Some of them have touched the conscience,
> And some have touched the body and spirit.
> Whatever I have done for the sake of desire,
> I have become repentant.

The desires that we run after, some of them wound our conscience, some of them wound our body, and some of them ruin our health. Ultimately, we will repent.

Therefore, giving our heart to transient things, to unstable things, such as seasons, and transient beauties, is meaningless. Rumi, in the spring season, watching a flower, which grows, smiling and dancing with the breeze, thinks of the relationship between this flower and the sun. The sun speaks to the flower as follows:

> "Oh smiling flowers! Oh green grass! I will see when I pass over you. Now you are quite joyful because you don't think of your end. Humans, youth, beauties are similar. Beauties open like a flower. They are proud of the beauty of their body. They look at the mirror and they love because they receive power from the spirit hidden in them. It gives life to them and makes them happy."
>
> The spirit speaks to the beautiful who are proud of the beauty of their body as follows:
>
> "You live because of my light. What is the reason for this pride? Through the power that I give you for one or two days, you move, you feel happy, and you think that this material life will never end. Your joy is so big that it cannot fit in this world. Wait and see after I leave you. Those who have loved you very much will bury you in a grave where your body is eaten by ants and snakes. Is there anyone who is content with death? Even those who are content with death will plug their nose so they don't smell your body."[84]

Another Turkish poet, Ziya of Adana, says,

> The sun of beauty ultimately sets.
> I am in love with the Eternal One.
> I do not love those who are fleeing.

After briefly mentioning the concept of transient love, *Ishq Majazi*, we have to elaborate the concept of divine love. Therefore, the question that is posed needs to be answered. How can humans love God, who is not seen, not known, and not understood thoroughly? In fact, God's Messenger, Prophet Muhammad, referring to this ambiguity, says,

> O Lord, we have failed truly to know You, as Your Glory meints.

The Prophet of Islam, despite his closeness to God, confesses that he has not understood God as He merits. Therefore, for ordinary people it is hard to understand, and if they do not understand, how can they love? Ali, the cousin and son-in-law of the Prophet, says, "I don't worship a God whom I don't know." Of course, God is not a material entity to be seen by the eyes. We cannot see Him as we see creatures. As another Turkish poet, Muallim Naci, says,

> The mindful know that there is one God,
> Although His personality is not understood.

In order to love God, first of all, we have to feel His existence with our reason, conscience, and submission. We have to accept His existence. How beautifully it is said in the following poem by Ibrahim Hal al-Din:

> When you read a book,
> You ask who the writer is.
> When you see a nice building,
> You wish to know who the builder is.
>
> Have the heavens and the earth no owner?
> When one thinks of it, one understands,
> That everything proves to us
> That there is a great and Almighty God.

The Creator of this universe, including our planet, has adorned the universe with beautiful works of art, has hidden Himself behind his works, and has made His works as a veil for Himself. We cannot see Him, but His works are obvious. Everything has been created beautifully. The world is ruled by unchangeable rules. The Creator is majestic and unique. Rumi, in one of his poems, prays to the Lord as follows:

> O Lord who gives life to my life, lift the veil on your face.
> O You who join me in my grief and my problems.
> O My Lord, wherever I am, You are with me.
> O Beloved who is with me in the night.
> O the one who hears my supplications all the time.

> O My Lord who has sent the fire of love to all atoms of my
> body. You are exalted from all shapes and all bodies, and you are
> purer than all spirits.
> You have no image or shape,
> but you are the magnet of all my shapes.
> All my existence runs toward You and annihilates itself in You.

As Rumi mentioned in the above poem, we cannot think of the nature of God who is beyond any shape or image. Also because the Prophet of Islam commanded his community, "Reflect on the blessings of God. Do not reflect on (the person of) God." Therefore, we can understand God by means of His Beautiful Names and attributes, and, through His art we can feel. Everyone looking at this art will understand and feel God according to their level of understanding and also according to the grace of God. Without grace and the bounty of God, we cannot find a way from our heart toward Him. Therefore, humans understand God through God. In everything, His power and His art are evident, but to see them depends on the bounty of God. If He does not allow you to see, you will not see. Therefore, as human beings we have to pray to God to show us His power, His art, and His beauty. God has created us as the most honorable creatures in the entire cosmos. As human beings, our existence is not limited to this bodily life. We have become human beings by means of the Trust that has been bestowed on us. As Rumi says, "All those who live on the earth eat and drink, move and travel. All our bodies are in fact a shadow. The reality of our existence is beyond the limit of this body." As the Turkish poet and mystic, Yunus Emre, says, "There is an 'I' in me beyond me." There is also a tradition in which God says, "I wanted to be known, therefore, I have created humankind." The desire to be known is hidden in the concept of love. God does not need to be known and loved, but He loves to be known and loved.

The question is in what way we can love God. We have five known senses, but, in fact, we have a sixth sense as well. We can conceptualize and feel God through this sixth sense. Humans have become different than animals through reason, heart, light, and inner sense. The inner eyes in humans are called the "eyes of the heart," or *Basirah*. These eyes are stronger than the eyes in our head. Rumi says that, "You have two heads. One belongs to the worldly life, which is made of dust. The other belongs to the heavens. It is a pure and spiritual head." Through this spiritual head and spiritual eyes, we can understand reality. Accordingly, what is not understood through the five senses can be understood through the spiritual head and the spiritual eyes, can be felt and tasted through the eyes of the heart. No one can deny the love of God except those who lowered themselves from the level of humanity to the level of animals, and have no senses beyond the five biological senses.

To love God is to give thanks to God. If we think deeply, we will see and feel that God loves humankind, because He has given to us what He has not given to any other creature. Not loving God, despite His unlimited bounties, is to be ungrateful. In fact, there is a human need for love and faith. The person who has abandoned this spiritual need becomes ungrateful, not only to God, but also to all creation, for he has abandoned his real duty. This creates emptiness in the spirit, and such people feel that they are missing something important. Through thinking, one will understand that there is a strong relationship between God, the Creator, and man, His servant. This state is hardly understood. Mostly, we take refuge in God when we are bored, when we grieve, or when we face a disaster, even in joyful times because God is closer to us than ourselves. The Qur'an says, "He is closer to you than your jugular vein."[85] Those who act according to the command of their conscience, remember God frequently, work for humanity, do good deeds and commit their actions perfectly regardless of the nature of their duty, and those who pray to God exceedingly are the happy people who have reached this level of closeness to God.

God is not something material. Therefore, closeness to Him should not be understood in a material or physical sense. This closeness has nothing to do with space and distance. The closeness is through the senses, love, and attributes. As the verse states, "I have blown into him (Adam) a part of my spirit."[86] The human being, who has become the reflection of this verse, is the one who is close to God; and for this reason God commanded the angels to bow before Adam. The verse says, "Surely, We have made you a vicegerent on the earth,"[87] which indicates the superior level of humanity among all creatures. There is a relationship between humankind and God through this special creation of humankind. This is because God has created humankind and made them His vicegerent on the earth. He has given human beings superiority over all other creatures. Rumi, describing the situation of a man who feels alone in this life and has been left by all his friends, says,

Don't feel alone. There is a hidden One here.[88]

The One who is referred to by Rumi is the One who cannot fit within the heavens and earth because of His majesty, but can fit into the heart of the believer because the heart of the believer can be larger than the universe as long as it is attached to God. In another poem, Rumi says,

There is another soul in your soul. You seek for that soul.
In the mountain of your body, there is a highly valuable element. You seek for the mine of that element.
O mystic who looks around, if you search for Him
Don't look for Him outside. For Him, look inside.

The soul of our soul is the spirit which came from Him. The search for the soul is the search for God. To understand God is to love God. But what is love of God in the heart of the servant? This is a feeling in the heart, and the sense of the servant cannot be described in words. It is a subtle, joyful, and pure sense. This leads humans to exalt God over everything, to seek His pleasure before everything. When we fulfill our duties to God we find relaxation in our inner self. Therefore, those who are friends of God and feel friendship with God stay in the state of pureness having that ritual ablution not only at the time of the five daily prayers, but they always think of Him as much as they can. They remember Him with their hearts, they feel Him in their inner sense, and they work hard to have excitement toward Him. The servant will find God's power, His art in everything and in every event and will be amazed. When people smell a beautiful flower's fragrance, they will see the art of God. When people eat fruits, they think of the creation of these tasty fruits from this soil, and they are amazed by the bounties of God that have been given to them and give thanks. Those who travel toward God have to believe in the ultimate justice of God. If they see some injustice in their society, they believe that sooner or later, His justice will prevail, here in this world or the other.

The goal of the mystic is to understand and love the One who has created humankind. The love of the servant for God is not described through inclination, limitation, or encompassing because God cannot be encompassed or limited. In the Sufi tradition, love is described as annihilation in the Beloved. Therefore, love cannot be described, understood, limited, or defined by borders. At the same time, there is nothing more clear and certain than love in the heart of the lover, as long as the lover feels and understands. It is well-known that when something is not understandable, we try to explain it. Through this explanation, we avoid any ambiguity. When it comes to the concept of love, there is no need to explain it. Rumi explains in his following poem:

> Whenever I need to explain the concept of love and think of it,
> I feel repentant when I become influenced by love.
>
> My pen moves over the paper, and the pen would not dare and splits.
>
> Reason, as far as the explanation of love is concerned, is like a donkey stuck in the mud.
>
> Finally, love has provided the explanation of love and the lover.[89]

Similarly, Rumi, in the beginning of his *Mesnevi* says, "Someone asked me, 'What is love?' And I told him, 'When you become like

me, you will understand.'" Therefore, love cannot be counted or measured. In reality, it is an attribute of God. Allegorically, it can be
related to the servant. The Qur'an says, "He loves His servants. They
love Him" (5:54). In fact, to speak of love is not love because love
is a state of experience that cannot be explained in words. There is
no doubt that as a result of knowing God, finding him in our hearts
through the utmost efforts and long contemplations, prayers, good
deeds, and help to others, one will be able, even at the lowest level, to feel the secrets of existence. Through this discovery, the person may reach a high level of spiritual state and can feel an indescribable joy of the spirit. Therefore, one can say that the spiritual
enjoyment, which comes from knowing and loving God is beyond
all pleasures. The goal of all lovers of God is to reach that level.
Here lies the spiritual flavour that few can feel. It has been said that
those who feel this state and have reached this level have annihilated their wants and they have no grief at all. Their hearts have
become busy with spiritual flavour. Even if they are thrown into
fire, they will have no feeling of fire because of their utmost joyful-
ness that they have been experiencing. Even if the whole of paradise is offered to them, they will not look at it because the joy that
they have is even higher than paradise. Rumi describes the state of
such mystics in the following poem:

> O My Lord, who is my rest for my soul when I am in grief,
>
> O My Lord, who is the treasure of my spirit when I hunger
> in poverty,
>
> What the imagination cannot attain and understanding and
> reason cannot reach, since all beauties come from You to my
> spirit, You are my Pole Star.
>
> My Lord, because of Your grace and bounty I look down on
> worldly things. How can the transient world, riches, wealth
> deceive me? My Lord, through Your utmost generosity, if You
> give me countless properties and You put before me all Your
> hidden treasures, I will prostrate from my innermost being and
> put my face on the ground and say, "My Lord, for me, Your
> love is worthier than all of this."[90]

The beloved of all Muslims is the Prophet of Islam. In fact, not only Rumi, but all saints have love and respect for the Prophet of Islam. Moreover, they love not only the Prophet of Islam, but all messengers of God. Rumi has a special place in his heart for the Prophet of Islam because he proposed a high level of ethics for humanity, such as freeing slaves and taking care of the poor. Historically speaking, there is no historical personality like Muhammad who brought freedom to slaves and the lower classes. Therefore, not only Muslim saints but philosophers like Thomas Carlyle and the German poet Goethe have fallen in love with Prophet Muhammad because of his service to humanity throughout his life. In their books, they have expressed their reverence for Prophet Muhammad. Very recently, Michael Hart has written a book about the hundred most influential historical personalities and ranked Muhammad number one.[91]

Throughout the history of Islam, Muslim scholars and poets have expressed their love for the Prophet of Islam. These poems and writings have constituted a tremendous amount of literature about the love of the Prophet in Islamic literature. Rumi is one of the prominent Islamic mystics and poets, who wrote on the same subject. When he writes about the Prophet, his poetry receives an excitement and warmness because the poem involved in the love of the Prophet is illuminated by his light. For example, in the following poem, he speaks of the love of God, and he immediately jumps to the love and remembrance of the Prophet.

> We hear all the time the voice of divine love from right and left.
>> With the influence of this voice we are ascending to the heavens.
>> Who has the capacity to watch us?
>> Before coming to this world we were in heaven.
>> We were friends of the angels.
>> There is our real homeland, and we will return to it.
>> How distant are the pure pearl of the divine and the dirty world of the soil. Without thinking of your honor, you came to this lower world. Pick up your properties and tie up your burden. This place is not ours. We have to migrate.

The young chance is our friend. Sacrificing the soul is our job. And the head of our caravan is Mustafa, the Prophet, of whom the whole universe is proud.

Mustafa, peace and blessings be upon him, is so high a being that the moon did not dare to see his face and split.

The fragrance of the wind of this spring comes from his blessed hair. The shining of our imagination comes from his beauty, which reminds us of the newly rising sun.

In these poems, Rumi remembers the Prophet and his love. He speaks of the Prophet sometimes with the name of Ahmad, sometimes with the name of Muhammad, and sometimes with the name of Mustafa. These are honorable names of the Prophet. As well known, every saint in Islam has his own way and focus on specific things. As far as Rumi's way is concerned, love, love of God, and love of humanity because of its manifestation of God's love are all emphasized. Because of Rumi's great love for humanity, he tolerated the mistakes of people. Therefore, one has to consider Rumi's love for the Prophet from this perspective. The well-known title of Prophet Muhammad is *Habib Allah* or the Beloved of God. The Prophet is the ideal model of all human beings. Therefore, his love for the Prophet is based on this principle. In his famous poem, Rumi says,

I am the servant of the *Qur'an* as long as I live. And I am the soil where the foot of Muhammad stepped.

With this Rumi expresses his deep love for Muhammad. Therefore, Rumi can be considered one of the great poets who emphasized the love of the Prophet in his poems. In some of his poems, he dedicates the entire *ghazal* to the Prophet. These are called *na't* in which the attributes of Muhammad are narrated. In some cases, Rumi, while speaking about various things, suddenly refers to the love of the Prophet. For example, while speaking of the relationship between the heart and love, Rumi refers to Prophet Muhammad and his great Companion Abu Bakr. Rumi says,

Heart and love have become friends, like Ahmad and Abu Bakr
became friends in the cave. These two friends' names were different, but their spirits were one.[92]

In another poem, Rumi expresses Prophet Muhammad's light,
as enlightening the whole world:

The light of Muhammad has become distributed in millions of
pieces and has encompassed the whole world.

The Prophet was like the lightning of that light.

When it strikes, all veils of unbelief are torn, and thousands of
monks are influenced by Muhammad and run toward him.[93]

In another poem, Rumi speaks of unbelief in the light of Prophet
Muhammad:

When Muhammad's light came, unbelief put on its black clothes.

When the period of the eternal kingdom came, the unbelievers hit the drum to prevent death.

The whole face of the earth had become green. The heavens
envied the earth and tore its sleeve. The moon had become
split. The earth received life and became alive.

Last night, there was a big commotion among the stars
because a peerless star had descended to the earth.[94]

Rumi speaks of the love of the Prophet in his monumental work,
the *Mesnevi*. He says the following:

If the face of Muhammad is reflected on a wall, the heart of the
wall will become alive.

The wall, through his blessed reflection, will have such great
happiness that even the wall will be rescued from hypocrisy.

It would be a shame for the wall to have two faces while the
pious and the pure have only one.[95]

In another poem, Rumi speaks of Prophet Muhammad's inter-
cession in this world and in the other world.

The honorable Muhammad, peace and blessings be upon him,
is the intercessor in this world and the other.

This world is the world of religion and the other world is the world of paradise.

He shows them the way in this world, and in the other world, he shows them his moonlike face.

Muhammad's secret and evident prayer was to say,

"O my Lord, show my followers the right path. In fact, they don't know."

With his blessed breath, the doors of the two worlds were opened.

His prayer had been accepted in both.

No one like him has come to the world, and no one like him will come.[96]

According to Rumi, as indicated in one of his poems, all Muhammad's words came from the ocean of reality. He says,

His words totally are pearls from the ocean of reality
Because his heart was united with the ocean of truth.[97]

In another part of his *Mesnevi*, Rumi narrates miracles of Muhammad in several of his poems with great enthusiasm.

It has been narrated from Anas, son of Malik, that a certain person became his guest.

He (that person) related that after the meal Anas saw that the table napkin (was) yellow in hue,

Dirty and stained; and said, "O maid-servant, throw it into the oven at once."

Thereupon the intelligent (maid) threw it into the oven, which was full of fire.

All the guests were astounded thereat: they were in expectation of (seeing) the smoke of the (burning) napkin.

After a short time she took it out of the oven, clean and white and purged of that filth.

The party said, "O venerable Companion, how didn't it burn, and how too did it become cleansed?"

He replied, "Because Mustafa (Muhammad) often rubbed his hands and lips on this napkin."

O heart afraid of the fire and torment (of Hell), draw nigh unto such a hand and lip as that!

Since it (the Prophet's blessing) bestowed such honour upon a lifeless object, what things will it reveal to the soul of the lover!

Inasmuch as he (the Prophet) made the clods of the Ka'ba the *qibla*, do you, O soul, be (as) the dust of holy men in (your) war (against the flesh).

Afterwards they said to the maid-servant, "Will not you tell (us) your own feelings about all this?

Why did you (so) quickly cast it (into the oven) at his behest? I suppose he was acquainted with the secrets, (But) why did you, mistress, throw such a precious napkin into the fire?"

She answered, "I have confidence in the generous: I do not despair at their bounty.

What a piece of cloth? If he bid me (myself) go without regret into the very essence of the fire,

I, from perfect confidence (in him), will fall in: I have great hope of them that are devoted to God.

I will throw myself, not (only) this napkin, because of my confidence in every generous one who knows the mystery."

O brother, apply thyself to this elixir: the faith of a man must not be less than the faith of a woman.

The heart of a man that is less than a woman is the heart that is less (in worth) than the belly.[98]

Rumi in a poem in his *Divan-i Kabir*, speaks of the influence of the Prophet of Islam on his Companions and how they were amazed by his personality and teachings.[99]

In another poem from his *Divan*, Rumi speaks of the light that Muhammad brought to humanity and how people that were bewildered in the darkness of unbelief came to life with the light brought by Muhammad.[100]

In another poem, again in his *Divan*, Rumi speaks of Islam that Muhammad revealed to humanity and the strength that remained in this religion even after centuries.[101]

In the *Mesnevi*, Rumi speaks of the Prophet of Islam and the Qur'an, which have remained unchanged as a promise of God. This displays the strength of Islam and its prophet, according to Rumi.

Rumi wrote these poems seven centuries ago in the time of turbulence and almost total destruction of the Muslim world by the Mongols and Crusaders. Mosques were destroyed and thousands of Muslims lost their lives. Despite this horrible destruction, Rumi was not a pessimist. As seen in his poems, he spoke of love and hope and believed that Islam will remain as a religion forever. He suggested that Muslims will face that kind of oppression from transgressors with patience and hope.

BELIEF AND UNBELIEF

There are many different religions and creeds in our world inhabited by billions of people. All over the world, there are mosques, churches, and synagogues. Since the earliest times of history, people of many different colors and many different nations have been worshipping in innumerable houses of worship, praying to idols that they themselves made in countless temples. It is an undeniable fact that humans have a need to worship. A person who does not believe will surely feel an emptiness inside. After losing his religious faith, Tevfik Fikret, the well-known Turkish poet of the twentieth century, felt the need to believe and complained as follows, "All is empty, earth is empty, sky is empty, heart and consciousness are empty, I'd like to hold on, but there is no point in front of me." Mehmet Akif (the author of the Turkish national anthem) said, "A faithless, rusty heart is nothing more than a burden in the chest."

Even today, no matter how materialistic they have become, people are still unable to stay away from religious belief. Russia is a most recent example of this fact for the whole world. Religion, which was banned by the communists, could not be eliminated. Despite all efforts, the view that says "Religion is the opiate of the masses" proved wrong.

How did Rumi view these "religious feelings" the inevitable spiritual need of human beings? Since Rumi saw humans as beings that carry the Divine Entrustment, he loved people no matter to which faith or creed they belonged, and therefore respected all religions. It is for this reason that behind the coffin of that great saint, not only Muslims but also Christians and Jews shed tears. As Aflaki writes, a preacher in Konya, when speaking of Christians, said, "Praise be to God that He did not create us among the Christians." When they related this statement to Rumi, Rumi said about that preacher, "He is wrong himself and also makes others go astray. He is weighing himself with the balance of the Christians and boasting because he happens to be one gram heavier. If he came and weighed himself with the balance of the prophets and saints, then he would realize his real value."

Since everything, all beings, reflect the manifestations of Divine Attributes, events that seem to be contradictory are based on a supreme wisdom our minds may not comprehend. Everything is under God's control; everything comes from Him. The followers of all religions and creeds are carrying out His orders and walking on the line of destiny that He has drawn. We have no right to criticize anybody in this regard. Every follower of a creed has known his belief as right and walked on that path although it is wrong with respect to other creeds. Rumi explains this matter in the following couplets of the *Mesnevi*:

> In the world there are invisible ladders, (leading) rung by rung up to the summit of Heaven.
>
> There is a different ladder for every class, there is a different heaven for every (traveler's) way.
>
> Everyone is ignorant of another's condition (in) the kingdom (which is) wide and without end or beginning.[102]

Since God's predestination in the eternal past and His will are manifested in people's way of worshipping and believing, those who remained outside the "path of guidance" are people who walk on the "path of misguidance" and are all known to God. Therefore, the Holy Qur'an does not begin by saying "Lord of the Muslims" but "Lord of the Worlds" (Lord of all beings, everybody, and everything other than God). We have to know very well that God alone creates guidance and misguidance. Everything depends on His will and predestination in the eternal past. If God wills, He can guide a misguided person to the true path. He also can misguide someone walking on the true path to the path of misguidance. This is God's will that no mind can grasp. It is also true that as much as finding the true path or going astray from the true path is a result of predestination in the eternal past, with God's permission, our effort and endeavors also have a role in it. It is for this reason that the gnostics have said, "The predestination of the eternal past loves effort." If one pays attention, one can see and sense that God leads everyone to success in the field where he spends his effort. If a person's soul is rotten with evil, bad deeds and inappropriate attitudes emerge from him. If a person's essence is good, good deeds and pleasant acts emerge from him. That is to say that the goodness or badness of the deeds depends on the goodness and badness of the essence.

There are many common beliefs among the religions of the world. For example, murder, theft, and lying are vices in all religions. Considering these common aspects of the religions, Akbar Shah, the great Turkish-Mongol ruler of India, wanted to invent a new composite religion by merging all religions and creeds, but the great saint Ahmad Sirhindi prevented this attempt and helped millions of Muslims in India, Pakistan, and Java to preserve their faith.

Rumi also viewed faith and unbelief differently and explained these notions differently:

> With the eye of the heart, look at the believer and unbeliever.
>   They don't have anything but the cry 'O Lord!' and the wail
> 'O Ever-Alive!' according to their own beliefs.[103]

If we view this sky as the dome of a great house of worship, under that dome there arise many mosques, churches, and synagogues. In many different ways, in many different houses of worship, in many different religions, and with many different words, people of many different colors all pray to the unique and peerless God and ask Him for his help. How glorious, how great, how mighty is He that His Holy Name is pronounced in many different languages. He knows all languages, understands what everybody says, listens to the prayers of His servants who pray to Him with their hands open, no matter where these people might be on earth or in which house of worship. He even knows what goes through their minds and hearts. In a couplet from the *Mesnevi*, Rumi explains how God, the Most Merciful, the Most Compassionate, protects His servants, declaring, "Whatsoever the soul which is in man and woman strives to do, the ear and eye of the soul's King are at the window."[104]

As Rumi states, the Muslim who prays in a mosque with open hands, a Christian who makes the sign of the cross in the church, and a Jew who prays in a synagogue all turn to God. If we get stuck in the formalities and are overtaken by appearances, we categorize them as Muslim, Christian, and Jewish based on their beliefs and the houses of worship they attend. However, in the sight of God, no matter to what religion or creed they belong, they all are His servants. Therefore, Ziya Pasha says, "In the sight of God, the Muslim and the fire-worshipper are one." That is to say, both are His servants. "Infidelity, too, is wisdom in relation to the Creator, (but) when you impute it to us, infidelity is a noxious thing."[105]

Do you not see that the moth flies into the flame of a candle—whether in a mosque, church, or synagogue—without making any distinctions between them? God has opened up His table not only to the Muslims, but also to non-Muslims and even to those who deny Him, and He feeds them all generously. He does not distinguish between them as believer or unbeliever, in terms of keeping them alive. In another poem, Rumi says, "Know well that belief and unbelief are like the white and yellow of an egg. There is a membrane that separates them. Therefore, they do not mix with each other. With God's grace and favor, when the mother hen takes it under her wings, both belief and unbelief vanish and the chick of unity cracks the egg and emerges."

Rumi, who saw not the outer aspects of the religion but the truth of it, reveals in one of his quatrains: "Know this well that the lover of God cannot be a Muslim, in the sect of love there is neither faith nor unbelief. In the lover there is no body, no mind, no soul, no heart; and if a person is not like this then that person is not a lover of God."

These issues should not be misinterpreted. Rumi means that if the lover of God cannot reach the view of unity and believe that all people who worship in mosques, churches, and other houses of worship in many different ways actually turn to God, plead to Him in many different languages and that the essence of all religions is the same, then that person cannot be a true Muslim. Such a Muslim's understanding of Islam is still in the imitation stage; he has not yet been able to ascend to the realization level. That is, that person could not become a Muslim in the true sense. In yet another quatrain Rumi says, "You are both the unbeliever and the unbelief and you are worse than these two. You are both the believer and the belief, and you are the head of the two." We should know that this is another way of expressing the same belief. Just as the farmer is called *kafir* (unbeliever, one who covers the truth), since he hides the seed inside the soil, a person who does not know what is in him and covers the truth is also *kafir*. By the same token, a person who knows what is in him is a holder of faith, a believer because in the Noble Qur'an it says that, "Wherever you may be, God is with you."[106] A person who is not aware of the Divine Entrustment in him is an unbeliever, and a person who is aware is a believer.

When we read couplets that contain the words "belief" and "unbelief" in the poetry of Rumi and other Sufi poets who consider these Sufi views, that is, the view of unity, we should not be confused and misinterpret them. For example, let us examine this couplet by Rumi: "My unbelief, faithlessness, is the mirror of the faith in you. O son, you observe both belief and unbelief in me."[107] In this couplet there is an implicit reference to the Prophetic Tradition: "A believer is the mirror to another believer." Rumi means to say that whatever you believe in you, see it in me because I am your mirror; you watch and see the belief and unbelief in me. Rumi does not count the faith of those who worship in ostentation and those who value the form more than the spirit as faith. He wants them to advance their faith from imitation to realization. In a quatrain he says, "As long as the Islamic seminary and minaret are not torn down, the spiritual states of the lovers of God who walk on the paths of truth, in sincerity and without ostentation, will not attain stability. No servant of God can be considered Muslim until worship done for a gain and faith that is based on imitation are viewed as unbelief and until the faith of the seeker of truth, which is seen as unbelief by those who cannot comprehend the truth, is viewed as true faith." In this quatrain, the theme is that the faith of those who do not rely on the love of God and who do not raise their faith from imitation to realization is not real, according to Rumi, but is unbelief.

While immature Sufis accuse the lovers of God who do not give the first priority to formalities of unbelief, the lovers of God view those who do give such priority as unbelievers because they do not penetrate into the essence and know the truth. Therefore, Rumi says, "Don't you know that our unbelief is the spirit of Islam?"[108] Rumi reminds us frequently that it is wrong to call someone an unbeliever by just looking at his outer aspects. In another quatrain, Rumi says, "If you walk without seeing, the path is the very essence of the mistake. If you rely on your eye thinking that you see everything, this is the arrow of calamity. How would you know the true place of people in the madrasa and the church and where they actually are just by looking at their form, in a metaphorical way, without knowing their essence?"

As seen in the above examples, Rumi transcended faith and unbelief; he attained love and unity and found God and truth. He explains this matter very clearly and very well in the following quatrains, "Outside the world of faith and faithlessness there is a place. It is not the place for every young, immature, and beautiful person. To attain that unique place and extraordinary level one has to sacrifice his life and heart as thanks for attaining that place." This spiritual level is not a rank that any servant can be blessed with attaining. In another quatrain Rumi tells of the gnostic who attains this level: "There is a plain outside of unbelief and Islam. In the middle of the plain is our love. When the gnostic arrives in that plain, he puts his head on the ground and prostrates because in that plain there is no unbelief and Islam."

In the following poems, Rumi explains how he overcame the obstacles of unbelief and faith, *yaqin* (certainty of faith) and skepticism with the love of God and attained God and truth:

> "And if he speaks of infidelity, it has the scent of (the true) religion, and if he speaks of doubts, his doubt turns to certainty."[109]

> "I melted like salt in the sea of clarity, the sea of spiritual joy. There remained no unbelief, faith, yaqin or skepticism in me. There appeared a star inside my heart. Such was the star that the seven heavens and everything within them vanished inside it."

When you hear Rumi's views on religion, faith and unbelief, do not suppose that he is putting forward new ideas, that is, carrying out reforms in the area of religion and faith. These views are not only held by Rumi. But the fact remains that since Rumi was a great and very talented poet in addition to being a great saint, he explained this very difficult to understand matter in a beautifully clear manner. Other poets also showed interest in this issue. For example, Hafiz of Shiraz (d. 1390) says, "There is no difference between the Ka'ba and the temple of idols. Wherever you turn you are with God, and whatever you see is His Power and Art." Another poet writes, "Sometimes I seclude myself in church, sometimes I sit in the mosque. O God, I am looking for you house by house." While yet another poet says, "O God, I throw into the fire and burn this religion and this creed that does not lead me to You. Instead of a creed I make Your love my guide. Until when can I hide Your love? All my aim is You, I want You. I have nothing to do with religion or creed." Do not consider this poet as irreligious and creedless. He means to say, "O God, I have taken Your love to the forefront, I throw into the fire and burn this religion and this creed that does not lead me to You." When the Turkish poet and mystic Yunus Emre said, "The creed of love is religion to me," did he mean to say "I have no religion"? And was it not Yunus Emre who brought the love of God to the forefront and sincerely proclaimed to God that he was not aspiring to paradise?

> What people call "Paradise! Paradise!"
> Is a few houses and houris.
> Give them to whoever wants them
> But I long for You.

These views that center around the belief in unity and divine love are not mere individual attempts. It is because of this tolerance in the Islamic view that Muslims have looked at the religion of the people in the lands they conquered with respect; they did not interfere with their beliefs nor touch their churches. It is due to this belief that Mehmed II, the Conqueror, who was a young man in his early twenties, showed respect to the Byzantine patriarch and reinstated him as the patriarch.

I would like to end this section with a couplet by Hafiz of Shiraz. As commonly known, Jesus said, "If someone slaps your face, turn the other cheek." The people of Ta'if stoned the Prophet and made his holy feet bleed. If Prophet Muhammad had used his authority as a prophet, he could have made stones and fires rain on them from the sky, or he could have devastated them with hurricanes and strong winds. However, the dear Prophet prayed to God, "O Lord, do not punish these people because of me; forgive them, they are ignorant people, they do not know what they are doing." This is because the prophets knew very well that one could not hate people created by God without upsetting Him. Contrary to a common misconception, unbelief is not only denying God. Unbelief is turning one's back on Islamic principles. Unbelief is not living Islam. Hafiz of Shiraz expressed this idea in his couplet: "Let us be loyal, let us take the blame, let us be looked down upon. But let us still be content and happy with our state. Let us not feel offended by anyone because in our Law, being hurt, upset, and offended is unbelief."

SALVATION

We all are longing for a perfect, flawless human being. How difficult it is to find a perfect human being in our day. When we see flaws that arise in those valuable people whom we respect and love, we are disillusioned, torn down from inside, and we feel an urge to love people and accept them with their both good and bad sides. We say, "Flawless humans cannot be found." But in this regard we should not be completely hopeless. Though in this world people turn to materialistic values by losing spiritual values, it is still possible to find superior people, flawless people, and perfect people even if they are one in a million. They are the suns of the spiritual world and the world of humanity.

For a moment let us suppose that the sun of this perceived material universe darkens until it extinguishes; everything on the face of the earth will be destroyed and life will stop. But how about the suns of the spiritual world? We live because of them; we realize our humanity because of them. When they retire from the face of the earth, spiritual life will stop and human beings will lose their humanity. Grudge, anger, lies, hypocrisy, envy, jealousy, lust, and many other evils will cover the earth and people will start eating each other like beasts. It is known that once Diogenes, a philosopher of Sinop, a city on the shores of the Black Sea, walked on the streets with a lamp in his hand in broad daylight looking for a human being. Were there not any humans around him? Indeed, there were plenty, but the philosopher was seeing them as wolves, foxes, rabbits, and pigs disguised in human form. In his opinion there were no human beings on the streets; the streets were full of animals in human form.

One day Rabia al-Adawiyyah (an early woman mystic in Islam) came out into the street in ecstasy without properly covering herself according to the tradition of that era and walked in the market place. When she ran across the great saint Hasan al-Basri, she covered half of her face. When her ecstasy subsided, they asked her the reason why she came out without proper covering, and she replied, "I didn't see any human in the streets. I saw some foxes sitting in front of the stores, many wolves walking down the street, and some dogs that were snarling at each other. In this herd of animals, I saw a half human, and I covered half of my face." With the following couplet, Rumi reminds us of Diogenes, who was looking for a human being with a lamp in his hand in broad daylight: "Yesterday a shaykh took a lamp in his hand. He said, 'I am tired of devils and beasts. I seek a true person.'"[110]

A philosopher likens people to buildings. The sides of the buildings that face the street are beautiful, clean, and decorated. Their rear sides are poorly maintained and contaminated. Somebody whom we call "a nice person" is one whom we view from one side and see his good attributes. However, there may be many bad attributes of a person whose good side we see and like. Similarly, people whom we consider bad and hateful can have many good attributes. Therefore, people are both good and bad. Rumi does not view people from one perspective; he considers them from all sides. He seeks ways of salvation for humankind. He strives to cleanse them from their flaws and make them true human beings. In the *Mesnevi*, Rumi says,

> The human body is like a jungle where predators roam. We have to be very careful and watchful not to be victimized and torn into pieces. In our body there are thousands of wolves, thousands of pigs, clean, dirty, beautiful and ugly, thousands of attributes. If one of these attributes in us overweighs we come under the influence of that attribute. . . . Sometimes the wolf in man takes control of the city of the body and it acts; then the attribute of wolf appears. Sometimes, the human becomes a beautiful person like Joseph with a face as beautiful as the

moon. Goodness, evil, hate, grudge keep on flowing from heart to heart through secret channels. Every moment there is a different thing that emerges in the heart. The human sometimes turns into a devil, sometimes into an angel, sometimes into a trap, and sometimes into a beast.[111]

It is clear that Rumi views human beings comprehensively, considering all of their attributes. Thus, the human being is neither absolutely good, nor absolutely evil. Rumi says, "Sometimes angels envy our cleanliness and sometimes the devils run away from our evil." He also says in the *Mesnevi*, "Since there are many devils who have the face of Adam, it is not well to give your hand to every hand."[112]

Considering man's habits and attributes, Rumi says in one of his poems, "They have made this physical form and appearance of man by bringing together many opposite attributes. They have drawn this form in the workshop of sorrows. They have kneaded his clay with sadness. The human being sometimes becomes a devil, sometimes an angel, and sometimes a wild beast. What a mysterious creature is man that different habits, virtues, goodness and evil have come together in him."[113] After seeing humankind in this manner with an eye that sees the truth as a creature that has gathered both good and evil attributes in itself, Rumi seeks ways to salvation for them.

How can humanity be saved? How can those wild beasts in the jungle of the body be annihilated? How are we going to overcome the animal within us and regain our lost humanity? How are we going to do away with our bad habits? According to Rumi, our passions, anger, and lust have taken our humanity prisoner. How are we going to liberate our humanity from the captivity of these beasts? Rumi gives us some suggestions: "Throw away the passion, envy, and grudges from the heart. Change your bad behavior and bad thoughts. Denying everything harms you, deny little. Affirmation is, on the other hand, useful. Increase your affirmation."[114] Rumi wants us to get away not only from bad behavior but also from adoring the world and striving to gain material prosperity, and to be courageous: "Until when are you going to think about this soul that flutters within needs? Until when are you going to worry about this world that is full of hardship and struggle? All that the world can take from you is this body. Count yourself, your material existence, this pile of flesh that is going to decay and feed the ants and the worms as garbage and do not worry so much."[115]

It is not that Rumi does not want us to work, but rather he does not want us to love the material world because in another place Rumi says, "What is the world? The world is the state of being unaware of God. It is not richness, wealth, possessions, and having children." Although human beings are not the largest, the strongest, or the most powerful creatures in the outer world, or the universe of material, they became the masters of the universe due to their mind and intelligence, and they overpowered the strongest and the most courageous animals. They use the huge elephant as a servant although the elephant could easily throw them with its trunk and trample them under its feet. Human beings put the most dangerous predators—lions, tigers—in a cage like helpless birds. But unfortunately humans have been defeated by the animals inside; they have been overpowered by them. The masters of the material universe, the brave, capable, resourceful, and strong humans who keep all animals under their command, fly in the skies, go to the moon, invent radios, television, attain dazzling successes—how surprising it is that they have surrendered to the animals inside. They have become the slaves of the wolf of anger, the snake of lust, the dog of the *nafs* (ego and desires). In order to teach us a lesson, in the following lines, Rumi complains of the dog of the *nafs* as follows: "I thought that if I put the chain of repentance around the neck of the dog of the *nafs*, if I make it old that way, maybe I could eliminate its rebellion. But whenever it sees a decaying corpse, it breaks the chain and runs for the corpse. I do not know how I am going to deal with this dog of the *nafs*. I do not know what I should do to this dog of the *nafs*."[116]

According to Rumi, humankind is a poor slave that seems free and independent. People have invisible handcuffs on their wrists and chains tied to their feet. A human is a slave that is forced to serve both his or her desires and the animals in him or her. It is for this reason that real freedom is to be free from the influence of the internal animals. Our Great Prophet viewed this internal struggle, man's battle with his lower self (*nafs*), as "the greatest jihad" and described it as the greatest battle for the sake of God in the path of independence. According to Rumi, in order for us to win this battle, we need first to find ourselves and know where we came from and what we are. The moment we get to know ourselves the good news of our freedom will reach us. As Rumi puts it, we first need to take off the bond of body from the spirit. We need to turn our head to the heavens because our place is not this dirty soil. We are like the animals with our flesh and blood but we are not animals.

Rumi maintains that we need to cleanse our body that has become contaminated with desires. In the *Mesnevi* he says, "O defiled in body, frequent the tank: outside the tank, how shall a man be cleansed? The bodily pure one who has been banished from the tank becomes distanced also from his spiritual purity. The purity of this tank is infinite; the purity of bodies is little weight. A man can purify his body, but the purification of the heart is not easy."[117] According to Rumi there are two great enemies that prevent humankind from attaining true humanity: one of them is lust, the other one anger. "Anger and lust make a man squint-eyed; they change the spirit (so that it departs) from rectitude."[118] Humankind has been created in the middle level. Above them are the angels and below them are the animals. Human beings are close to the angels with their mind and knowledge. They are close to the animals with their anger and lust. Rumi explains that the person who becomes a slave to his selfish desires and lust is far away from the true path: "If you are taken by lust and desires of the self, let me tell you that you will go empty- handed and without any gains. If you give up lust, you will see clearly why you came to this world and where you are going."[119]

According to Rumi, in order for us to be saved, we should first turn inside ourselves and see our mistakes. We should cleanse the house of the heart from dirty thoughts. We should keep it as clean as a house of worship. We should endure the calamities that strike us. We should believe that everything comes from God and nothing happens without His will, and for this reason we should not complain of diseases, poverty, and sorrows. We should see the trouble that comes from the Beloved as a remedy. "O heart, there is you and there is His trouble. How pleasant is it to be troubled by Him. His trouble is your remedy. Therefore, endure the pain and sorrows that come from Him; do not complain or lament. This is His will and His command is this. If you trample your material desires under your feet, you will kill the dog of the self, and this is the real sacrifice."[120] We are created from the soil, and we live on the soil. With our bodies we are tied to the soil, and like animals we also eat and drink, but in us there is a Divine Entrustment (*amanah kubra*) that is not in the animals, and therefore our heads are in the heavens. In our physical composition and our body we resemble animals, but we are human in our spirit and the Divine Entrustment that is in us. We take the food that nourishes our body from the soil. The nourishment of our spirit is above, in the heavens. The nourishment for our spirit and for our humanity is the holy light of God that fills the earth and the heavens. In the *Mesnevi*, Rumi explains this idea: "Man's original food is the Light of God: animal food is improper for him. But, as a result of disease, his mind has fallen into this (delusion) that day and night he should eat of this water and clay. (He is) pale-faced, weak-footed, faint-hearted—where is the food of Heaven which has (starry) tracks? That is the food of the chosen ones of the (Divine) sovereignty; eating thereof is (done) without throat or implement."[121]

So, in order to conquer bad habits and animalistic feelings that are hidden in us, Rumi advises us to nourish ourselves with heavenly foods and discover the ore, the entrustment that is in us. In order to open our hearts' eyes and to escape animality and attain humanity—in other words, to let our good habits come up and our humanity be dominant, that which is hidden in our body (our animalistic side in physical terms)—we need to contemplate God, who created the whole universe, and who is the possessor of all creatures, to feel Him in our hearts, to know that we are always in His presence, no matter wherever we may be. If we realize His power, art, and greatness by looking at the works of art He has created, and frequently remembering Him, we descend to our hearts. We find Him there, gain His holy light, and shine with His holy light. Our eyes as well as our hearts shine with Him, and we come to realize that we are not alone. In the *Divan-i Kabir*, Rumi says, "There is someone hidden here. Do not think that you are alone." Also in a couplet in the *Mesnevi* he says "When Man receives light from God, he is worshipped by the angels because of his being chosen (by God)."[122]

For human beings to discover what is in themselves, Rumi offers a variety of metaphors and examples. He says that the jug that finds a secret passage to the sea of unity ceases to be a jug and becomes a sea: "The great rivers kneel (in homage) before the jar into which there comes a channel from the sea."[123] Human beings are created from soil, but when Adam became subject to Divine Manifestation and was charged with the Divine Entrustment, he gained superiority and became the most honorable and the most superior of all creatures. Rumi indicates this truth in the following couplets from the *Mesnevi*:

> When the earth of Adam became God's courier, God's angels laid their heads (in worship) before His earth. . . . He is the Ruler and (the One who said) God does what He wills: from the very self of pain, He creates the remedy. Then it has become certain that You exalt whoever You will: He said to an earthly creature, "Unfold your wings." To the creature of fire He said, "Go, become Iblis (Satan): be gone under the Seventh Earth

with (your) imposture! O earthly Adam, go you above (the star)
Suha; O fiery Iblis, go to (the bottom of) the earth."[124]

While we try to recognize the Divine Entrustment in us, we
should also push the devil that is in us to the deepest corners of our
self and imprison him. For us to save our humanity that is a slave
of our animalistic nature, it is necessary to think and realize where
we came from and where we are going. Rumi discloses this truth
to us in the following couplets:

> I am not of the same order as the King of kings—far be it from
> me!—but I have light from Him. His light illuminated me in
> (His) self-manifestation. Homogeneity is not in respect of
> form and creation, that is to say, we are not homogeneous with
> Him in form and essence. We have relations with Him, since
> we are reflections of his names and attributes: water becomes
> homogeneous with earth in the plant. Wind (air) becomes
> homogeneous with fire in consistency; wine at last becomes
> homogeneous with nature because it gives enjoyment to
> nature. Since our genus is not the genus of our King, my ego
> has passed away for the sake of His existence. Inasmuch as my
> ego passed away, He remained alone: I roll at the feet of His
> horse, like dust. The soul became dust, and the (only) signs of
> it are the mark of His feet on its dust. Become dust at His feet
> for the sake of this mark, in order that you may become the
> crown on the head of the lofty. Let not my form beguile you:
> partake of my desert and spiritual fruit before my departure.
> Oh, there are many whom the form waylaid: They aimed at the
> form (of the holy man) and (in reality) struck at God. After all,
> the soul is joined to the body, (but) has this soul any likeness to
> the body? The sparkle of the eye's light is paired with the fat;
> the light of the heart is hidden in a drop of blood; joy (has its
> seat) in the kidneys, grief in the liver; intellect (bright) as a can-
> dle, inside the brain in the head. These connections are not
> without a how and a why, (but) as regards knowledge of the
> why (our) minds are impotent. The Universal Soul came into
> contact with the partial (individual) soul, and the (latter) soul
> received from it a pearl and put it into its bosom. Through that
> touch on its bosom the (individual) soul became pregnant, like
> Mary, with a heart-beguiling Messiah, Not the Messiah who is

(a traveler) on land and water, (but) the Messiah who is beyond (the limitation of) measuring (space). So when the soul has been impregnated by the Soul of the soul, by such a soul the world is impregnated.[125]

When the human realizes his or her essence in this way, he or she will try to appreciate that essence and find his or her humanity. According to Rumi, real humanity, the love that we feel for God who created us by realizing our humanity and sensing the essence in us, will destroy all our bad habits, cleanse, and raise us spiritually. Our realization of where we came from and who is in us will rescue us from all vice. What great happiness it is for a believer to be aware that we live with Him and to feel that He is with us wherever we may be. In a couplet in the *Mesnevi*, Rumi says, "We have to come to know (that) we are not this body: beyond the body we live through God."[126]

REASON

Rumi considers reason, which is the faculty of thought, cognition, and comprehension, from two points of view. According to Rumi, reason is the faculty of man that can sometimes be very valuable and sometimes serve no use. He elaborates his views of two stages. At the first stage, reason is a very valuable divine gift that distinguishes humans from animals and lets them attain humanity. They defeat their lower self (*nafs*) with reason and become superior beings by escaping from their bodily desires. Reason is a holy light in the heart; truth and falsehood can be distinguished with it. By the same token, our Prophet says, "Whoever is foolish, that is, has no reason, is our enemy." Explaining this Prophetic Tradition, Rumi says,

> The Prophet said, "Whosoever is foolish, he is our enemy and a ghoul who waylays (the traveler).
> Whosoever is intelligent, he is our soul, his breeze and wind is our sweet basil."

> (If) intelligence reviles me, I am well-pleased, because it pos-
> sesses something that has emanated from my emanative activity.
>
> Its revilement is not without use, its hospitality is not with-
> out table; (But) if the fool puts a sweetmeat on my lip, I am in
> a fever from (tasting) his sweetmeat.[127]

Rumi composed many other couplets that emphasize the importance of reason. He lets us know that reason stops selfish desires
and is the opposite of lust.[128]

Rumi expresses in metaphor that selfish desires and lust are
feelings that belong to our body and that, as a divine gift, reason
remains like a strange guest in our mortal body. Most of the time
the lower self (*nafs*) overpowers reason. The reason for this is that
the dog of self is in rebellion in its own home: "You are in this body
store selling all stuff. There are two valuable elements hidden under
your store . . . Be quick to dig before the end of this lease of the
rented house without you having gained any profit from it."[129]

Rumi expresses the struggle between reason and the self with
the following verses. Like a psychologist, he explains the feelings one
by one with metaphorical expressions and warns us:

> The (carnal) nature desires to take revenge on its adversary: rea-
> son is an iron chain upon the flesh.
>
> It comes and prevents it (the flesh) and restrains it: reason is
> like a police inspector controlling its good and evil (actions).
>
> Reason that is allied to faith is like a just police inspector; it
> is the guardian and magistrate of the city of the heart.
>
> It is mentally alert like a cat; the thief remains in a hole, like
> a mouse. Wherever the mouse gets the upper hand, no cat is
> there, or (at least) there is (only) the (unreal) form of a cat.
>
> What cat (is to be compared with the reason)? Faith-reason
> in the body is the lion that overthrows the lions.[130]

In another couplet Rumi compares a man with reason to a spiritual guide carrying the torch that shows the true path and guiding
those who have remained in darkness and lost their way: "The
intelligent man is he who has the lamp: he is the guide and the

leader of the caravan."[131] Rumi continues to praise reason: "If intelligence displays its face in visible form, day will appear dark beside
its light. And if the shape of foolishness became visible, beside it
the darkness of night would be radiant."[132] And: "The rip made by
foolishness and ignorance does not admit to being patched up: do
not sow the seed of wisdom there, O counselor."[133] The *Mesnevi*
contains a parable about Jesus' running away from the fool:

> Jesus, son of Mary, was running toward the mountain as if he
> were running from a lion that wanted to shed his blood.
> Somebody ran behind him and asked,
>
> "What is wrong? There is no one behind you. Why are you
> running as fast as a bird flies?"
>
> Jesus was running so fast that he did not even turn around to
> answer the man because of his hurry. The man ran a little bit
> more after Jesus, and he called out again,
>
> "For God's sake, stop for one moment. Why and from whom
> are you running away? I want to know."
>
> Jesus said:
>
> "I am running away from a stupid person. Don't stop me; let
> me get away."
>
> The man said,
>
> "Aren't you the Messiah who opens the eyes of the blind and
> the ears of the deaf?"
>
> Jesus:
>
> "Yes, I am."
>
> The man asked again,
>
> "Aren't you the one who makes a dead man jump like a lion
> that has just found its prey?"
>
> Jesus:
>
> "Yes, I am."
>
> Upon this, the man said,
>
> "O pure and clean spirit! Who are you afraid of when you
> possess so many miracles?"
>
> Jesus said,
>
> "I read the Greatest Name that God has granted me to a
> blind person, and his eyes opened. I read it to a deaf man, and
> his ears started to hear. I read it over a rock like a mountain,

and it split and fell into pieces. I read it over a dead person, and he came back to life and arose. And I read it to a stupid man a hundred thousand times, but it did not help."[134]

After explaining from many different perspectives that reason is a great gift for man, Rumi provides us with a metaphor to show us that, after all, reason cannot take us further on the path to God, the path of love. He likens reason to the Archangel Gabriel and says, "While the Prophet was ascending toward God during the Night of Ascension (*Mi'raj*) with the guidance of Gabriel, they came to a point where reason said, 'O Ahmad, if I take one step further I will burn. You leave me here, from this point onward. You proceed further, O king of spirit, this is my limitation.'"

According to Rumi, there comes a time when reason is no longer of use. How is it that reason that defeats the self, benefits us in many ways, raises us to the level of humanity, makes us attain faith, is thrown away like an old fashioned lamp? *'Aql*, the Arabic word for reason, comes from the same root as *'iqal*, which means "watch-chain." Like the watch-chain that ties the watch to the vest, if you try to pull and extend something beyond its range, it breaks. Therefore, Ziya Pasha, speaking of the life of paradise, said, "The comprehension of its higher concepts is not necessary for this little mind because this scale cannot handle that weight." The Dutch Erasmus (d. 1536), one of the greatest thinkers of the Renaissance era, maintains in his work *Praise to Folly* that reason is sometimes useless. The great poet Fudhuli complains of reason in one of his couplets: "I seek guidance from reason, and reason gives me misguidance." Rumi stated that reason cannot be called reason when it becomes an obstacle to attaining the greater truths: "When your mind becomes an obstacle for you on the path of God then that is no more a mind. It is a snake and a scorpion."[135] Rumi describes as a mischief-maker the faculty of reason that he once praised very much and that took us toward good and humanity: "The mind that is a mischief-maker takes the spirit to evil."[136] "Sell reason and mind and buy excitement," he says. "What you call reason and intellect are a guess and an illusion but excitement is insight. Sacrifice reason in the presence of Mustafa (the Prophet of Islam) and say 'Hasbiy Allah' (God is enough for me).[137] Wherever, in whatever matter, you see a selfish interest, run away from it, drink poison, and pour the Water of Life Everlasting on the ground. If somebody praises you, insult him and curse at him. Give your capital to the bankrupt person. Leave security and go where there is fear and danger. Leave your reputation and dignity. Be publicly disgraced. I have already tried the mind that thoroughly contemplates and calculates the future; from now on I will try to adopt craziness."[138]

In the *Mesnevi*, Rumi refers to the well-known tale of Moses and Khidr as narrated in the Qur'an,[139] explaining that although Moses was a prophet, he could not make sense of some of the things Khidr did: "Acts that were trivial for Khidr bewildered the mind of Moses. When Moses saw those things, he could not make sense of them. Those acts seemed inopportune and untimely to Moses because Moses did not have that spiritual state (of Khidr). If Moses' mind could not make sense of the matters of the Unseen, the matters that happen beyond, then how can that mouse mind of yours make sense of them?"[140]

In other verses in the *Mesnevi*, Rumi discusses the faculty of the mind:

> The foresight of this mind is up to the grave. But the mind of a "possessor of heart" sees things that are to come until Judgment Day and the blowing of the Trumpet. This mind goes no further than the grave and soil. This foot cannot go beyond to the field where there are amazing things. You give up on this mind and on this foot and walk. Seek an eye for yourself that can see the unseen world and be saved.[141]
>
> When the human being escapes this mind that is full of desires, passions, and aspirations, he finds hundreds of thousands of amazing minds.[142]
>
> In love, there are many bright and beautiful things other than what can be comprehended with this mind. In God there are many minds other than yours with which He manages the infi-

nite heavens and countless worlds therein. You obtain the nourishment of this world with this mind. With the other mind, you
transcend the seven heavens. If you let go of yourself in the love
of God, escape from the self, and abandon the mind, God gives
you ten times this mind, even seven hundred times.[143]

I have presented some of Rumi's views found in the *Mesnevi*
regarding the real reason that will lead us to God. Here I also find
it useful to borrow a few couplets from the *Divan-i Kabir* discussing
the same subject:

> Reason is a chain around the feet of those who set out on the path
> of God and the lovers of God. O son, break this chain, the path
> is perfectly visible. Reason is a bond and the heart is an illusion.
> The body is taken by arrogance and pride. The soul hid itself
> behind a curtain and does not show itself. Under these circum-
> stances, with these heavy burdens, how can you proceed toward
> the truth? The path is invisible and hidden. It is hoped that if you
> give up reason, the heart, and the soul, you will be able to see the
> path of complete understanding and perception of God.[144]
>
> Yesterday reason ran away from our assembly barefooted
> because we are out of the realm of reason and assumptions.
>
> You are submerged in thoughts, you are looking for a remedy
> for your illness while in fact the thing that increases your illness
> and annoys you is your being submerged in thoughts. The
> thoughts are preventing you from proceeding on the path to
> God. If you want to attain God and truth, leave thoughts and
> increase the excitement. You are not a man of thoughts, but a
> man of clarity, a man of heart. Thought turns into a dragon on
> the path that leads to God. O soul, be crazy, be insane, why are
> you relying on reason, why are you tying yourself to reason?[145]
>
> I grabbed reason by its ear and said, "O reason! Get out;
> today I am saved from you. O reason, take your hand off me.
> Today I attained insanity, and held on to it."[146]
>
> May the people with reason be far from the lovers of God.
> May the smell coming from the drain of a bath remain far from
> the zephyr. If someone with reason comes to our assembly, do
> not let him in, but if a lover of God comes, welcome him and
> say, 'Welcome, you have honored us' to him hundreds of times.

> Love shies away from the light of reason. It is a very bad thing to become old at a young age.[147]
>
> You have two heads. One is the head of earth that belongs to this world; the other is the spiritual head that belongs to the heavens.[148]

What Rumi describes as the reason that provides us with material benefits, makes us superior to the animals, is apparently the reason that is our material mind, which Rumi calls "the head of earth." At the first stage, Rumi praised this kind of reason, and then he found it reason to be insufficient, rejected it, and left it behind. After saying that it is crazy to carry this material reason, he began describing the other, spiritual reason that is in our other head that belongs to the heavens. It is clear that we can attain God and truth only through the reason in the pure head that belongs to the heavens.

BEAUTY

The concept of beauty that leaves an impression on us, caresses our soul, changes us spiritually, and gives us an indescribable and sweet excitement has intrigued man since the earliest ages. This is the science of aesthetics. Philosophers and scholars have interpreted the meaning of beauty according to their understanding. Many books have been written on this subject to explain beauty in a scholarly and scientific way. Rumi, on the other hand, expresses beauty not in terms of reason but in terms of the heart, love, and faith.

According to Rumi, all beauty and the beautiful refer to God who is beautiful. All beauty that we see in this world is the minute particles of God's beauty because God is the Absolutely Beautiful. True beauty, complete and comprehensive beauty is His. He manifests His attribute of beauty in everything He creates. In the stars that shine in the heavens during the night, in the moonlight, in the sunrise and sunset, in the seas, heavens, forests, mountains, rivers there is beauty. In the flowers, butterflies, creatures living in the depths of the sea, and in the birds that fly—in everything—there is beauty. The physical and spiritual beauty in man who is the most honorable of all the creatures cannot even be listed. Similarly, the beauty in the works of art that humankind has produced is impossible to frame.

Rumi, who is familiar with the secrets of the heart, clarified the reason for the fascination and admiration that we feel when listening to a beautiful voice or observing a beautiful landscape, even if we cannot explain exactly our attraction and merely say, "I like this." According to Rumi, the admiration that we feel for beauty brings us closer to that Most Beautiful of the Most Beautiful, God. Through the fascination and admiration that we feel for beauty, our heart enters a different state, and we feel a sweet and indescribable excitement. For example, when a *nay* (flute), a violin, a piano, or any other instrument is played with emotion, we come under its influence. A beautiful poem, a play that deals with courage, self-sacrifice, affection, and compassion touches us. When we listen to a hymn that is sung properly according to its rules, our personality changes. At that moment we come out of our body and go to a different world. Our spirit is freed from the prison of our body, and we leave our physical existence. At that moment it is as if we have become a new person. We are in the presence of our Beloved Lord as pure and spotless people who have slipped away from our ambitions, bad habits, and sins. At that moment we are taking spiritual nourishment at the *Maida al-Asuman*, the heavenly table of God, possessor of favors, where He bestows upon us beautiful voices and divine melodies. When this voice that we like becomes silent, we return to our old state by falling from the sky like birds with broken wings. We want the divine melodies that take us beyond to continue. The artists that produce these divine sounds are people who sense something from beyond and express it in different ways. Artists have a spiritual sense that not everybody has. Sometimes even the artist has no idea about his own spiritual power. Some fascinate us with their voices, some with their instruments, some with the works of art they produce, and some with their beauty and manners. Regarding this matter, Rumi says the following: "Beautiful faces are mirrors of God's beauty. Loving them is the echo of loving and seeking God. It is contemplating God."[149] There is a point where we have to be very careful: To avoid polytheistic thoughts, we should think of God's Beauty in spiritual terms. In fact, Rumi warns us in this matter: "Transcend the glasses of forms and beauties of faces, and do not be taken in by them. The wine may be in the glass, but it is not the glass itself."[150]

Can mortal and transient beauty really be the same as God's beauty? Divine light can be seen on this body that is a pile of flesh and bones. Sunlight falls on the wall. The wall shines brightly. But the wall is not the sun. A poet expresses this feeling as follows: "The sun of beauty of the beautiful eventually sets. I do not like mortal beauties. I love the Beautiful to whom there is no end and who never sets." To avoid polytheism, Rumi tells us to see and love beauty and not the beautiful: "You go to visit a friend. But your going is not only for seeing his physical form and outer appearance. It is for his appearance to show closeness with love and affection to you. In reality, you did not go to see your friend. In spirit you went to the universe of formlessness and infinity. But you did not have the slightest idea of this goal since you are unaware."[151] In a quatrain Rumi says, "O God, after learning of your love and getting to know you, my eye stopped seeing the beautiful of this world." Also in the *Divan-i Kabir* he prays for beauty: "We Sufis came to Your neighborhood. For Your holy sake give us something from Your beauty."

Because all beauty is the manifestation of God's beauty, the fascination that a beautiful face awakens is not of itself, its material beauty. It is of the Most Beautiful of the most beautiful who gave it that beauty. For this reason, to be absorbed by outer beauty and not think of the Creator is a vice and among the greatest of sins. Seeing beauty that mesmerizes us, we should remember the Qur'anic verse: "Look closely, how high is the Glory of God who is the Most Beautiful of those who give form and create shape."[152] All beauties belong to Him. To find the Creator, who is the Most Beautiful of the most beautiful, in the beautiful faces and to be fascinated by It, is a favor and grace of God to true believers. In the *Mesnevi*, Rumi says, "I am the foundation of both reason and divine ecstasy. Now we realize that the beauty which we saw in forms and fantasies was the reflection of our beauty."[153] Since the admiration felt toward the beautiful is a bounty of God to the believers, the true human concentrates on the spiritual aspect of beauty rather than the physical aspect of it, and the Giver of that beauty from whom he accepts everything. God has been creating "living glasses" that will serve the wine of spirit, the wine of Mansur (al-Hallaj).

Why do we like beauty and the beautiful? According to Rumi, beauty and the beautiful not only make us closer to God but also remind us of the beauty in the world of spirits. Just as there is an expression of longing in music, in beautiful voices and divine melodies, there is also a memory of the world of the eternal past in beauty and the beautiful. In this regard Rumi says, "In my ear nothing remained except for the noise of love. No reason or no idea remained in my spirit except for the beauty of the world of the eternal past." According to Rumi, there is a predecessor to this life in which we live. Before we came to earth, our spirits were in the world of spirits. There were indescribable beauties in the world of the eternal past. It is for this reason that we love beauty that we see here. This beauty reminds us of the beauty in the world of the eternal past. Rumi mentions this in both the *Mesnevi* and the *Divan-i Kabir*. He says, "My universe, my world is illuminated with the holy light of the eternal past. My happiness is because of the Greatest of the Great, the Most Beautiful of the Beautiful." Rumi expresses the same truth in the following poem:

> Do you know where you came from? You came from God's private and sacred territory. Do you not remember that spiritual world, all of that beauty? You forgot them and became bewildered in this world. Your head is spinning and you give your life in return for a fistful of soil. What a cheap barter!

> Return that soil. Know your value; you are not a slave. You are
> the king, the sultan, and you have no idea of this. Many beau-
> tiful faces secretly came down to earth from the heavens for
> your sake.[154]

Have these beautiful faces that we see in this world come down from the heavens to remind us of the beauty of the world of eternity? What a sweet and pleasant allegory in a metaphorical sense! In the world of spirits there were the most beautiful, the most perfect, and the most flawless samples of all the things that we see in this world. All the things that we see and like in this world—a beautiful view, a beautiful face, a work of art, music—remind us of the beauty in the world of spirits in the eternal past. Our Great Prophet also mentioned beauty in some of His Traditions: "Verily God is Beautiful and loves beauty."[155]   In another Tradition: "The green fields, rivers, and beautiful faces relax one and make one rest." And: "Seek wisdom near the ones with beautiful faces."

According to Rumi, beauty takes us from ourselves, frees us from the prison of the body, and brings us closer to another realm, to God. Thus we find God within the impact of the fine arts on sensitive people. God's Beauty is manifested in the beauty of the masterpieces of the great artists that mesmerize and fascinate people. This is because all works of art are works of humans who carry the Divine Entrustment and are subject to Divine Grace no matter to what country or nation they belong. Human beings exhibit in the masterpieces that they produce themselves, their humanity, their feelings, and their thoughts. However, God is the one who grants all artists the power to produce works of art. Just as no mosquito can ever move its wings without His permission, no masterpiece can be produced without His commitment. He is the one who allows the masterpieces to be produced, gives the artists that inspiration, that power, and that talent. Yet that great unique and peerless Artist conceals Himself. Can anybody know the intricacies of the abilities, talents, beauty, and the joy of the beauty bestowed by God upon humans who have been created as the most honorable of all creatures? The famous scholar of aesthetics, Charles Lalo, says, "Just as the beautiful view of the sunset brings to a villager's mind the idea of dinner, which is not at all aesthetic, it brings to the mind of a physicist the notion of the analysis of light, which is neither aesthetic nor unaesthetic but is only possibly true or false. A sunset is only beautiful for people who feel beauty."

Rumi reveals the notion that not everybody is able to perceive beauty as follows:

> For those whose eyes are illuminated with the light of gnosis, God has made the six directions of the house of the world subject to His signs. Wherever they look they see the Power and Art of God there.
>
> Those whose hearts' eyes are open receive spiritual nourishment from the gardens of God's Art and Beauty, perceive it no matter which animal or which plant they may look at.
>
> It is for this reason that the lovers of God were told: "Wherever you may turn, there is His Face and His Beauty."
>
> If you are thirsty and drink a glass of water, you see God in the water.
>
> But the person who is not a lover of God sees his own form in the water.
>
> Whom does the lover see in the water when his existence is effaced in God?
>
> Just as the moon shines on the water and is seen there, lovers of God, too, see God's beauty in the faces of the beautiful.

Those whose eyes of the heart are open see God's art, power, and beauty in everything, in every atom, and they say, "The world is the mirror to the beauty of our true Beloved. Every atom is a witness to His beauty." According to Rumi, if a lover of God sees the art of God, who is the Most Beautiful of the Beautiful, and sees His power in creating the beauty in the faces of the beautiful that he sees in this world and is not fascinated by it, and if he is taken over by animalistic thoughts, watches them with a different eye, does not look at the beautiful beautifully, is taken by lust, and his glance becomes contaminated, then that lover of God loses God's love. He descends to the depths, exits the realm of humanity, and becomes someone resembling animals.

Let us conclude this section with a couplet by a lover of God: "O God, You manifested Your beauty in the form of the beautiful. Thus in the eye of the lover, you are watching Your own beauty."

WOMEN

Some people maintain that except for anatomical differences, all the differences between men and women are a result of the way women are brought up, that is, a result of social influence. Those who oppose these views believe that the differences result from creation in the mother's womb and in the differences of the genes. According to scientists, sociologists, and psychologists, the dispute over nature versus nurture is resolved more easily. They state that one's personality is formed as a result of the joint influence of these two factors, that is, nature and upbringing. Thus, there is no clear-cut distinction between men and women. Men and women are equal in terms of responsibility for their deeds in this life, but they have been created differently. What are these differences in creation?

Scientific studies have shown that the female embryo's heart beats faster, and girls mature faster. Newborn baby girls react differently under certain conditions. For example, they react more intensely when the sheet on them is removed, and they have stronger reactions to touch or pain. It has been determined that twelve-week-old baby girls look at human pictures longer than at colorful geometric shapes. It should also not be forgotten that female babies show more interest in other people than baby boys do. Baby boys look at colorful geometric shapes longer than they do at human pictures.

In IQ tests, men and women usually get the same average scores. Nevertheless, sociologists and psychologists have studied the reasons for the phenomenon that women are not as predominant as men in the areas of science, technology, and the arts, in terms of new inventions and discoveries. They reached the conclusion that women are not as entrepreneurial as men because they are afraid of making mistakes and are affected by negative criticism.

Men and women are not exactly the same in terms of biology. The nature of women is different in terms of physiology and psychology. However, this does not mean that women are superior to men or that men are more important than women. Women and men are like nitrogen and oxygen in the air. The air is not composed of only nitrogen or only of oxygen. It is the combination of these two elements that forms the air. One does not consider whether oxygen is more valuable than nitrogen. Every creature that lives on the face of the earth needs both oxygen and nitrogen to breathe. Thus, we can conclude that both sexes are equal to each other and complete one another. We are humans and we unite in humanity. Just as we are not separate, we cannot live apart either. We need each other. A poet expressed this truth as follows: "Women need men, the young need the old—in terms of knowledge and experience—the bow needs the arrow, every member of the world needs the other."

Rumi's views on women are completely Islamic views, as is the case in all other issues. In this book, I have tried to explain Rumi's views on various issues with examples from his works so that one does not have the impression that his holiness has brought new, innovative ideas to religion. This great saint who says, "I am the slave and the servant of the Qur'an, I am the dust on which Prophet Muhammad steps," cannot be outside the Muhammadi path. He has not deviated from the Islamic path one iota on the issue of women, nor on any other issues. Any beliefs, life styles, or behavior that contradict Rumi's views are un-Islamic heresies and innovations. In fact, Rumi put the Islamic views, which were blurred with other beliefs originating from different regions, back on track. He did not make any changes in Islamic beliefs because Islam does not need reformation.

Since Rumi explains selected issues in his own way by giving examples with a deeply meaningful, beautiful, and pleasant narration, it would be better for us to understand the fundamentals of the Islamic religion through his views. Some people who do not understand Islamic principles claim that women are looked down upon and are given fewer rights than men in Islam. For us to understand this issue better, it will be beneficial to review briefly what kinds of rights were given to women in different parts of the world before Islam and what Islam has introduced in this regard.

When we review briefly the status of women in different parts of the world before the emergence of Islam, we see the following: In the ancient Indian judicial system, women had no rights in marriage, inheritance, and other transactions. In the Vedas, the holy book of the Hindus, women are described as creatures that are worse than hurricanes, death, or poison. At first, the Buddha, founder of Buddhism, did not admit women to his religion because they were creatures that followed their feelings. When his close friend, Ananda, asked him, "How are we going to treat women?" he answered, "You shall never look at them." "What if we have to look?" "Then you shall not speak with them." Ananda continued this line of questioning: "What if we have to speak?" The Buddha replied, "In that case you should be very careful with them." Ananda used to feel sorry for women and protect them. On his insistence, after much hesitation, the Buddha admitted women to the religion, but pointed out that this was very dangerous for Buddhists. Once he said to his dear friend Ananda, "If we had not admitted women to our religion, Buddhism would have continued unchanged for many centuries. But since women have come among us, I do not think that this religion will survive for long."

In the Jewish judicial system, man was the ultimate authority in the family. Jewish women were like servants in their fathers' homes. If the father wanted, he could sell his daughters. In the Jewish judicial system, a woman was a damned being because she could deceive and lead to evil. In ancient Iran during the Sassanid Empire, there were no rights or value given to women. It was legal to marry one's sister. In China, the ancient Chinese did not count women as human beings; they did not even think that it was necessary to give them a name. They would call women not by a name, but with a number like "1, 2, 3, . . . " Women were referred to as "pigs."

In Ancient Greece and Rome, societies with which Western cultures are fascinated, women had no rights. Women were considered to be merely childbearing machines. They were not seen as worthy of love and affection because their anatomy was considered to be inferior to that of men. Affection between men was very common. While women were doing all the household work, men would enjoy themselves.

Around the time Islam emerged, the status of women was heart-breaking in the Arabian Peninsula. Women were deprived of any marriage, childbearing, or inheritance rights. Adultery and fornication was very widespread. A daughter was a financial burden and a moral disgrace to the family. The father, who had unlimited say in his family, did not see any harm in killing his daughter, often burying her alive. Islam came to rescue women, who were looked down upon and were denied all rights. It banned the burying alive of baby girls. It ordered that love and affection be shown toward women. Fifteen centuries ago, at a time when women were looked down upon all over the world, our Prophet said, "There is no doubt that women are counterparts, similar, and equivalent to men." The chapter of the Qur'an, *al-Baqara*, says, "Just as men have rights over women, women have rights over men" (2:228). In his well-known Farewell Sermon, the Prophet reminded us of women's rights: "O people, I recommend you to observe women's rights and fear God in this matter. God entrusted women to you."[156] Because the issue of women is a topic on which many ideas have been put forth, much has been said, and more particularly since some people claim that women are not valued in Islam, I have presented briefly the views of different nations and different religions on the subject of women. I hope that this subject will be understood better before I go on to present Rumi's view on women.

Rumi's view of women centers around two points. On the one hand, Rumi has considered the higher aspects of women and glorified womanhood; on the other hand, he very realistically described their human weaknesses, passions, and inclinations. Those who read Rumi's works carefully will notice that he often makes some light-hearted jokes or exaggerations for any topic to be better understood. In fact, in the story[157] that begins with the caliph of Egypt falling in love with a female servant of the sultan of Mosul and goes on to depict the relationship of the young commander ordered to take the beautiful female servant to Egypt, he points out how much that female servant is addicted to physical pleasures and says, "That sweet beauty with a face like the full moon was amazed by his power of manhood."[158] Then when describing the meeting of the same female servant with the caliph, he continues the story: "When the female servant saw the weakness of the caliph who was afraid of a mouse, she started to laugh out loud."[159]

Again in the story, he tells the tale of a woman who has intercourse with a donkey. This story starts as follows: "A woman, due to the excessiveness of her lust and abundance of her ambition, made a donkey used to herself."[160] This story resembles very much the story of "The Golden Donkey" by the Latin author Apuleius (125 – 180 CE). Rumi wanted to teach a lesson using this tale, which was being spoken about among the public at that time. It is for this reason that, when Rumi tells this story, he recites the following couplet: "When the inclination of lust and the desire of lust make the heart deaf and blind, it sees even the donkey as Joseph, a piece of fire made up of light."[161]

These stories in the *Mesnevi* are not told to belittle women, but to show the nature and inclinations of human beings. Yet, at the same time as women are able to be so weak, if they had not been created with more sensitivity than men, and if their hearts were not filled with love and affection, then human beings could not have multiplied and populated the Earth. It is known that for a woman to give birth to a child is as difficult as facing death. Many young women have lost their lives when giving birth. After bringing a child into the world, it is not easy to bring that child up. A woman is faced with countless difficulties; she sacrifices her sleep and feeds the child with her own milk. It is for this reason that the Prophet admired this duty of women and glorified them, and that Paradise has been placed, not under the father's feet, but under those of the mother. The Prophet, who honors women and sees them as honorable individuals, ordered us to avoid women who are slaves to their feelings and who cannot overcome their sensuality.[162]

God has put more love and affection into women's hearts than into the hearts of men. God has created women with this nature so that they may endure the difficulty of childbirth and motherhood. Women are more patient; they endure pain and suffering better than men. Women live longer than men. They resist illnesses better than men. These qualities are a gift from God to women. Moreover, when a woman keeps her feelings under control and overcomes her sensual desires, she leaves men behind on the path of God and attains the truth faster than men.

The fact that the love, affection, and mercy in women are plentiful is a gift from God not only for their children, but also for their spouses. Many great men, artists, and inventors are indebted in their success to the care, affection, and love of their spouses. Does the fact that women are weaker in physiology and more sensitive than men mislead men and women? Does it lead them astray from the true path? No. Rumi attaches importance to the dignity of women, as did the Prophet, whom he deeply loved and to whose rights he was wholeheartedly committed. The Prophet said, "If one falls in love with a woman, if he does not reveal his love to anybody, and stays chaste, and if he dies in this manner, he is counted as a martyr."

Rumi criticizes and accuses men who want to take advantage of women's emotional vulnerability. He says the following in the *Mesnevi*: "Whoever does something bad to his wife, know that that person becomes his own wife's panderer (he sells his wife) because the punishment for a bad deed is to be subjected to an equivalent mischief. The punishment of a crime is the equivalent of that crime. If you attract someone else's wife toward yourself for some reason, you are a cuckold just like him and even worse than him."[163] This should not be misunderstood; Rumi did not want to belittle women by pointing out their human weaknesses. Are passions and sensual desires only limited to women? Are men cleansed of these feelings? Women are human and so are men. This duality, having both good and evil feelings, is what it means to be human. Even though these feelings are natural, they lower one when one acts out of emotion. When one realizes one's humanity, then these feelings honor one. Does the Qur'an not say, "Verily we have created the human being in the best pattern and then we abased him/her to the lowest of the low"?[164] Like Rumi, most famous authors and philosophers of the world have discussed the issue of women in their works.

What did the great Rumi say about women centuries before the above-mentioned famous philosophers? Let us read his description of women in this section very carefully:

> God has created woman for man to rejoice with her and to accompany man. Thus how can Adam be separated from Eve? How can he live without Eve? Even if a man exceeds Rustam, son of Zal, in bravery, or Hamza, the uncle of the Prophet, in courage, he is still the slave of his wife's orders. Even the Prophet, who enraptured the world with His beautiful and sweet words, would plead with his angered wife, "Talk to me, O little pink-white one!"
>
> If water is poured on fire, it extinguishes it. Water is superior to fire in terms of form and appearance. But put water in a bowl, the fire boils it. If a pot becomes an obstacle between the two, fire annihilates water and turns it into vapor.

> Externally you are superior to woman, just as water is superior to fire. But in reality, you are taken over by her. You are defeated by her, and you need her. You cannot do without her; you want her and you love her. Such an attribute can only be found in humans. Love is little in animals. This is because of their specific nature.
>
> In a Prophetic tradition our Prophet said, "Women usually dominate intelligent people and people of heart. But ignorant and crude people dominate women because they treat them very roughly and harshly. Mercy, generosity, and love are rare in such people because their animal nature is dominant. Love and affection are human feelings. Anger and lust are animal feelings.[165]

Rumi's description of woman as "creator" in other writings should not lead us to false ideas. Here he is referring to women's honor as mothers and their ability to bring children into the world. Have not women given birth to the distinguished men of the world, even to the prophets? As mothers, women not only give their milk to their babies, but also their love, courage, patience, and endurance. The truth is that if there were no women, there would be no life nor humanity. The following Tradition of the Prophet is a testimony to how honorable a being a woman is: "I was made to love three things from your world: Women, nice fragrance, and prayer, which is the light of my eye." The fact that our Prophet mentions women before prayer shows how much importance he places on women.

POETRY

It is surprising that although Rumi always expressed his feelings and views through poetry and has gained the admiration of the greatest poets of the East as well as the West, he did not see himself as a poet and is almost ashamed of being called a poet. In reality, one can hardly call a lover of God like Rumi a "poet." The late Ziya Pasha sensed this and said, "To call such people of high spiritual states 'poets' is to undermine their maturity, perfection, and superiority and offends them spiritually." The truth is that the word "poet" cannot describe Rumi. We have to find other words and other expressions to describe him. In his book *Fihi Ma Fih*, Rumi expresses his feelings in this matter:

> I have such a habit that I do not want anybody's heart to be broken because of me. For example, some people accidentally hit me during whirling. And some friends scold those people and try to prevent them. I do not like this. I have told those friends a hundred times, "Do not say anything to anybody because of me. I am pleased with those who hit me." I want to make people happy so much that, when friends come to visit me, I recite poetry so that they will not be sorry and bored. Then for some time I stop the poetry, and they become sad and want me to recite poetry again. And I cannot refuse them, so I recite poetry. Otherwise, where am I and where is the poetry? By God, I am away from poetry. In my sight there is nothing worse than poetry. What is this situation like? Upon the request of his guest someone has taken an animal's stomach and is washing it. This act of his and his enduring the dirty smells is to fulfill the request of his guest because he knows that his guest likes the meal prepared from the animal's stomach. In our hometown—the city of Balkh—there was no occupation or craft more disgraceful than poetry. If we had not come here and had stayed in our hometown, we would have followed their ways. We would have worked the way they wanted. We would have been occupied with teaching, giving lectures, and classifying books, and we would not recite poetry.[166]

Rumi is submerged in such love and rapture that in his sight poetry is left very much behind. He is intoxicated with never-ending spiritual sensation, excitement, and joy, and says, "I don't know this and that. I am intoxicated, enraptured with the glass of love." Rumi, who does not see himself as a poet although he is counted among the greatest poets of the world, is actually right. He could not compare himself to other poets because he says, "What value does poetry have for me so that I may talk of it? I have an art, a talent different than the arts and crafts of other poets. I am a lover of God."

The poems of the poets who are not lovers of God are a product of thought and imagination. Their goal in composing poetry is to gain fame. In other words, the poets of the world write poetry to make themselves known, and the poets of God write poetry to make God known. It is for this reason that most of the saints have written poetry. But none of the saints have produced as much poetry as Rumi. Comparing the saints with each other is contradictory to good manners, and it is not right. But we can say this much: Since Rumi was a great saint as well as a great poet, his influence has been great. Rumi himself is a poem. He is a poem of God to the Community of Muhammad. If the poems that poured from his blessed lips had not been written, we could not have known Rumi. Thus, whoever wants to know Rumi should go into his poetry. His love, faith, excitement, feelings, and thoughts are all in his poetry. If there were no *Mesnevi-i Sharif*[167] and *Divan-i Kabir*, there would have been no Rumi. Rumi, who is God's poet from beyond, is at the same time a great poet himself. But he is a different kind of poet and recites a different kind of poetry. He does not want those poems that are recited by the tongue. He pleads, "O word uttered by the tongue! When will I leave you, when will I be free of you so that I may find my real Sultan with the light of the sun of gnosis and seek refuge in Him? When will I call out to Him from the heart? O Lord! Before death comes, save me from knowledge and actions. Save me especially from words that do not come from the heart but that are just uttered by mouths."[168] In another poem Rumi says,

> My words and my statements are curtains to my states.
>
> My heart, which is like a rose garden, is ashamed of my thought, which is like a thorn.
>
> O Lord, give my spirit a tongue other than this one so that I may be liberated from the bonds of faithlessness by proclaiming unity.
>
> Even if for one day only, may I be enraptured and not care about the good or bad and recite the attributes of God in my heart without any tongue or lip [169]

If one pays close attention, one will see that although Rumi very eloquently expresses his feelings, views, and love with poetry, he still feels that he cannot communicate his feelings for God properly. In this regard, he finds poetry inadequate and desires to call out to his Lord from his heart without tongue or lips. Just as our Prophet beseeched God, "O my God, whose existence is known and felt! We have failed truly to know You as Your Glory merits." It is not that Rumi does not like poetry and poets, but he finds poetry inadequate. He is saying, "O my God! I am incapable of expressing You and Your Love in a way suitable to Your Glory. O my God! I cannot express what I feel about You with words and poems."[170]

MUSIC AND WHIRLING CEREMONIES

Let us hear Rumi's views on music and whirling from his own blessed mouth:

> Wise men have said, "We have taken these beautiful sounds and melodies from the whirling of the heavens. These pleasant sounds that people produce with musical instruments or their voices are taken from the rotation of the heavens. We all were components of Adam. We heard those melodies while we were in Heaven. Although entering this cage of the body made of mud and water and dressing in clay may have caused doubts in our spirits and misled us, we nevertheless still remember some of those melodies. It is for this reason that music and whirling is nourishment for lovers of God. In whirling, there is peace of heart, a connection to God and hope of finding the Beloved. When we listen to those beautiful sounds, the imagination in our hearts strengthens; those imaginings even take on forms from breath."[171]

In the above couplets, Rumi explains that man's fascination with music even from very early ages is an expression of the longing felt for God. It is a fact that even from the very early ages that history records, men have been very much influenced by music. Women who heard the sound of the magic flute of Krishna, a dark and handsome young man who is the equivalent in Indian mythology of Apollo, were spellbound and left their homes and ran to the forests to see Krishna. This way they would be relieved of fear, sorrow, and tiredness through the influence of the music. The last hero of Greek mythology, Orpheus of Thrace, would play such pleasant melodies with his lyre that even the predators would come out of their caves and lie down by his feet to listen to his music. When he began playing his lyre, not only animals but also even the trees would shake with ecstasy; the rocks would tear away from their places and roll down toward him.

Prophet David's voice was very beautiful and affecting. It is narrated that when he began reciting the Psalms, the rivers would stop flowing and listen to him. The birds would fall on the ground, the trees would prostrate, and even the animals would become tame. In ancient times, people explained beautiful voices that excited their spirits with myths since they were not aware of the unseen and did not know that music was a memory of the melodies heard in Heaven. As Rumi says, in music there are sounds that come from the beyond. Some things awaken in our hearts when we listen to the music. Beautiful voices and melodies take us away from ourselves. We forget ourselves. It is as if we enter a secret and mysterious world that we do not know and cannot really understand. It is as if we escape the cage of the body and strike our wings toward the heavens to be cleansed. We become a different being. Someone who longs for his Eternal Beloved from Whom he was separated and who feels the disparity of the exile in this world is crying inside. So then what is the whirling that Rumi refers to, the whirling that he describes as nourishment for the lovers of God?

Whirling (*sama*) means listening to music, moving with the excitement induced by the music, and entering into ecstasy and whirling. According to Sufis, whirling has different effects on people's spirits. It enhances one's love of God and produces many spiritual states. These spiritual states clean the vices in the heart and finally open the eye of the heart. In a way, whirling is an expression of the love and excitement a lover of God feels for God in the form of turning. Thus whirling saves the dervish from himself, his existence, and makes him spiritually closer to God. It is as if the chick in the egg of the self is trying to hatch out of the eggshell; the spiritual bird imprisoned in the cage of the body is striking wings to rise to the heavens, and the Divine Entrustment that is stuck in the mud is attempting to emerge from the mire. Whirling is to find God in one's heart through the influence of the music and to turn like a moth in this excitement. This whirling is not the mere turning of the body. This whirling is turning with the heart, spirit, love, faith, and with all one's physical and spiritual existence.

In this kind of whirling, the lover of God escapes his imaginary existence, his ego, and he is annihilated in God. The annihilation of the particle in the whole is like the shivering and whirling elevation of an atom to the sun. When a true *samazan* (whirling dervish) who has cleansed his heart of desires, is in a state of ritual purity and is dressed in a *kafan* (shroud-like garment), whirls to the spiritual tunes of the music, he is no longer self-conscious. The spectators may watch the dervishes whirl, but they are not aware that the dervishes themselves are not there. Only the images of the whirling dervishes are seen. Their real existences have escaped and gone to the beyond. If you think these words are memorized sentences, common clichés, or frequently repeated views on whirling, you will be wrong. If you do not feel tense, if your mind is not preoccupied, and if you are at peace, during a whirling ceremony when the dervishes are floating in tune with the spiritual music in the whirling hall you also will experience the whirling in your spirit. That whirling and that harmony take you from yourself, and you also go to the beyond. When you feel all this outside the whirling, what would you have felt if you had participated in the whirling? Many people have explained the whirling. Many nice things have been said about the whirling. But the one who best explained, felt, and made others feel the whirling was Rumi himself, as in the following ode:

Do you know what the whirling is? It is hearing the voices of the spirits saying "Yes" to God's question "Am I not your Lord?" It is deliverance from ego and reunion with the Lord.

Do you know what the whirling is? It is seeing the Friend's states, hearing the secrets of God from across the curtains of the unseen.

Do you know what the whirling is? It is escaping one's existence, continuously tasting the everlasting existence in the absolute non-existence.

Do you know what the whirling is? It is making one's head a ball in front of the Friend's kicks of love and running to the Friend without head and feet.

Do you know what the whirling is? It is knowing Jacob's sorrow and remedy, it is smelling the smell of the reunion with Joseph from Joseph's shirt.

Do you know what the whirling is? It is swallowing Pharaoh's spells just like Moses's staff every moment.

Do you know what the whirling is? It is a secret from the Prophetic Tradition: "There is a moment for me with God where no archangel or no prophet can come in between God and me." It is reaching that place without any means where no angel can fit.

Do you know what the whirling is? It is, like Shams-i Tabrizi, opening the eyes of the heart and seeing the sacred lights.

Let us now carefully read the following *Mesnevi* couplets and understand Rumi's views on music and whirling:

It was clapping hands because it escaped death and was dancing in the air like the branches and the leaves of trees.

When the branches and the leaves come out of the prison of soil they raise their heads above the ground and become friends with the wind and start to dance with it.

When the leaves break out of the buds on the branches they climb up to the top of the tree. Each leaf and each fruit sings the graces of God with the tongue of the bud.

Without mouth or lips, every branch, every leaf, every fruit recites praises and remembrance of God.

They say, "God who has a lot of graces and favors has nourished our root and from the root a strong tree grew, it grew wide, erect and high."

And when the souls that had been in water and mud were saved from the swamp of water and mud, their hearts were filled with joy.

They dance to the tune of love and attain perfection as the moon when it reaches the full moon stage. Their bodies move and dance. But in what state are their spirits? Don't ask in what state their spirits are.

And when it comes to those in whom there remained no material body and who completely turned into spirits, do not ever ask about them. There is no way to explain them [172]

Whirling is not confined to Rumi or to the Mevlevis. It is related that whirling ceremonies were arranged as early as the time of Abu Sa'id Abu'l-Khayr (d. 1049). There has been no exhaustive study on how whirling—acknowledged by almost all Sufis and accepted as a result of ecstacy—is perfomed by different Sufi orders. But it is known that the Gulshani branch of the Khalwati order has adopted the Mevlevi way of whirling.

The question of whether whirling that is based on music and dancing is religiously acceptable or not has been and continues to be a matter of much debate. Even today there are people who do not associate whirling with Rumi and maintain that he did not whirl. These people who do not study Rumi's works, historical accounts from Rumi's age, such as Sipehsalar's work and works by Sultan Valad, claim that Rumi had nothing to do with the whirling ceremonies and that these ceremonies were later attributed to Rumi. Some others see Rumi as a reformist because of his inclination toward whirling and music. All these views are mistaken. Rumi, who professes himself the slave of the Qur'an and the soil under the feet of Prophet Muhammad did not deviate even minimally from the Prophet's path. On the contrary, he tried to correct the heresies caused by local beliefs and customs and to restore the Tradition of the Prophet, whom he loved so much.

Those who carefully read the *Mesnevi* see how Rumi fought against the false beliefs of Mu'tazilites and against the views of those strongly attached to the letter of the law without any regard to the spirit of the law, and how much he tried to advance his followers from the initial stages of imitation to realization. Islam does not prohibit music. In fact, in the Glorious Qur'an the beautiful voice is praised while the ugly voice is renounced.[173] It is narrated that the Prophet permitted some of the dances that he watched.[174] It is also well known that when our Prophet and his Companion Abu Bakr left Makka and honored Madina, some of the women of Madina greeted them, singing the poem *Tala al-badru alayna* ("A full moon has risen over us") and playing tambourines. Similarly, history books record that when the first mosque was being built, the Companions were carrying stones and bricks, and our Prophet helped them in this effort. While working, the Companions sang poems in chorus, and our Prophet joined them in this singing. These poems were also recorded by historians.

When the Prophet, who explained, "There is an ornament for everything and the ornament of Qur'an is the beautiful voice (with which it is recited)," conquered Makka, he recited the chapter of the Opening (*al-Fatiha*), or Victory (*al-Fath*) melodically while riding his camel into Makka.[175] Music increases the asceticism of an ascetic. According to Dhu al-Nun, "Music is a divine influence that leads the heart to search for God. Those who listen to it from their hearts eventually attain God." Sufis who consider the effects of music and poetry on the human spirit and the ecstasy and excitement it generates have analyzed whether music is lawful or not. It is narrated that Anas, Abd Allah bin Ja'far, Abd Allah bin 'Umar, among the Companions, and many others from the Followers, held that music was lawful. Imam Shafi'i maintains that music is permissible as long as it does not undermine the honor of manhood and that prohibited music is the kind that is performed with bad intentions and instigates evil.[176] Ankaravi, commentator on the *Mesnevi*, writes, "Imam Ghazali commends that wherever the lover of God who longs for union with God looks, he sees God's Power and Beauty there. In every pleasant sound that reaches his ear, he finds

God's grace and favor. Therefore, music increases the longing, fervor, and love of the lover of God and sets his heart on fire."[177]

The following event is related in one of the last sections of Ibn al-'Arabi's book entitled *Futuhat al-Makkiyyah*:

> Shaykh Ja'far relates, "We were on the road for the pilgrimage to Makka with Junayd of Baghdad. On our way, we climbed Mount Sinai. We sat on the ground where Moses sat. We came under the influence of that blessed place, Mount Sinai. There was a singer with a beautiful voice with us. Junayd asked the singer to recite something. He recited such a touching couplet that when Junayd heard it he went into a state of ecstasy and began whirling. We, too, were enraptured and started whirling. We reached a state where we did not know whether we were on earth or in the heavens. There was a church nearby. There was a priest in seclusion there. He came out of the church and called out to us. We did not reply. He then called out again, 'O Muslims, answer me.' We were in such a state that none of us was able to answer. The priest could not help but call out again, 'O Muslims, reply for the love of God. Why are you silent?' Again there was no reply from us. Afterwards we became tired of whirling and came to ourselves. We told Junayd that the priest had called out to us but we did not reply, although he urged us to reply for the love of God. Junayd asked us to call the priest. We called him. He came and greeted us. He asked, 'Who is your shaykh?' We pointed at Junayd. The priest asked, 'Is what you did a custom of yours? Does it have a place in your religion? Do all of you whirl?' Junayd replied to him, 'Whirling is for some people in our religion. That is, not all Muslims whirl. Only some of us do.' The priest asked, 'What is your intention in whirling? Do you whirl in order to plead for something from God? Or do you whirl in order to find happiness and joy inside yourselves?' Junayd replied, 'We whirl to feel the pleasure of the spiritual address of 'Am I not your Lord?' that occurred in the world of spirits.' The priest asked again, 'What purpose do these beautiful sounds serve?' Junayd replied, 'These beautiful sounds remind us of the eternal call and take us from ourselves. When these beautiful sounds stop, we again come to ourselves.' This explanation touched the priest, and he embraced Islam there."[178]

The Sufis who lived during or close to Rumi's time viewed whirling as lawful for appropriate people. They also whirled. Abu Hamid al-Ghazali (d. 1111) allocated a separate section on music and whirling in his masterpiece *Ihya' Ulum al-Din*. His brother Ahmad al-Ghazali (d. 1123) was very fond of music and whirling.[179] Aynu'l-Quzat al-Hamadani (d. 1138) would join Ahmad al-Ghazali in whirling. It is also related that Sanai (d. 1127), 'Attar (d. 1227), his vicegerent Majd al-Din (d. 1219) and Awhad al-Din Kirmani (d. 1237) all whirled. Fahr al-Din Iraqi (d. 1289) also whirled very ardently.[180]

How did Rumi whirl? As Sipehsalar writes, at first Rumi was devoted to the order and path of his father Baha al-Din Valad. He was mainly occupied with teaching, preaching, asceticism, and self-mortification. He had never whirled before he met Shams.[181] Thus, based on this account of Sipehsalar, we can say that Rumi did not think of whirling before meeting Shams because he devoted himself to teaching and preaching and perhaps because religious men, the scholars and shaykhs in Konya, did not whirl. In fact, Aflaki writes that Rumi esteemed whirling only after meeting Shams. His whirling caused the bigots, who only considered the crust of the religion, to criticize him, and they even called him crazy.[182] Some consider this account not very sound. However, since Rumi was attached to the order and path of Sultan al-Ulama Baha al-Din Valad and since there is no account of Sayyid Burhan al-Din Tirmidhi whirling, the argument that Rumi did not whirl before meeting Shams gains strength. It is also fair to say that although Sultan al-Ulama and Sayyid Burhan al-Din did not whirl, they had a favorable view on whirling and accepted its practice because Najm al-Din Kubra, Sultan al-Ulama Baha al-Din Valad's shaykh, counts whirling as one of the fundamentals of his order when he explains the conduct of the Kubrawiyya order in his work entitled *Adabu't-tariqah*.[183] According to Najm al-Din Kubra, three conditions have to be observed for the whirling to be lawful and acceptable:

Place: Whirling cannot be done everywhere. Whirling should not be performed on a crowded street, a dirty place, or any place where one's heart will be distracted from God.

Time: Whirling cannot be done at any time. Whirling should not be done when the meal is ready or when the prayer time is approaching or where there will be a hostile reaction from outsiders.

Company: People attending a whirling ceremony should be noble-spirited, clean-hearted, and good-willed people, like the descendants of the Prophet. Whirling is not to be done in the presence of the people who undermine whirling, cause boredom in the assembly, have an arrogant attitude, simulate ecstasy, and cannot understand the value of whirling.

According to Najm al-Din al-Kubra (d. 1221), if these rules are not observed, the whirling will not yield the spiritual joy expected from it.

Whirling can be performed in a group as well as alone. Rumi's whirling was mostly induced by coincidences. A truly beautiful sound that he heard, a deeply meaningful and touching word or an exciting event was enough to move him, and he would begin to whirl, as he describes in the following poems:

> Whirling is the business of the spirit that cannot stay in one place. Do not sit there lazily, stand up, jump. Is there any reason to wait? Do not stay here thinking; if you are a man, then go where your beloved is.[184]
>
> Whirling is the comfort of the people whose spirits are alive. Only the one who is the spirit of the spirit knows this.[185]
>
> O Lover of God, when you start whirling, you leave the two worlds. This world of whirling is out of the two worlds. The ceiling of the seventh heaven is at a considerable height. But the ladder of whirling reaches and exceeds this ceiling.[186]

Rumi felt whirling very strongly and very importantly. He loved whirling so strongly that he did not observe the whirling conditions of time, place, and company. Since his whirling depended more on the ecstatic state that came over him rather than the place and time formalities, he was observed to whirl almost anywhere such as in schools, homes, gardens, and streets. The quality of the participants in whirling, as well as the spectators, were also largely ignored. One day when Rumi was passing through the jewelry bazaar, he heard harmonious hammer beats coming from the shop of Shaykh Salah al-Din. He entered into a state of ecstasy and began whirling. During the whirling, Rumi recited an ode beginning with the following couplets:

> In that jewelry shop a treasure came to be discovered. What a beautiful appearance, what a beautiful meaning, what beauty, what beauty!
>
> How beautiful is the jewelry bazaar! The secrets of Jacob are also very beautiful. The spirit of Joseph burns with the love of God and increases the ardor of Jacob.
>
> With the love of God, hundreds of Laylas became Majnun and broke their ties and chains. Against this fire even the patience of Job cannot withstand.[187]

SORROW

There are many poets and philosophers who talk about sorrows and sadness and deny the existence of joy. They claim that our happiness is but an illusion. Others have considered our sorrows as natural. Shaykh Sadi writes, "Everybody suffers from sorrow, from problems as determined by his destiny and in his own way. No one is given the certificate of perfect happiness." Rumi, in contrast, considers agony and sorrow from another perspective, saying, "There is nothing holier or more powerful than sorrow." He considers agony not as a calamity but as bliss and divine grace. In the honorable *Mesnevi*, the *Divan-i Kabir*, and his other works, he frequently declares that sorrow is a means and sometimes a test for man to mature and attain perfection. But there is a subtle point in Rumi's view on sorrow. The notion of enduring the difficulties and calamities of life, having patience with heartache, and reaping the sweet fruit through bitter patience was not adopted by Rumi. The essence of Rumi's approach is not to endure difficulties silently, uncomplainingly, but rather to love the agony.

It is a religious duty to accept God's predetermination and to have patience in the face of calamities that are a result of one's selfish actions. Does not God commend in the Qur'an: "God is with the patient"? Prophet Muhammad has brought good tidings for the faithful who are patient in the face of difficulties. He tells us that God gives sorrows only to those whom He loves very much. The hardest of the agonies is given first to prophets, then to saints, and lastly to select believers. He also revealed, "Patience is half of faith," and "patience and endurance against calamities is worship." Therefore, a believer who is smitten by many difficulties and problems is slave God's whom He loves very much. Since the sad man has heard these tidings, is he then expected to accept them silently, not complain about them, and smile like a stoic philosopher while his heart aches? No, Rumi says that agony is in reality not agony but a grace of God and happiness that comes in the disguise of agony. He therefore maintains that instead of endurance and patience one should love the agony. Sensing this truth, Fuzuli pleaded to God in the tongue of Majnun, "Do not deny your help to the people with difficulties. That denial gives me a lot of sorrows and difficulties."

There is no doubt that being patient and being content with all the pain and suffering that God gives is a great virtue. It is related that the great saint Shibli was once jailed. Some of his friends came to visit him. Shibli asked them who they were. They replied, "We are your friends, and we came to console you." Shibli was very angry with those who came to console him and started throwing stones at them. When they ran away from him, Shibli shouted after them, "You are liars. If you had been my real friends, you would have congratulated me on my calamity and you would have patience with me." The Qur'an says, "Be patient with the judgment of your Lord. Verily you are under Our watch."[188] In this way, believers who are stricken with a calamity know that when they are patient they will eventually attain their goal. They expect that when they go through the gate of contentedness, they will receive the reward for their endurance.

The state of one who goes through the gate of love, however, is quite different. They have no goal other than love. They accept pain as nothing other than a gift from the beloved. Even if a true lover of God is taken to hell because of a sin, they consider themselves fortunate that they are burning in the fire of the Beloved's judgment. In the following passage, Rumi explains the meaning of our pain and sorrows as follows: "The concerns and sorrows that come to the heart are like a guest that knocks at our door in the morning. The guest is capricious; he commands the host and is bad tempered and behaves in an unmannerly way. But the duty of the host is to treat the guest well. It is also to endure his unmannerly behavior and bad temper and show hospitality to him."[189] In another poem, Rumi continues,

> Every moment a thought and a worry come to the heart as a welcome guest.
> O my dear master, think of the thought (worry) that comes to your heart as a human being because it is thought and spirit that make one a human being.
> Do not be sad if the thought of worry cuts the path of joy because the worry that comes to the heart prepares other joys for you.
> Sorrow thoroughly sweeps and cleans the house of the heart so that a new joy and happiness arrives.
> It removes and throws away the dry leaves on the branch of the heart. This way it helps new, green leaves to flourish.
> Sadness takes out the root of the old happiness so that new joy comes all the way from far away.
> Sorrow tears off the rotten and decaying old root in order to strengthen the new root that is covered with branches and leaves.
> Whatever sorrow tears away from the heart, it surely replaces it with something that is better and more beautiful. In fact, it treats more favorably those who know that sorrow is the servant of the people of sound faith and maturity.

If the cloud and the lightning did not show a sour face, the vineyard would be boiled with the heat of the sun.

Fortune and misfortune, joy and sadness come from time to time, visit one's heart and then they leave. They are like stars that travel from house to house, from one sign of the zodiac to the other.

When the star of fortune comes to your sign of the zodiac as a guest, be sweet as the fortune itself, be vibrant and lively.

Do this so that when your star of fortune reaches the moon of truth, that sultan of hearts, it can bring gratefulness and contentedness from you to him.

For seven years, Job, who was patient and content with everything, showed hospitality to the guest of sorrow that was sent to him by God.

When tough and overwhelming calamities visited Job again and again, he never complained to God but on the contrary thanked Him in hundreds of ways.

When the calamities that followed one another took away Prophet Job's loved ones one by one, due to his great love of God, he never complained and did not frown even once.

Because of the love that Job felt for God, he showed such an attachment, faithfulness and obedience to God that he mixed with the calamity as milk with honey.

When new worries and calamities come to your heart, do not run away from them either. Instead run toward them and welcome them as a dear guest. Thank God for sending them to you and say,

"O my Creator, O God, protect me from the evil of the calamities you have given to me. Do not deprive me of the bounties that will come because of these calamities and make me attain them.

"O Lord, grant me the ability to thank you for this calamity. Let me not regret that I have not thanked You for them at the time and let me not miss this opportunity."

Treat well thus that sour-faced sorrow, revere and protect it, take all the bitterness it brings as sweet.[190]

As clearly seen, the lovers of God are telling us the same truths in many different ways and are trying to awaken us, the unaware. The couplets from the *Mesnevi* that I have quoted above can be summarized as follows: O lover of God, receive every sorrow and agony that comes to visit you with a smiling face so that when they return to the One who sent them to you, they do not complain of you. Treat them well so that they testify to God, "O God, I stayed with such and such of your slaves for a few days and he received me well, he did not complain about me to others, he was not sad; on the contrary, he showed me hospitality, and was patient with me. This slave of yours surely loves you. Protect him."

I would also like to present Rumi's view on sorrows with the following couplets selected from the *Divan-i Kabir*:

> Learn the secret of happiness from the Prophet, and be happy with whatever God gives you.
>
> If you are patient and content with whatever happens to you and do not complain, instantly the doors of heaven open to you.
>
> If the messenger of sorrows comes to you, receive him as an old friend and hug him. He is not a stranger to you; you surely have acquaintance with him.
>
> Do not show a sour face toward the adversity that comes from the Beloved, receive it with joy. Say, "Hello and welcome!" Show a smiling face and say nice words so that that unique, beautiful being removes its unpleasant cover and shows its beauty.
>
> Firmly grasp at the end of the cover of that beautiful being that came covered with sorrow. Never release it. Do not think about the dirtiness of the cover. The being under the cover is very beautiful, sweet, and faithful.
>
> ...
>
> The calamity of sorrow can see me not frightened or worried but only smiling. I do not invite sorrow in the guise of joy. On the contrary, I invite the remedy disguised as sickness.
>
> Be sure that there can be nothing sweeter or more sacred than sorrow. Its reward is infinite [191]

FREE WILL

I have noticed that in some books written about Rumi, in the talks on Rumi delivered on TV or on the radio,[192] the impression that Rumi was not completely on the Muhammadi path is evoked.

Some people try to introduce Rumi as deviating from the Muhammadi path, although he completely adhered to the Sunna and the Qur'an like other Sufis of Islam. I am not a scholar, only a lover of Rumi. The Rumi that I know and love is not the same Rumi as the one whom some scholars, who happen to have written a number of books, describe. I also cannot grasp how beliefs can change according to one's character. The Muhammadi path is a path for all saints. Every saint explains this path according to his own style of expression, sensation, and character. "Everybody means the same thing. But the words used are different." For example, while Rumi proceeds in this path with love, Shah Naqshbandi walks this path with asceticism and piety. But none of them can change this path according to his character. Furthermore, Rumi is a lover of God; he is not an expounder of Islamic law. It is common knowledge that an expounder is a scholar like Abu Hanifa and the three other founders of the four popular schools of Islamic Law. Rumi never claimed to be such a figure. He was never known as such either. He says, "I don't know much. I am intoxicated with the glass of love."

We also cannot reach the conclusion that Rumi did not belong to the *salaf* (righteous members of the early Muslim community) because such a conclusion would separate Rumi from our Prophet and his closest Companions and imply many untrue things. The path of the *salaf* is commonly defined as the path of our Prophet's Companions, in other words the path of the Qur'an. Rumi, who says, "I am the slave of the Qur'an as long as I live," followed the way of the *salaf*. This is the way of those who are not contaminated with materialist philosophy. The valuable scholar, Ismail Hakkı of Izmir gives the definition of the path of the *salaf* as follows: "The path of the *salaf* is the path of proving the principles of faith by deductive and narrative means as indicated in the Qur'an without indulging in deep thought and exclusive logical reasoning based on the perception of the universe that only results in controversial ambiguities."[193] In order to show that the *salaf* complied with the Muhammadi views on the issue of fate, I would like to quote a letter by Hasan al-Basri (d.

728) to the Prophet's grandson, Hasan and a few sentences from Hasan's reply. When Wasil bin 'Ata (d. 748), founder of the Mu'tazilites, departed from the lecture circle of the great saint Hasan al-Basri and began to spread un-Islamic views on the issue of fate, Hasan al-Basri became saddened and had doubts. So he wrote a letter to the Prophet's grandson Hasan. In his letter he said, "O grandson and most beloved of the Messenger of God, may the mercy of God be upon you. You, children of Hashim, are like a ship navigating on the ocean. You are stars that shine in the dark heavens. You are like milestones that show the true path. You are religious men who show their followers the path of salvation. O grandson of the Prophet, we are bewildered about the issue of predetermination and the execution of fate. There is a controversy. What is your view on this issue? You are the descendant of the Prophet, your knowledge is due to the inspiration of God." In his reply, Hasan wrote, ". . . I have received your letter about the issue of fate concerning which you are bewildered. My view on this issue is the following: Whoever does not believe in destiny and that good and evil come from God is a unbeliever. Whoever attributes the sins that he himself commits is a sinner . . ."[194] It can be seen from this letter that the *salaf* did not engage in philosophy.

Rumi followed the path of the Qur'an and held the exact view of the Sunnis (*ahl al-sunna*) regarding the concept of destiny. According to this view, the Creator of a person's deeds and other events that occur beyond one's control is God. God has given humans a "minute free will." With this free will, the human being attempts to act, to accomplish things. If a person's intended deed is compatible with the "divine (universal) will" of God, then God creates that deed and that event happens. The will, choice, and determination to act belong to man. In short, if man's will and endeavor is compatible with God's will, then that event occurs. Therefore, a believer believes in destiny while he rejects total determinism. Rumi renounced the views of the Mu'tazilites and Murji'ah (those who deny human responsibility) and proclaimed that a believer has to believe in destiny following the path of the *ahl al-sunna* or mainstream Islam. Belief in destiny (predetermination and execution of events by God) is one of the six principles of Islamic faith. But believing in destiny does not mean that one is to leave everything to fate, claiming, "This is my fate" for whatever happens. We can make our situation better or worse by using our "minute will." Otherwise, if we did not have the opportunity to change our destiny, in other words had we lacked free will, human beings would lead a predetermined life dictated by destiny, and no prophets would have been sent to show human beings how to struggle against evil. The following verse from the Qur'an clearly indicates this fact: "Whatever good comes to you it is from God and whatever evil comes to you it is from your self."[195] Based on this verse, Rumi says, "Whatever sorrow and sadness comes to your heart, it is because of your fearlessness and insolence."[196] There is a subtle point here: When we say, "All good and evil comes from God," we mean that both good and evil is created by God. But good is the grace of God and evil is the return for a person's deeds. The Traditions of Prophet Muhammad shed light on this issue: "Nothing can change destiny. Only prayers can prevent calamities, and only grace and generosity can prolong life."[197] The change of destiny by prayer is again fate. Just as an umbrella shields one from the rain, prayer shields one against calamities.

In accordance with the Sunna of the Prophet, Rumi clarified this complicated subject by his beautiful way of expression and superb sensations. According to Rumi, our "minute will," our choice and power to act, is nothing other than the manifestation of the "universal will" of God. Since nothing other than God possesses true existence and all "relative beings" are the manifestations of the one "absolute Being," the will ultimately belongs to the Unique and Absolute Being. The will found in relative beings is nothing more than the manifestation of the Absolute Being's will within them. Who are we in comparison to the Universal Will, the Absolute Being, God, so that we may speak of *ourselves* and claim that we can do this, and we can accomplish that? "O spirit of our spirit, who are we to claim that 'we are' in comparison to you. We do not exist, our existence comes from you, the Real and Absolute Existence who makes the shadows visible. Neither we nor our will exist. Your grace has heard what we have not said."[198]

Rumi explains the matter of free will and *jabr* (determinism) according to the *ahl al-sunna* belief. He finds the Mu'tazilah mistaken and the Murji'ah misled. We do have choice and power. And yes, even if we shoot an arrow, it is God who shoots that arrow. We only serve as a bow, that, a means. God said in the Qur'an to our Prophet, "When you threw (a handful of dust), it was not your act. . ."[199] If we shoot an arrow, that shooting is not from us. We are more like the bow. It is God who stretches the bow and shoots the arrow.

This explanation is not deterministic rhetoric but the meaning of God's Beautiful Name *al-Jabbar* or the Compeller. The purpose of mentioning God's name *al-Jabbar* is to seek refuge in Him. Our crying and lamenting is the sign of our powerlessness and incapacity. Our being ashamed of what we do is the evidence for our free will and choice. "If we had had no free will, would we be ashamed of what we do? Whence comes this regret, sorrow, and shame?"[200] "If you do not see the compulsion (*jabr*), do not say that you see it. If you do see it, then what is the sign of your seeing? On the contrary, in whatever you want to do, you see your own choice and power and you say, 'I did this' with no regard to the *jabr* of God. In whatever you do not want to do, you say 'This is the *jabr* of God', and you become a Murji'ah. The prophets are like the Murji'ah in the matters of this world, and the infidels are like the Murji'ah in the matters of the hereafter. The prophets have preferred to concentrate on the matters of the hereafter, whereas the ignorant focus on the matters of this world."[201]

The attitude of the prophets and saints, who are their successors in this world, is deterministic. They view everything as coming from God. Whatever hardship they face they say, "This is from God" and accept it the way it is. But in the matters of hereafter they use their choice and power. In contrast, the infidels who use their choice and power in matters of this world behave like the Murji'ah when it comes to the hereafter. Therefore, they blame God for all the evil they do. They say, "God makes us do these things." They view themselves as innocent. Rumi views man's free will as a bounty of God and recommends that we duly extend our thanks to God for this. The proper duty of giving thanks is not limited to just saying, "Thanks to God, with His Grace, we have free will, hence we can distinguish right from wrong, and we have found the path of salvation." The proper duty of giving thanks for the bounty of free will includes using that free will for the common good, for meaningful purposes, and good deeds. If we can do this, our power increases.

Trying to give proper thanks for the bounties of God increases one's power. But holding deterministic views is the denial of man's free will, that great bounty.

Thanking for the bounty of choice and power He has given enhances your power. On the other hand, believing in necessity causes you to lose that gift.

Believing in *irja'* is like sleeping on the road and deserting work. O walker of the path of God, do not fall asleep on the road before reaching your destination and arriving at the doorsteps of God.

O Murji'ah who will not take lessons, do not sleep anywhere else other than under the tree which bears fruit.[202] Lie under that tree so that the wind moves the branches of the tree and fruits and nourishment pour on the one lying underneath.

Believing in *irja'* is like sleeping among bandits. How can a bird whose wings have not yet grown strong enough escape them by flying?[203]

The deterministic view of the saints who have cleansed themselves of the self's evil and ornamented themselves in the manners of the Law and adopted the Qur'an as their code of conduct is praiseworthy. But it is a disgrace for the bearers of the *nafs al-ammarah* (the part of the self that forcefully commands evil). The famous *Mesnevi* commentator, Ankaravi (d. 1631) writes:

> One day someone related to Seriyy-i Sakati (d. 870) the follow-
> ing words and asked his opinion on them: "In reality we are
> like the door. Neither our motion nor our motionlessness is
> from ourselves."
>
> Seriyy-i Sakati replied, "The man who utters these words is
> either a saint or a heretical sinner," and added: "If he is on the
> Muhammadi path and acting according to the Qur'an and
> Prophetic Tradition, then he is a gnostic and a saint. But if he
> is someone who ignores his religious duties and views every-
> thing as lawful, then he is a heretical sinner."[204]

Since Rumi fought many un-Islamic beliefs and spiritual diseases, in his works he frequently brings up issues related to the
beliefs of the Mu'tazilah and the Murji'ah which contradict the *ahl
al-sunna* belief and damage many people's faith: "See what God
does and see also what you do. See both of them and know that
there are things that we do. This is apparent anyway. If you claim
that people do not act and it is only God who acts, then do not
complain to anyone, 'Why did you do this to me?' God's creation
brings our actions into existence. The actions that we carry out are
the execution of God's creation and His predetermination."[205]

> O son, God knows, understands, and grasps everything. His
> doing one thing does not prevent him doing something else at
> the same time.
>
> That lowly devil said to God, "You have misled me," and
> tried to conceal his sin.
>
> But Adam said, "We have done injustice to ourselves,"
> admitted his sin, and took it on his shoulders. And yet he was
> not unaware of God's predetermination as we are.
>
> However, because of his comportment, he took on the sin pre-
> determined by God upon himself, and he was forgiven for this.
>
> When Adam repented, God asked him, "O, Adam, wasn't I
> the One who created the sin that you committed and all the
> hardship that you faced?"

Adam replied, "I kept my comportment because of my fear."
And God said, "I forgive you for this."[206]

In order to prevent any doubts that might form when reading this passage, I would like to give the following explanation: According to the belief of the *ahl al-sunna*, in contrast to that of the Mu'tazilah and the Murji'ah, man has minute free will. God knows what we have done so far and what we are going to do. He is also the Creator of all our deeds. Good, evil, utility, and harm all come according to His judgment. He is also the One who activates or deactivates our free will. We should not tie the evil that comes to us by God's predetermination to destiny, but we should maintain comportment and blame our self for not using our choice and power to remove the evil in us and restrain our self, which dictates evil. Whatever God, who is Absolute Justice, creates has a very good reason. Both good and evil come to us by His judgment in order to better us and awaken us. "Do not say 'Why is this so?' It is proper the way it is. Look what happens at the end. Let us see what God does. Whatever He does, He does beautifully." Rumi provides another example in order to clarify this matter:

> O heart, bring an analogy for the free will and necessity to be distinguished from each other so that you may know what is free will and necessity.
>
> Think of a weak hand that shakes because of old age or illness, and a hand that you consciously shake. The shaking of both hands is with the creation of God.
>
> The shaking of both hands happens according to God's law. Know this. But these two shakings cannot be compared.
>
> You can regret it when you shake or move your hand. But when have you seen someone who regrets his hands' shaking because of illness?[207]

If someone who drinks coffee drops the cup and breaks it, he regrets his clumsiness or carelessness. But is the cup that drops from a healthy man's hand and breaks the same as the cup that drops from an old and weak man's hand and breaks? If the healthy man who acts on free will had taken proper care, he would not have dropped the cup. But one does not regret when the sick man drops the cup and breaks it. The cup's dropping from a shivering hand is beyond one's free will and control. Rumi repeats many times that man has free will:

> Yes, there is predetermination and execution. But there is also man's choice and power. Be mindful and do not be blind as the devil.
>
> Sometimes we hesitate between doing two things. Would there be any hesitation if we had no free will, choice and power?
>
> Would a man with two hands and two legs tightly bound hesitate whether he should do this or that? Hence we have a free will.
>
> In such a case, can anyone think of doing this or that? Can he say, "Should I dive into the sea? Or should I fly in the air?"
>
> All this means that the hesitation between doing two things shows that man possesses choice and power. Otherwise one who hesitates would be laughed at.
>
> O young man, blame predetermination and execution little. How can you put your blame on the shoulders of others?
>
> Is justice served when 'Amr is punished for the man killed by Zayd? Is justice served when Ahmad is beaten as a punishment for 'Amr's drinking of wine? Is all this sensible?
>
> Go around yourself and see your fault. Know that you are responsible for your actions and not your shadow. Instead of seeing others' faults, see your own faults. Blame yourself instead of blaming others.[208]

After explaining to us, the unaware, this difficult to understand and difficult to explain subject of predetermination, execution, and man's free will with many analogies, Rumi then seeks refuge in his much beloved God and begs Him for help:

> O God who gave us minds, please help us to understand this difficult matter, come to our help. In reality it is You who wills and acts. No one else can will and act.

Our requests and prayers come from You and also acceptance and bounties come from You. Who are we? You are the Eternal Predecessor and the Eternal Successor.

You say and You hear and You are. In all the things that we do that look so magnificent, we are still at the level of nought.

O God, You gave us commandments, You gave us duties and responsibilities, You willed our worship. Increase also our tendency to prostration. Give us the pleasure of worship. Protect us from the laziness of the belief in *irja'*; do not extinguish our enthusiasm with the laziness of *irja'*.

Irja' is the arm and wing of the saints, but it is the chains on the feet of the sinners.

See the belief in *irja'* as the water of the Nile. To the faithful it is water but to the infidels it is blood.[209]

REINCARNATION

Some people who have read certain of Rumi's poems in the *Mesnevi* and *Divan-i Kabir* have misinterpreted them and think that Rumi believes in reincarnation; reincarnation is an un-Islamic belief. As I have stated repeatedly, it would not be possible for a great saint who follows the Muhammadi path to adopt an un-Islamic belief.

Reincarnation is defined as the transmigration of souls into the bodies of others. Pythagoras and his followers were of this belief among the ancient Greek philosophers. Today, most Hindus believe in reincarnation, and therefore do not eat animal flesh believing that it might be carrying the souls of their ancestors and relatives. It can be seen clearly in the passages from the *Mesnevi* below that Rumi, like many other lovers of God, spoke of the belief of *dawriyya* (rotation). One should be careful not to confuse reincarnation with *dawriyya*. But what is *dawriyya*?

In order to understand this belief properly we first have to think carefully about some issues. According to the view of the gnostics, everything that we see in this universe is a place of the manifestation of the Divine Names and Attributes of God. In other words, everything is like a mirror. From gigantic creatures to microscopic ones, in everything His Art, Power, and Beauty is manifested. Like a sun, the Holy Light is reflected in every atom and in every being the manifestation of an Attribute or a Name of God can be seen. Everything in this universe is alive. Not only human beings, animals, and plants but also objects like rocks, soil, water, and minerals, which we consider to be inanimate, are actually alive. However, the naked eye cannot see their motion which is the sign of their life force. In the Qur'an, God says, "Everything in the heavens and on the earth praises and invokes God."[210] It is also for the same reason that the Prophet commanded, "Do not disturb your belongings unnecessarily." In his famous *Futuhat al-Makkiyyah*, Muhy al-Din Ibn al-'Arabi writes, "I can hear the praise of everything. Things that we normally consider inanimate invoke God more than humans, animals, and plants as they are less attached to the world." Since the dervishes want to abstain from disturbing objects during their invocation, they step only gently on the ground when they walk; the ground is laid below everyone's feet, carrying everybody on its head and serving all. Therefore, they do not want to hurt the ground on which they walk. When they want to drink water, they gently kiss the glass. When they grasp the spoon, they kiss its handle. When they finish their meal, they do not stand up without kissing the table. This is because everything carries a spirit. Everything provides a service. It is a debt for the served to reward and respect those who serve.

Dervishes who treat the objects that we consider inanimate with so much respect in order not to disturb them show even more respect for plants and animals. There have been saints who abstained from picking flowers, sensing their invocation of God's names, as well as gnostics who walked for hours to return an ant to its colony in order not to separate it from its community. It is related that Shibli bought a sack of wheat from the bazaar and brought it home after walking for several hours. When he emptied the sack he saw a bewildered ant running around. He thought that he had separated the ant from its home. So he took the ant and put it in a box. He took it back to the bazaar from where he had bought the wheat and released it there. Ferdausi, author of the *Shahname*, says, "Do not hurt an ant that is dragging a grain of wheat. It has a spirit and is alive. And life is a very sweet thing." We see that the ant is dragging a grain of wheat, and this convinces us that it is alive. We see the flowers grow, and this convinces us that they are alive. But the Qur'an and Prophetic tradition tell us that objects like rocks, minerals, and soil, all things that we consider inanimate, are also alive.

Today science has proved that there are plenty of things and actions that we cannot see with the naked eye. When inanimate objects are viewed with electron microscopes, they are magnified thousands of times, and their microscopic motion is revealed and can even be photographed. The soil samples brought back from the moon have the same molecular structure as those from Earth; this microscopic motion is not restricted to our Earth. Just as plants exhibit their living through their growth, blooming, and bearing of fruits, "inanimate" objects demonstrate their life by the rotation of electrons around a nucleus. Animals demonstrate their life with sound, motion, eating, and regeneration. But human beings, who are the most honorable among all creatures, prove their superiority not only with their intellectual faculties, like reasoning, reading, writing, speaking, and laughing, but especially through the Divine Entrustment that has been granted by Him. All the beings in the universe are places of manifestation for the Divine Names and Attributes, but the human being, the essence of the universe, is the place of the manifestation for *all* the Divine Names and Attributes.

God who existed before anything existed bestowed life on humans, animals, plants, and inanimate objects. God bestowed life on all the creatures in the universe that He created with one word, *kun* (be) and manifested in them His attributes, like the reflections of a spiritual sun in the mirror of the universe. All this happened without Divine incarnation (*hulul*) or unification (*ittihad*). That Supreme and Unique Universal Spirit bestowed the *jamadi*, or inorganic spirit on the objects that are considered to be inanimate, the botanical spirit on the plants, and the zoological spirit on the animals. However, the human spirit, which was blessed with the Divine Entrustment, is not like other types of spirits. The human spirit shall live after death. The spirit that is bestowed on human beings when they are still in their mother's womb will continue on to the Intermediate State (*barzakh*) and remain there until Judgment Day. On Judgment Day, when decayed corpses will be resurrected by God, the human spirit will reenter the body.

The *dawriyya* (rotation) poetry, which has been written or recited by many poets who, like Rumi, talk about the love of God, is the story of the Divine Light's separation from the Absolute Being— God, whose existence has no beginning. This story begins with the descent of the Divine Light from the heavens, and after going through many stages, its returns back to its origin. In other words, *dawriyya* poetry deals with the separation from the Origin (*mabda*) and the return to the Home (*ma'ad*). Those *dawriyya* poems that give an account of the separation from God in the eternal beginning and exile in this world are called *farshiyya* (earth) or *nuzul* (descent) *dawriyya*, and those that give an account of the return to the Origin are called the *'uruj* (ascension) *dawriyya*.

Now let us look at some *dawriyya* poetry composed by Rumi and try to understand it: "Man first came to the world of inorganic substances. From there he fell into the world of the plants. He lived in the world of the plants for years and never remembered his life in the world of inorganic substances. And when he transferred from the world of plants to the world of animals, he then forgot his life in the world of plants."[211] These verses illustrate the development of our physical being. In fact the human body, our material existence, is built through what we eat and drink. Our food consists of meat, vegetables, fruit, water, and inorganic substances, such as the minerals in our food. Man's seed was dispersed around different parts of the universe before it fell in the mother's womb. The mother and father prepare that seed from the food they eat, consisting of meat, vegetables, and minerals. Furthermore, when the seed develops in the mother's womb, it is nourished with the food that comes through the mother's food. In this way, humans came to into existence from the ranks of minerals, plants, and animals and became the 'essence of the universe.' Therefore, Shaykh Ghalib wrote, "Take care of yourself because you are the essence of the universe." In another poem, Rumi remembers this subject:

> I died after being inorganic matter and became a growing plant. I died after being a plant and appeared in the shape of an animal.
>
> I died after being an animal and became a human being. After all this why would I be afraid of decreasing and being incomplete?
>
> Let me make another move ahead and escape the state of humanity and spread my wings in the world of angels.
>
> I cannot stop even after becoming an angel. I have to proceed even further because everything other than God is destined to be destroyed.
>
> And in the end, I will be sacrificed from being an angel and become something that cannot be imagined.
>
> I become nothing by leaving all forms. I am completely effaced and say like Arganun[212], "We surely return to Him."[213]

When carefully read, we can see that in these verses Rumi describes the different stages of the development of the human essence. The physical being of humans comes from the soil. They obtain their food from the plants that grow in the soil and the animals that are fed from that soil. After being in those worlds, humans come to the world of humanity. But they do not lose anything by departing from these other worlds. On the contrary, they advance and develop. This is not to say that the plants and animals we see around us today will be humans in the future. Rather, what is being discussed here is that when humans attained the bliss of dying after the animalistic stage to become human beings, there remained no fear of death; humans are aware that they will not vanish with death. They will escape their physical existence and attain God. The sword will be freed from its sheath. The following quatrain by Rousseau, addresses this subject:

> When the spirit escapes the darkness of body
> And betakes itself on the road to its homeland
> That is when doubts and illusions fade
> And then the truth is known.

In the verses cited above, Rumi not only talks about departing from the world of spirits and descending to the lower plane, but he completes his *dawriyya* with the ascension and reunion with God. He is not content with saying, "I died after being an animal and became a man." His spirit did not find peace with this. When he says, "Let me make another move ahead and escape the state of humanity and spread my wings in the world of angels," he wishes to attain the state of an angel by escaping the state of humanity, understanding that the state of humanity has many obstacles, like the desire for fame, lust, anger, greed, love of this world, and passion; these chain one's hands and keep one far from God, making one's self a slave to materiality. Being an angel does not satisfy Rumi either, and he wishes to advance even further because elsewhere in the *Mesnevi* he says, "O brother, the door (path) of God is a door that is never reached. Hence, however much you proceed toward this door, you will not see it as being far enough and will not stop. Proceed ever more." "Every day there is a new departure for me and new distances to cover." This is the character and approach of Rumi.

Because of his character, Rumi does not stop even after attaining the state of an angel; he wants to proceed to become completely nothing, "something that cannot be imagined," leaving all forms. Here Rumi means the level of *fana fillah* (annihilation in God). At this point we face a subtle issue. The concept of nothingness that Rumi talks about is not the same nothingness that is the foundation of Buddhism. Leaving the world, dying before dying, and escaping the ego is not the selflessness that the Buddhists believe in. The nothingness that Rumi seeks is escaping the evil that is inherent in the state of humanity, killing desires like lust, anger, and love of the world and being annihilated in God. In other words, it is an escape from this shadow existence. However, the nothingness in the Buddhist belief is an attempt to escape all existence and to attain Nirvana. Akif Pasha expresses the Buddhist's view of nothingness in his following couplet: "In nothingness there is neither sorrow nor concern, nor the bitterness of pain or former hope lost. Therefore, all men seek this nothingness." The two following couplets of Akif Pasha might also have been inspired by Rumi: "Some people seek the eternal existence with a lack of sorrow; some seek nothingness due to sorrows and pain. I, on the other hand, am effaced in the dust under the feet of Muhammad, who is the King of Both Worlds, and hence I neither seek existence nor run away from nothingness." It is impossible not to remember Yunus Emre when speaking of existence and non-existence, when he says:

> I am neither happy with having
> Nor sorry for destitution
> I am overwhelmed with your love
> You are the One I seek.

The following ode explains *dawriyya* more closely:

> I stayed for some time in each of the nine heavens called the Great Fathers (Saturn, Jupiter, Mars, Mercury, Venus, Neptune, Uranus and the two Pole stars). I rotated for many years with the stars in the signs of the Zodiac.
>
> For some time I remained invisible. I was somewhere with Him. Those days I was in the country of *aw adna* (or even closer),[214] which is closest to God. There I saw what I saw.
>
> I received nourishment from God just as the embryo receives nourishment from its mother. Children of Adam are born once but I am born many times.
>
> I stayed in the robe of the body for many years. I have done many things. I have torn apart many robes with my own hands.
>
> I spent many nights with the ascetics in houses of worship. And I slept many nights with the idol worshippers in front of idols.

I am both one of the thieves running around and the agony of the lamenting sick. I am both the cloud and the rain. I keep on raining on the gardens.

O beggar, the dust of mortality has never reached my dress. I picked many roses in the garden of immortality.

My essence is not of fire, water, nervous wind, and decorated soil. I laugh at them all.

O son, I am not Shams of Tabriz. If you see me do not tell anyone, "I saw him." I am not him. I am pure light.[215]

In order to better understand the issue of *dawriyya*, which is difficult to understand and to explain, we have to grasp the fundamentals of *wahdat al-wujud*. According to this belief, existence is one. There is only one thing that exists, and that is God. There is no other existence than the existence of God. And it is impossible for anything else to exist. In other words, when there were no heavens, no earth, nothing at all, God, *al-Qadim* (the Primordial), existed. All the beings in this universe, visible or invisible, have appeared in the knowledge of God. Then they came into existence with God's manifestation of His Divine Will. In other words, they were created as a result of God's manifestation of His Person (Self). But in reality, all created beings and all universes consist of non-existence that has the illusion of existence; the real existence is only the existence of God. Prophet Muhammad described the state before the universe, whose existence is an illusion in a sense, as follows: "God existed and nothing else existed with Him." 'Ali was present there and he replied: "It is still the same way," pointing to this truth.

Here one might ask: How can this be true? How can one view this universe that was created *ex nihilo*? We live amongst all these creatures and we feel that we exist and live. Then how can we say that we do not exist? Also we came to possess some of the things that God created. We eat and drink. How can all this be considered to be non-existent? Is this at all possible? Is this because our existence is for all practical purposes non-existent and insignificant in comparison to the vast greatness of this universe?

Modern science has discovered that there are stars as far away as 60 billion light years from our planet. The spacecraft, the Spirit, only recently arrived on Mars and began sending images to the Earth. The universe is so vast that our world seems like a little blue spot among countless stars, and we are like particles of dust on an orange. Thus is the notion of nothingness, a way of approximating the truth as the poet says:

> If our earth is like a dust particle compared to the heavens
> Then along the same line of reasoning, man has to consider
> himself to be in non-existence.

No, this consideration is neither an approximation nor a delusion, but it is the truth of Rumi's interpretation of Islam. What kind of significance can our physical existence have when all the stars in the heavens do not have any significance at all with respect to the infinite greatness and power of God? In one of his quatrains Rumi says, "There is none other than Him in this world. There is neither anything ugly nor anything beautiful, neither anything visible nor anything invisible. Every arrow that is shot is shot with His Power. Every deeply meaningful word is uttered through His lips." When we look at the sky on a clear summer night we see billions of stars shining in the heavens. But when the morning comes and the sun rises with all its magnificence, we cease to see the beautiful stars that caressed our hearts with their twinkling and which comforted us. Where have all they gone? Have they disappeared in the infinite vacuum of space? They are still in their place, still traveling in their orbits, and still emitting light, but they are not visible anymore since the light of the sun overwhelms their light and makes them invisible. Similarly, if a sun of truth, a sun of faith, rises in our hearts, our eyes are dazzled with its light and we become unable to see anything other than God. Then we came to understand the truth of "Nothing exists but Him."

Other followers of the view of *wahdat al-wujud* describe this in the following way: Although existence is one, it has an inner and an outer aspect. The inner aspect of existence is a light that is the spirit of the universe, and the universe is filled with that light throughout. It is this light that gives life to everything, including those things that we mistakenly describe as inanimate. The Qur'anic verse, "God is the Light of the heavens and the earth" expresses this truth.[216] There is no limit, end, or peak to this light. It does not penetrate things and it does not unite things. This light is an infinite ocean of holy light that has no shore and whose greatness cannot be encompassed. Life, knowledge, will, and power exist because of this light. Everything comes into existence and sustains its existence through this light. The vision, sound, speech, motion, work, and influence of creatures come from this light. In fact, everything consists of this light. The characteristics of beings, the nature of things, their attributes, and power all come from this light. This light is unique and it is not more than one. It enlightens everywhere, like a sun. All things from the microcosmo to the macrocosmo, all the stars and countless worlds, everything is a place of manifestation and reflection for this light. As Niyazi Misri (d. 1696) has said,

> Look at the things in all six directions with a careful eye
> They are all a mirror where the Face of the Most Merciful is seen
> He is the Sayer, the Said, the Seer and the Seen
> Whatever there is, high and low, know that the Beloved is seen there.

After becoming familiar with these views, we understand that all the different stages, levels, attributes, and modes are His mirror and His place of manifestation. Since we could say that He is the Spirit of the Universe, in the Rumian sense, there is no one but He who is in the mosques with the pious and in the temples with the idol worshippers. Ziya Pasha spoke of this truth when he said, "In the sight of God, a Muslim and a fire worshipper are one." In other words, both of these different states are manifestations of His different Names; in this case, *al-Hadi* and *al-Mudhill*. The following ode by Rumi helps clarify this issue:

> O God, you are the Healer of the sick. You are the One hidden as the spirit within the boons and bounties.
>
> You make your servants sick so that they may pray to You because You are the purchaser and accepter of their lamenting and crying.
>
> Everyone in this world is seeking a remedy for his own hardship. However, the remedies of these hardships are seeking You because there is no doubt that You are the Creator of both the hardship and the remedy.
>
> The hardships that make one beg from others are veils, pretexts that are predetermined. Beyond this veil is Your door of boons, where one ultimately is destined.
>
> You first make the sick lament and cry so that they may find comfort and regain their health eventually. But in reality You are the One who is our illness and our lamenting. By God, You are the One who says "you are . . ."
>
> On this game field You are the ball. You are the player and the spectator. Slavery, lordship, and kingdom are all Your predetermination. Both the straight line and the curved line are drawn in Your school.
>
> Our bodies are like houses and our souls are like guests in these houses. O God, we do not exist. Our bodies and our souls are Your Shadow. In reality You are the spirit of our spirits who are guests in our bodies.[217]

Since God manifests himself in everything, expressions like "from inorganic substances, I transformed into plants, from plants into animals and from animals into man," which can be found in many places in the *Mesnevi*, must be interpreted as the developmental stages of our physical being, as previously mentioned. Transmigration of souls is not what is being talked about here. The notion of reincarnation leads to a denial of the Hereafter, which is contradictory to the fundamentals of Islam. Regarding this matter Rumi says, "You own a body without body. So do not be afraid of your spirit leaving the body. (Your real existence is beyond this physical body.)"[218]

According to the followers of reincarnation, there is no Intermediary State (*barzakh*) where the spirits after death will wait until Judgment Day, and reward or punishment for our deeds is manifested as coming back as a lower or a higher form of life. They further claim that the spirits are limited and constantly transmigrate from body to body. They do not adhere to the Islamic perspective that God manifests Himself in a different way in every instance. Instead, they believe that there is repetition in God's manifestation. Those who believe in reincarnation, who are unaware of the fact that the Divine Emanation spreads over all things and covers them constantly, believe that the spirit will cease to exist after going through many adventures and entering and exiting many bodies. Muslims, however, believe in the immortality of the human spirit, which is a Divine Entrustment. Therefore, we are not afraid that we are destined to vanish in the soil. Omar Khayyam (d. 1131), a Muslim philosopher, remembers our physical mortality and says, "Know that every breath you take is an opportunity, You are not grass that will grow again next year." He advises us to prepare for the spiritual world and not waste our time. Human beings do not want effacement; rather they want to live after death. They want to live on, even if it is in the hearts of others. Therefore, the great Turkish poet, Baki says, "All that remains under the dome of the heavens is the memory of a pleasant sound."

Can we remain tied to the elements (inorganic materials, plants and animals) that reach our bodies through what we eat and drink when our physical existence, our bodies are destined to decay and to be eaten by insects and worms in the grave? In the preceding ode, Rumi said, "My essence is not of water, fire, air, and soil." The elements belong to our bodies, which house our spirits. While the four elements make up the body, the spirit, which resides in the body, has nothing to do with the elements because the spirit is "Divine Breath." Indeed, in his famous *Qasidah al-Ta'iyyah*, the great Sufi poet Ibn al-Farid (d. 1235) pleads first to be delivered from the influence of false belief and delusion that originates from lowly desires and then begs God that He may keep him away from those who believe in reincarnation:

> O God, grant me the sign of the virtues and wisdom that will save me from the influence of false belief and delusion based on imperfect knowledge and hypotheses caused by lowly desires.
>
> O God, keep me away from the believers in *naskh* (reincarnation, transmigration of soul from one human body to another), *maskh* (transmigration of soul from one human body to an animal body).
>
> O God, mix me not with those who claim *faskh* (transmigration of soul from one human body to plants), and *raskh* (transmigration of soul from one human body to inorganic substances) and hence believe that in every transmigration the soul suffers the agony that it deserves.[219]

The belief in reincarnation, which is un-Islamic, causes us to lose our spirit, the existence of which we feel (our real self). I feel a Divine Entrustment which is within me. What is inside me is mine. It is not someone else's. It will not go anywhere else. When it exits this world it will only return to its origin.

Mahmud Shabastari (d. 1320), author of the *Gulshan-i Raz*, points out the inadequacy of the intellect in this matter and then says that belief in reincarnation comes from a narrowness of viewpoint and hence it is *kufr* (infidelity) and has no substance to it:

> Know that the whole universe is filled with the light of God. He is hidden in the universe since He is apparent. In other words, the fact that He is as apparent as sunlight causes Him not to show Himself and to remain hidden.
>
> The light of God neither goes from one place to another, nor does it change from one state to another. That light neither changes nor assumes a different form.
>
> You think that the universe sustains its existence with its own existence and that its existence is everlasting with its own essence.

Whoever possesses a mind that is inclined toward long reflection, it takes its owner to many mind-boggling places, surprising and misleading him.

Because of long, useless reflections of the mind, some have been taken by philosophy and some by the belief in incarnation (*hulul*).

The intellect does not have the ability to see the light of truth. So, go and seek another eye, the eye of the heart, to see Him.

Both eyes of the philosopher are cross-eyed, and therefore he cannot see God as one.

The belief in reincarnation is caused by the narrowness of the point of view and hence it is infidelity and has no substance to it.[220]

When Shaykh Muhammad Lahiji (d. 1464) wrote commentaries on these verses, he followed the conduct of many gnostics and referred to verses in the *Mesnevi* to explain these difficult-to-understand, esoteric truths. Although it may be repetitious, for blessing's sake, I cannot proceed without including the following lines from the *Mesnevi*:

Since the existence of the soul is felt and is so close to ourselves, it remains unnoticed. Man is like a jug whose mouth is dry although it is filled with water.

How can you see the colors of red, green, and pink where there is no light?

But since your intellect and thoughts are lost in colors, these colors prevent you from seeing the light itself.

Whenever the night covers the colors, then you come to understand that seeing colors depends on light.

Outside, it is impossible to see the colors if there is no light. The same holds true for the colors inside you.

The colors on the outside can be seen with the light of the sun and stars. The colors of the inner world can only be seen with the shining of the light of God.

The light of your eye is the light of the heart because the light of the eye comes from the light of the heart.

The light of the light of heart comes from the light of God. But this light is completely different from the light of the intellect and light of the senses.

At night since there is no light, you cannot see the colors. This you came to understand as the opposite of the light.

First the light is seen and then the colors. You can understand this clearly with the disappearance of light.

God created sorrows and difficulties as the opposite of comfort and peace of mind, so that comfort and peace of mind will be appreciated (understood).

Every hidden thing becomes apparent with its opposite. And since God has no opposite He remains hidden.

You recognized the light with its opposite because when something becomes apparent it makes apparent its opposite as well.

In the world of existence, the light of God has no opposite making it apparent through its opposite.

Of course our eyes cannot see and encompass Him. But understand that He sees and encompasses us with the parable of Moses and Mount Sinai.[221]

The last section of the previously quoted material refers to the Qur'anic verse, which reads, "Eyes do not comprehend Him, but He comprehends all eyes. He is the Subtle and the Aware."[222]

The light of the existence of God is manifested constantly and without interruption. This manifestation is not in the way that believers in reincarnation understand it to be. There is no repetition in creation. Since everything is a mirror for the manifestation of God, every mirror constantly shows us something different from His Attributes and Acts. This manifestation is never separated from the Ultimate Emanator: "Sunlight is never separated from the sun, so how can the emanation be separated from God?" The following couplet by Aziz Mahmud Hudayi (d. 1628), a well known Turkish mystic, illustrates this truth very clearly: "His manifestation became a veil for His manifestation, Does anyone with eyes ever seek evidence for the existence of light?" This truth cannot be comprehended only with reason. Reason can take one only half the way. As

Rumi tells us, "The philosopher has relied on his mind and killed himself with thought. Let him run and go away. He has already left the treasure of truth behind. You tell him, 'Run and go!' The faster he runs the farther he gets from the desire in his heart."[223]

Why are we going far away? Is God not closer to us than our jugular vein?

> God is closer to man than his jugular vein. And you are trying to shoot your thought far away like an arrow.
>
> O, you who draws his bow and shoots his arrow, the prey is close by and you are shooting your arrow to a distant place.
>
> The farther one shoots his arrow, the more distant he remains from the invaluable treasure of the truth.[224]

The following lines, composed by a gnostic, reveal the same truth:

> That Beloved is always with you and never far away from you, even for a moment.
>
> Even though you are living your life unaware and separated from Him, He is never separated from you.
>
> In order to see the sun of His face open your eyes and look carefully because His sun is never covered and is visible to the eye.
>
> But even if there is no obstacle other than His own light it is only possible to see His face again with His light.

As discussed above, all the things that we consider to exist do not exist in reality. They only seem to exist. Just as the star becomes invisible when the sun rises, nothing other than God remains visible at the time of Divine Manifestation. Indeed, Rumi confirms this notion in the following couplets:

> O spirit of our spirit, who are we to claim that we exist? We simply are non-existing ones. The real existence that makes mortals seem to exist is You.[225]

When one admits that there is only one existence, namely God's existence, then *hulul* and *ittihad* become impossible; for both of these conditions to occur, there must be two existent beings and yet there is only one existing entity, and that is God.[226]

As is widely known, the gnostics tell us of four journeys that are necessary to make in order to orient one's self to God, to attain the truth, and to open the eye of the heart: The first journey is spiritual advancement from the station of the self to the "apparent horizon" (*ufq al-mubin*), which is the end of the level of heart. On attaining this level, the lovers of God throw away their excessive love for materialism, the world, and riches from their heart. They raise the veil of plurality (*kathrat*) from the face of the unity (*wahdat*). In other words, they deliver themselves from the perception of plurality. They see unity in everything. This journey is called the journey *to* God. (*sayr ilallah*).

The second journey is completed by assuming the conduct prescribed by the Qur'an and attaining the "highest horizon" (*ufq al-'ala*), which is the end of the level of Unity (*wahdaniyyah*). In contrast to the first journey, in this journey the veil of unity (*wahdat*) is lifted from the face of the plurality (*kathrat*). In this journey, plurality is seen in unity, whereas in the first journey unity is seen in plurality. This journey is called the journey *in* God (*sayr fillah*).

The third journey leads to deliverance from all dualities, esoteric or exoteric, viewing all the power and acts in God and attaining the level of "the very union itself" (*'ayn al-jam'*). This journey is called the journey *with* God (*sayr ma'allah*).

The fourth journey is the level where one returns from God to the people in order to guide them to God and this is a state where unity is seen in the form of plurality, and plurality is seen in the form of unity. Similarly this level refers to returning from the state of union (*jam'*) to that of separation (*firaq*), or from intoxication (*sakr*) to sobriety (*sahw*). This journey is called the journey *from* God (*sayr anillah*).

The great Sufi poet Mahmud Shabastari explains that all the spiritual levels that believers go through in their spiritual journey, where they walk on the path of Islamic Law to attain the truth, have nothing to do with reincarnation: "The meaning of this is not rein-carnation. These states are appearances of Divine Manifestations. Someone was asked, 'Where is the final destination?' He replied, 'It is the return to the origin.'"[227] The gnostics have described the descent of our spiritual existence from the level of unity (*ahadiyyah*) to the level of humanity (*insaniyyah*) as the "semi-circle of descent," and the ascension of our spiritual existence from the level of human-ity (*insaniyyah*) to the level of unity (*ahadiyyah*) as the "semi-circle of ascension." Gnostics who journey to God have thought of the journey *to* God and the journey *in* God as attaining the level of union (*jam'*), the level of sainthood. Furthermore, they have viewed the journey *with* God and journey *from* God as the level of separa-tion (*farq*), the level of plurality, and the level of inviting and guid-ing the people to God. There is a subtle point here: It is by no means a regression or descent for a gnostic to go from the level of unity (*jam'*) to the level of separation (*farq*). On the contrary, it is the per-fection of the knowledge of God and obtaining the license of being of service to humanity. This is the highest level for a saint; they will bear the title of spiritual guide (*murshid*) and guide the people to God. As Sadi explains, "Dervishhood is walking on the path of God and serving other people. It is not tied to beads, prayers, or dervish clothing."

In this sense turning from God to people is a higher state than turning from people to God; the most glorious and honorable per-sonality of the universe, our most beloved Prophet commands, "He who serves is the lord." While in the first level the issue is the salvation of the individual seeker *salik*, the issue in the second level is to save humanity. In the first level, the *salik* has cleansed his self and attained the level of sainthood. With the grace of God he has escaped evil and saved only himself. However, in the second level, he has been charged with the duty of cleansing people from their bad behavior and habits and has attained the bliss of living for oth-ers. He has obtained a diploma of spiritual guidance.

It is for this reason that a Gnostic attaining the level of separation after the level of union will see the one truth and one Being in all he sees in the plurality. He will attain the joy of viewing God, not in just one mirror, but in countless mirrors and everywhere. The gnostics who reach this level have obtained full spiritual freedom and are released from all attachments. The sultan of the Gnostics, Ibn al-Farid, mentions this subject in his famous ode *Qasida al-Ta'iyyah*: "Don't count me among the *muqarrib* (those who are close to God). The attribute of being close to God is the attribute of a servant at the level of union (*jam'*). I do not see myself as separated from Him. The view of separation is a sin for me. When I attain the level of union, there will be no difference between far and distant, union and separation, friendship and animosity, beginning and end. All will be the same for me."

The following couplets by Rumi explain that the human spirit does not necessarily need a body in order to live:

> The people say, "Such and such person has died." But you say, "O, those who are unaware, I have not died. I am alive." My body may be lying in loneliness and dryness, it has fallen asleep. But in my heart, the eight gates of heaven are opened.
>
> Why would one worry if the body lies in dirt when my spirit has fallen asleep in the rose garden?
>
> The spirit will never notice this in sleep. It does not matter whether he sleeps in the rose garden or whether he sleeps next to the furnace in the bath.
>
> The spirit walks in the world of spirits, crying: "If only my people knew my happy situation."[228]
>
> If the spirit does not want to live without this body, whose place will be the palace of the heavens?
>
> If the spirit did not want to live without this body, then who would receive the spiritual nourishment as promised by God: "Your nourishment is from the heavens."[229]

I would like to conclude this section with the permission of God with the following couplets by Rumi concerning resurrection. In these couplets, the great saint explains that the parts of human bodies that have already decomposed and mixed with soil will come together on the Day of Resurrection by the command of God. Every spirit will recognize its own body, will enter only its own body, and thus will be resurrected. It is a contradiction to the Qur'an to think that the resurrection will occur in spiritual terms only.[230] As Rumi says,

> The Spirit will reenter every body that raises its head from the stone. The resurrection of the body will occur in physical terms. What can lie beyond the Power of God?
>
> If the spirit was able to live in many different bodies, as believers in reincarnation suggest, then which body would the spirit enter on the Day of the Resurrection? With which body would the spirit enter the Presence (court) of his Lord?

In a Prophetic Tradition it is related that on the Day of Resurrection, a command will be given to every body: "Stand up!" The breathing into the *sur* (Trumpet) is the command that comes from God saying, "O humankind! Raise your heads from your graves!" Just as intellect and thought return to everyone when they wake up in the morning, so too will the spirit return to everybody that raises its head from the earth.

> The spirit recognizes its body on the Day of Resurrection. The spirit enters that ruined place which is its own, just like a buried treasure.
>
> Every spirit will recognize its own body and will enter that body. How can the jeweler's spirit enter the tailor's body? The spirit of the scholar will go to the scholar and the spirit of the tyrant will go to the tyrant.
>
> Just as the lamb recognizes its mother and the mother her young in the morning, so too has God's Knowledge given the spirits a similar knowledge.
>
> A foot can recognize its shoe, even in the dark; then O, beloved, how can the spirit not recognize its own body?[231]

CHAPTER III

Rumi's Influence

R umi has gained recognition far beyond all other people of heart, thinkers, and poets in the Islamic world. Whenever you take any book about Sufism in your hand or whenever you encounter people speaking of matters concerning Sufism, you surely will come across Rumi's couplets, views, and opinions. Rumi is known not only in Turkey and other Islamic countries, but he also is recognized in the West, in books about Sufism that are written in Western languages. Rumi is loved by everyone since he is a great spiritual guide and a perfect human being who knew how to express his feelings and opinions sincerely without any ostentation and arrogance, the way he felt them in his heart. Both his *Mesnevi* and *Divan-i Kabir*, as well as others of his works, have become sources of divine wisdom, a spring of gnosis for every believer who loves God and the truth and has a share in divine love. For centuries his books have been speaking to every poet, every writer, every sensitive person, and to every dervish no matter what order they belong to. Since Rumi loves all people, he has opened up his blessed heart to everybody. He addresses everyone in his writings. Everyone, according to his or her talents, understanding, taste, and inclination, benefits from Rumi and finds himself or herself in Rumi's feelings and ideas.

RUMI'S INFLUENCE ON TURKISH POETS

Rumi is not *Mevlana* (our Master) of Turks and Muslims only; he is *Mevlana* of many peoples and nations. It is for this reason that today his shrine has become a place of pilgrimage not only for

Muslims but for people of many different creeds. Rumi, who has had such an influence in the area of Sufism, has also influenced Turkish literature deeply for the past seven centuries. Poets of classical Turkish literature, Sufi poets like Yunus Emre, and most of the contemporary poets have been influenced by Rumi. Yunus Emre expressed Rumi's impact on him when he said, "Ever since Mevlana Hudavendigar (our master, our lord) looked at us, his blessed glance has become the mirror of our heart." Other poets of the same era, such as Gülşehri and Aşık Pasha, also were influenced by Rumi. Poets of the classical period, such as Sheyhi, Nesimi, and Ahmed Pasha, were also affected by Rumi, and, as we shall see shortly, some, like Ibrahim Hakkı of Erzurum (d.1780), have made poetic translations from the *Divan-i Kabir.* In his famous book of biographies that deals with the lives and works of well-known poets up to his time and is counted as the literary history of his time, Latifi of Kastamonu, one of Turkey's famous biographers of the sixteenth century, begins his book with Rumi and describes him as the "sultan of shaykhs."

Other classical Turkish poets influenced by Rumi have inspired the development of a *Mevlevi* literature. Since the sixteenth century when the *Mevlevi* literature began to develop, many poets began using terms particular to the *Mevlevi* order in addition to the usual Sufi terms. This can be observed more clearly among the poets of the seventeenth century. For more information about the *Mevlevi* poets, the interested reader is referred to Sakib Dede's *Sefine-i Mevleviyye*, Esrar Dede's *Tezkire*, and Ali Enver Bey's *Semahane-i Edeb*. One of the poets who was an admirer of Rumi and wrote odes for Rumi, although he himself was not Mevlevi, is Nef'i, a seventeenth-century Turkish poet. In his Turkish *Divan*, Nef'i dedicated the first ode to Rumi following the ode he composed for the Prophet. He thought of Rumi before the sultans and viziers and described each verse of the *Mesnevi* as "a world of gnosis." Also in Nef'i's *Divan*, which contains his Persian poems, are odes written for Rumi. In one of these odes, he introduces Rumi as "the saint familiar with divine secrets." Nef'i, one of the most famous poets of Turkish classical *divan* poetry and one of the masters of lyrical forms like the *qasida* (ode) and the *hicviye* (satire) loved Rumi, but he did not devote himself to his path. Nef'i is not the only one who admired and wrote odes for Rumi. After the seventeenth century, among Turkish classical poets who composed *divan* literature, it became a custom to write odes for Rumi. But in the Islamic world and among the Muslim Turks, there have come many saints other than Rumi. Why did Turkish poets mostly remember Rumi? The fact that Rumi was a great saint as well as a great poet has increased the love and respect felt for him. The poets that have read Rumi's books and have become his admirers are so many that writing only their names would fill up pages.

Among the poets who have been influenced by Rumi we should not forget Sultan Divani, Fasih Dede, Neshati, Shaykh Ghalib, and Esrar Dede. In particular, Shaykh Ghalib wrote his masterpiece *Husn-u Ask* under the influence of the *Mesnevi*. He confesses this when he says, "I took its secrets, its intrinsic meaning from the *Mesnevi*." Let us remember this most beloved couplet from *Husn-u Ask* (the Beauty of Love). When describing the member of the tribe of *Bani Muhabbat* (Children of Love) he wrote, "What they wear is the sun of July and what they drink is the flame that burns the world." This couplet must be inspired by the following couplet of the *Mesnevi*: "Our dress of the daytime is made of the light of the July sun and our bed and blanket at night is made of moon-light."

In addition to Shaykh Ghalib, among the poets who have been influenced by Rumi, one has to count Nahifi, Keçecizade Izzet Molla, Enderunlu Fazıl, Akif Pasha, Pertev Pasha, and especially Ibrahim Hakkı, the author of the *Marifetname*, whose translation of Rumi I shall quote below, Hersekli Arif Hikmet, Shaykh Nazif Efendi, Shem'i, Shaykh Jalal al-Din Efendi, Leyla Hanım, Shaykh Abdulbaki Bey, Ahmed Remzi Dede, Tahir al-Mevlevi, Tokadizade

Shekib, Neyzen Tevfik, and Yahya Kemal. If one were to collect the eulogies for Rumi that began with Rumi's son Sultan Valad and have been written for the last seven centuries, these would comprise a monumental collection of volumes. Although the manuscript *Mecmua-i Medayih-i Hazret-i Mevlana* (Collection of Eulogies of Rumi) compiled by Vasif-i Mevlevi can give us an idea of this matter, the eulogies it contains are too few with respect to all the existing eulogies. In the *Mevlana Şiirleri Antolojisi* (Anthology of Poems about Rumi) recently published by Mehmet Önder, some eulogies by our contemporary poets have been included. In this anthology there are poems about Rumi that were written by modern Turkish poets such as Halide Nusret Hanım, Arif Nihad Asya, Yaman Dede, Kemal Edib Bey, Feyzi Halıcı, Nezihe Araz Hanım, Bekir Sıdkı Erdoğan, and other poets. I would like to give an example of these eulogies, a poem of Bekir Sıdkı Erdoğan, an esteemed poet of our times, entitled "Mevlana":

> O Master!
> Who is the lord of the kingdom of happiness!
> There are secrets in you.
> There is rapture and the dance of the universe.
> Everyone enters your dervish lodge ignorant.
> Everyone comes out knowledgeable.
> O Friend who is the key to the secret of beauty!
> O Full Moon who is filled with enthusiasm through divine light!
> O infinite Beyond!
> O true Spring that never fades!
> Tell me, what are your secrets?
> Everyone enters your dervish lodge ugly.
> Everyone comes out beautiful.
> Your shrine is the house of the lovers of God.
> The whole universe is in rapture.
> The whole universe is Mevlevi...
> The earth revolves, space revolves, the universe revolves.
> The whole universe is dancing around the sun.
> In a great universe all the wind,
> A whirling starts such that the earth and the sky

All disappear
And the most beautiful meaning becomes apparent...
O Friend who is the Master of Love!
O Beloved who is the sultan of the throne of hearts!
Your character has penetrated into every heart.
Your appearance is on every face.
Every door is a page-by-page commentary on the Mesnevi.
Whichever the lover knocks on
He comes across Mevlana.

RUMI'S INFLUENCE ON MUSLIM PHILOSOPHERS

Here two examples will be given to illustrate the influence of Rumi. The first example is Ibrahim Hakkı of Erzurum (d.1780), the great Turkish Islamic scholar, and the second example is Muhammad Iqbal. To elaborate on this further, I will give examples of Rumi's poems found in the *Marifetname* by Ibrahim Hakkı. He was born in Hasankale near Erzurum in the eastern part of modern Turkey, was a great scholar and a famous Sufi, well-known and respected in Anatolia and even throughout the Islamic world. His book *Marifetname*, similar to an encyclopedia, is a work that encompasses diverse subjects and many areas: religion, literature, Sufism, geography, history, cosmography, biology, fashion, and much, much more. There are also a great number of Turkish, Arabic, and Persian poems that could comprise an anthology of poetry. The author of the book himself is a great poet in addition to being a great scholar. He authored a *divan* (collection of poems) that contains his own poems. His poems that are cited in *Marifetname* come mainly from his *divan*.

Ibrahim Hakkı devoted himself to Rumi's poetry, memorized many couplets from the *Mesnevi*, identified with many poems he selected from *Divan-i Kabir*, translated them in verse into Turkish with much effort, joined his voice with that of Rumi, and with these divinely inspired poems with the fragrance of faith and divine love, and answered the spiritual needs and joys of millions of Muslim

Turks. He made lovers of God shed tears, and enraptured and excited them. Should we not call this great saint Ibrahim Hakkı Mevlevi
instead of only Ibrahim Hakkı Erzurumi? Following are several examples that show how Ibrahim Hakkı was influenced by Rumi. The
first example:

> When we start to fight the night we turn it upside down. We
> extract salt from the sea of night.
>
> Those who see the truth of night will not want to sleep and
> run away from it. Pure and clean spirits "revive" the night.
>
> They will not sleep, but spend the night in worship. They
> plead to God. The night is the tulle and veil of the unseen
> beloved, the beloved of spirit.
>
> How can the day be equivalent to the night? In your view the
> night is like a dark pot since you have not tasted the sweetness
> of the dessert cooked in that pot and you have not understood
> the truth of the night.
>
> The day is the time for material gains and profit, but the love
> of the night has a very different pleasure.
>
> The night came and prevented me from trade and profit, it
> bound my hands, and I could not do anything.
>
> Until dawn the foot of the night remained bound, too.[1]

Ibrahim Hakkı interprets this poem in his own words:

> This struggle with the night has been peace and war
> The sea of the night has become a plane for us.
> It does not want sleep and runs away from it
> If this eye beholds the spectacle of the night.
> Many with hearts full of holy light and many pure spirits
> Have become servants of the Lord of the night.
> The stopping place of the unseen beloved is the night
> For the lover the day cannot equal the night.
> The darkness of the night is a dark pot for the eye
> If the tongue has not tasted the dessert of the night.
> Although the venture of profit and business is during the day
> Another happiness is the heart of the love of night.
> When the night bound my hands from every task
> Hakkı revives the night by praising God till the morning.[2]

The second example:

When the person who is a lover of God and has a strong desire (for God) in his heart goes to the door of the heart and the heart does not open its door to him, of course, there is a reason for this. Do not be sad that the door is not opened. Go, sit at the door and wait because that Beloved that conceals herself comes out either after midnight or right before dawn. The spirit that separates itself from everything and seeks only God is something that is rarely found and it is a wondrous spirit. The eye that sees a world other than his own is a possessor of the glance (*sahib-i nazar*). It has a pleasant nickname. Such a person becomes the closest friend of the spirit and never fears death. At the time of death he has a particular pleasure and indescribable joy. If his foot hits a stone, a pearl falls into his hand. When his spirit comes up to his mouth (to leave the body), he meets it with a sweet-lipped person. Be silent! Do not reveal the secrets everywhere. In the assembly of people who are not good-spirited there may be Abu Jahls present.[3]

The translation of this ode in the verse of Ibrahim Hakkı is as follows:

Whoever has joy and happiness on the inside
    And keeps waiting at the door of the heart, he has a reason
    He waits at the door of the heart till his Beloved comes
    When the beloved comes, he shows respect; the spirit has good manners.
    The spirit that is far from everything and has become a seeker of God
    Has sacrificed himself for love; he has an amazing inclination.
    The gnostic that sees His face in everything
    He became a possessor of the glance (*sahib-i nazar*); he has a pleasant nickname.
    Whoever is a lover of God and is loyal in divine love
    At the time of his death he has a festival.
    If his foot touches the stone, a pearl enters his palm
    Not to worry even if the spirit comes to the mouth, he has sugar lips.

O Hakkı! Remain silent! Say your words in secret phrases
Because there are many Abu Lahabs in the assembly of
impure souls.[4]

The third example:

When the address of "Come!" reaches the spirit from the
Almighty Creator of this universe and all beings, the Possessor
of Majesty and Beauty, how can the spirit not open its wings
and fly? When the waves' sounds reach the ear of a fish that got
separated from the crystal clear sea and ended up in a dry place,
how can that fish not jump at once into the sea that is its real
homeland? When the falcon hears the "Return!" command
from the drum and its wooden mallet, how can it not leave
hunting and return to the sultan? How poor, how evil and how
astray is the person who cannot find and love such a pleasant,
beautiful, friendly, life-granting Unique Being? O bird of spirit! You have been cleansed of sins. You escaped the cage of your
desires and ego. Your spiritual wings have spread. Come now
and fly, fly to your real homeland from whence you came in the
first place. Travel from the bitter water to the Water of Eternal
Life. Move from the ranks of those who sit at the entrance and
take your place at the head sofa of spiritual assembly. O spirit,
you go! Go so that we, too, may be able to attain the world of
reunion from this world of separation.[5]

Translation of this ode in Verse:

How can the bird of spirit fly when that Holiness of Majesty
    Addressing with elegance and justice saying "Come!"
    Why wouldn't the fish throw itself into the water
    When the sounds of the waves of the crystal sea come to its ear?
    Why wouldn't that falcon fly to its sultan and stop hunting
    When the drum and the wooden beetle give him the news:
"Return!"
    Amazing sweetness has this love of the Life-Giver,
    Whoever is content without it is evil and astray.
    Fly at once and reach your master, O bird of spirit!
    Freed from this cage, may your wings and arms spread.
    Travel from this confusing soil, drink the Water of Eternal
Life.

Find clarity of chest in your heart, sitting among the ranks of
those who sit at the entrance is enough.
Give the world to the worldly people, O Hakkı, come to the
world of the heart.
Since that is world of separation and this is the world of
reunion.

The second example is that of Muhammad Iqbal (d. 1938),
who is one of the greatest geniuses of the East and was influenced
very much by Rumi. He studied a long time in the greatest cultural centers of Europe, and after graduating from Cambridge University
in England, he earned his doctoral degree in philosophy from the
University of Munich in Germany. Iqbal is a great poet, a great
philosopher, a great scholar, and a great human being. There are
those who think that Pakistan deserved to be named Iqbalistan
since this great patriot, who attained God's mercy without seeing
Pakistan established, played an important role in the foundation of
Pakistan. After gaining much knowledge of Islamic sciences in his
country, during the time he stayed in Europe he got to know the
greatest scientists of the West and analyzed in depth the doctrines
of the most famous philosophers. After having read the books of
world famous philosophers, scholars, poets, and writers of both
East and West, he chose Rumi as his guide by accepting his views
on action and love.

Iqbal saw in Rumi the aspects that everybody could not see
easily. From Rumi he understands that "The gate of God is a gate
without an end. Wherever you reach on this path never say, 'This
is enough,' don't stop, go further." In one of his poems, Rumi also
says, "Every day I need to set out on a new journey and cover new
distances." In these views, Iqbal found his own views. According
to Iqbal, life is not only to live and to exist but also to develop and
attain perfection. It is even to surpass perfection. Life is composed
of a constantly running flow, progression, and change. Human
beings have come to the world to work and accomplish something.
The value of human beings is measured by their work. The Holy

Qur'an says, "For humankind there is nothing but what they do and earn."[6] Human beings are obliged to work and earn their living. Man has been created to worship. But this worship cannot be done by retreating to a lone corner and sitting there in idleness. It is achieved by working and benefiting one's self as well as one's relatives and nation.

Both Rumi and Iqbal renounced the fatalism that had infiltrated Islam in later stages. The idea that one should not worry and leave one's concerns to God, that whatever is the judgment of the fate will come to be is not an Islamic belief. A human being's work and struggle may not lead one to success all the time. Human beings should not be discouraged by their failure, should not let themselves go, and become idle. They have to keep on trying and struggling. Therefore Rumi says, "To work without any gain is better than sleeping." Iqbal also wrote, "Even if you produce something rarely, since it is the result of hard work it will be counted as a good deed even if it is a bad one."[7] In all his books Rumi rejected fatalism and recommended conscious initiative, work, struggle, and endeavor. In Rumi's books the wind of action and life always blows; it is not tranquilizing but awakening: "If the tree had mobility, if it could move from one place to another with its head and foot it would not have to suffer the chastisement of the saw and endure the wounds of the axe."[8]

Rumi constantly recommends action and struggle. In eight couplets of a poem Rumi says: "Don't stay idle. Travel from yourself to yourself." This notion of traveling from one's self to one's self and seeking one's self in one's self forms the core of Iqbal's system of thought. According to Iqbal, the real purpose of life is for every human being to realize his or her self, to find himself or herself in himself or herself, using the power hidden in himself or herself to serve the progress and advancement of the universe. The human being has to realize the Divine Entrustment in himself or herself, rely on it, by its power achieve great things, and, as related in the Qur'an, he or she has to be God's vicegerent (*khalifah*) on earth.[9] Iqbal's view on life is the view of knowing one's self. Since he makes one aware of what is in one's self, he is called the "prophet of the religion of self." Just as Abd al-Rahman Jami (d. 1492) says about Rumi, "He has a (holy) book but is not a prophet," the poet Garami said regarding Iqbal, "He brought news to people as to what was in them; he served the duty of a prophet but he cannot be called a prophet."

The reason Iqbal devoted himself to Rumi and made him his spiritual guide was because Iqbal was able to relate to Rumi's thoughts and views and thus found himself in Rumi. Rumi advises one to discover what is in one's self and to fall in love with one's self. He says, "O those who are unaware of the truth, I want to fall in love with my self."

In another poem he says, "You are another version of the divine book. You are a mirror of the Beauty of God that created the universe. Whatever exists in the world, it is not outside of you. Whatever you ask for, ask for it in yourself, seek it in yourself." Iqbal expresses the same thought in his poetry: "In your self there is an existence from God's existence. In your self there is a manifestation of God's manifestation. I do not know where this pearl that was obtained would have been found if His sea did not exist."[10] Rumi expresses the same view in one of his honorable couplets as follows: "Whatever pearl you seek, there is another pearl inside that pearl because all the atoms are saying, 'There is a treasure hidden in me.'"[11] In another couplet Iqbal says, "Don't look left and right, look at yourself. Do not be sad that your skirt is empty. In your chest a full moon is hidden."

How can one find one's self? How can one feel what is in one's self? How are we going to find the "I" which Yunus Emre describes as "the 'I' inside me"? The famous Mevlevi poet, Esrar Dede, once said, "All the time I have been saying 'I, I,' I have meant You." Mansur al-Hallaj felt what was in himself, entered a state of ecstasy, lost control, and cried, "I am the Truth." The great Sufi Sarraj said, "Since the real existence belongs to God, no one has the right to say 'I' except for Him." As a matter of fact, how can this mortal being who is doomed to perish, made up of skin, nerves, flesh, and bones say "I"? As commonly known, there are two "I"s in the human being. One is the *"rahmani* I" (*rahmani*: attributed to God who is the Most Merciful), the other is the *"satanic* I," or *"nafsani* I" (*nafsani*: sensual, malignant). The *"nafsani* I" misleads one; it prevents one from finding the real "I" and attaining the truth. As Vizeli Kaygusuz says:

> I found this path, this way,
> *Nafs* was a curtain, an obstacle for me.
> I read, understood, and came to know that
> *Nafs* was a curtain, an obstacle for me.

The "sensual I" acts like a curtain or veil for us. Rumi says: "As long as you remain in yourself, they will not give you a way to you from you. They will not let you find your real existence. But once you take your self under your feet and efface your self, they will not let you out of their sight. And if furthermore you can save yourself from desiring the bounties of this world and the hereafter, they start to point at you with their fingers as a complete human being." Rumi expresses this truth in another poem as follows: "As long as your existence is with you, do not sit comfortable because you are still worshipping idols. Let's suppose that you tried and managed to crush the idol of presumption (i.e., not having complete knowledge and guessing). But thinking highly of yourself and having pride because you crushed that idol becomes yet another 'uncrushed' idol for you."

The self that Rumi is talking about in these lines is the corporal self. The fact that a person who crushes the idol of presumption thinks of himself highly shows that he has yet to attain truly *yaqin* (certainty; complete faith). According to Rumi, a human being will attain the truth as soon as he realizes his own value and finds the real *"rahmani* I": "If I had known my own value and my own greatness properly, I would have pulled my skirt away from the dust, soil, and worldly dirt and, being lighter spiritually and cleansed from sins, I would rise to the heavens and put my head over the ninth heaven." As Rumi expresses in this quatrain, by knowing oneself and one's value, a person can get to know the Divine Entrustment inside, that is, the *"rahmani* I."

Iqbal explains the *rahmani* ego, whose existence was related in the Qur'anic verse: "He is with you wherever you may be,"[12] in the following couplet: "There is a beloved hidden in your heart. If you want to see it, come and let me show it to you."[13] Rumi mentions the same truth in one of his couplets: "There is someone hidden here, do not think of yourself as alone."[14] In another couplet: "We have come to know that we are more than this body. Beyond this body we live with God."[15] How are we supposed to find the hidden beloved, the *rahmani* self that both Rumi and Iqbal talk about? After a person has developed his character and raised it to perfection, after he has become an ideal model whom people would point to with admiration, after he has found himself, he will foot the presence of God with God's grace.

When the atomic self is merged with the universal self, will it lose itself there? According to Iqbal the drop that will fall into the ocean will not be lost but will still make its existence felt in the ocean. To attain God is not for the self to be effaced in God's existence, that is, to attain the level of *fana fillah* as conceived by other Sufis. According to Iqbal, it is to find God in one's self, in one's heart. The holy light of God joins the individual's candle instead of putting it out. Thus, one attains perfection by finding himself in the presence of God. The following couplet by Iqbal is of interest: "If you want to see and sense God clearly, try to see yourself even more clearly."[16] Here Iqbal is referring to a Prophetic Tradition. Elsewhere he says, "In the sight of a religious man, the person who denies God is a unbeliever. But in my sight, the person who denies himself and what is in himself is even more of a unbeliever."[17] According to Iqbal, one becomes more of a unbeliever with the denial of the self that is closer to him. Is God not closer to us than ourselves? The Qur'anic verse, "We are closer to him (man) than his jugular vein"[18] expresses this truth.

What difference is there between the realization of self and the realization of God? Here Iqbal emphasizes the importance of realizing the self that is in us. He maintains that the realization of God is possible only after the realization of the self. When one becomes absorbed in one's self by what the elders call *tafassuh al-daruni*, an inner checking, or concentrating all one's attention on a point, one establishes a connection between oneself and God who is the Supreme Being. And when one feels and thinks that one is in His presence and seen by Him, one begins to experience the joy of worshipping. Iqbal says, "The servant's worship is through his turning his eye to God. His living is with feeling the Divine Entrustment in him and seeing himself without curtain." One approaches God when one prays, performs daily prayers, pleads to God, concentrates all one's attention on a single point, gives charity, and does good deeds ordered by God. At such a moment, the person becomes unified with God without losing his or her own existence and personality and transcends the dimensions of time and space. A supplication that is offered not with compulsion but one that comes from the bottom of the heart makes one closer to God so that one finds God in one's self and one's self in God. In this kind of worship, self-absorption, searching, and finding one's self, Iqbal sees God and the servant as two beings standing next to each other. While keeping in mind the difference of "God-ness" and "servant-hood," between the Creator and the creature, he maintains the existence of both.

The meeting of the mortal human being with God who is eternal and infinite is far away from the suspicions of incarnationism (*hulul*) and unification (*ittihad*). It is not the finite self's losing itself in the infinite Self. According to Iqbal, this is the entering of infinite Self into the heart of the finite self. It is living this following Divine Tradition: "I do not fit into the earth and heavens, but I fit into the heart of my believing servant who loves Me." This is not an atom getting lost in the infinity, but it is the coming together of two beings that love each other. The spiritual union with the Beloved cannot be described. God says, "I sit next to the one who remembers me." But this state cannot be explained with logic or intelligence. A gnostic of God describes this indescribable state as follows: "Every night before dawn we go to the neighborhood of the Beloved. We hide this going even from ourselves because we are strangers even to ourselves. In his neighborhood both the mind and the soul become tough curtains which come in between. They will not show us the Beloved. Therefore, when we go to the Beloved we leave behind both the mind and the soul." When describing this state Iqbal says, "I know neither myself nor Him but I know that I am submerged in His love."

This union is far from the stain of the incarnation (*hulul*) doctrine. What Rumi expresses as, "Unity (*tawhid*) is not incarnation. It is the effacement of your ego, your escaping from the corporal ego and finding the *rahmani* ego", Iqbal expresses as follows: "Our union is a union in a state of separation. The resolution of this knot is not possible without a glance. The pearl is submerged in the sea but the seawater is not the water of the pearl." To find the self that Rumi, Yunus Emre, and Iqbal talk about is not something that anybody can achieve. It is what the perfect human being can achieve.

According to Iqbal, if one really becomes a lover of God, one overcomes all obstacles on the path that leads to the "I." The greatest obstacle on the path of God, the path that leads to "I" is fear. Fear is the opposite of love and is an attribute that harms religion and faith. If one fears someone other than God, he commits a form of *shirk* (associating partners with God). Even fearing God is not reconcilable with the love that is felt toward Him. The following line of Yahya Kemal, a well known Turkish poet, is an echo of Iqbal's feeling: "He does not feel ashamed of himself, and he is ashamed of others." Those who are not ashamed of the "I" in themselves and are ashamed of those around them and want to avoid others' criticism are not enviable people. Rumi expresses the same truth in one of his poems as follows: "If you are the lover of love and seek for love, take the sharp dagger and cut the throat of shame. Know that shame is a big obstacle for those who walk on the path of God. This word is sincere advice. Take it with joy."[19]

According to Iqbal, the shortest path to "I" is love. For the traveler to God, a love that never ends, one that deepens and increases at every moment is necessary. In Iqbal's view, as is in Rumi's, love is a key that opens every door. To develop the "I" love is a foremost prerequisite. The lover is not lost in the sea of love. On the contrary, the lover finds himself in the sea of love and gains strength. With the ability to love that God has granted to humanity, humanity will attain its horizon of humanity. According to Iqbal's view, humans have been exiled to the world due to a grain of wheat. A sip that they will take in this world from the wine of divine love will take them back where they came from. He values love so much that he says: "If a Muslim is not a lover of God, he is an unbeliever." Iqbal believes that the "I" that exists in the human being as the Divine Entrustment gains strength with love:

> There is a point of light whose name is "Divine Self" that is a spark of life beyond our body that is nothing but a fistful of soil. Love saves the "I" that is in us from mortality. It makes it livelier, more burning, and brighter. When his ore catches flame and flares up with love, the hidden possibilities in his heart develop and rise. His creation catches fire from love. It learns to enlighten the world with love. Love is not afraid of the sword or the dagger because the essence of love is different from the four elements. It is not of water, wind, or soil. The rocks cannot withstand the glance of love; they fall into pieces. The lover of God eventually becomes God from head to toe. Learn how to love and be a lover. Seek a beloved for yourself, ask for an eye that cries like Noah and a heart that is patient like Job. From a fistful of soil, alchemy comes out. Put your head to the door of a "perfect man." Like Rumi, light up the light of the heart, awaken its candle. Spread the fire of Tabriz to Anatolia.[20]

Let us take a few examples of the poetry of Rumi, who spread the fire of love in Iqbal's heart seven centuries later and thus not only spread the fire of love to Anatolia but also to Pakistan. In these lines we can see clearly the influence of Rumi on Iqbal:

> Love makes the dead bread wine of the soul, it makes the mortal soul immortal.[21]
>
> Because of love, bitterness becomes sweet. Because of love, copper becomes gold. Because of love, turbid wine becomes clear. Because of love, troubles become the remedy. Because of love, the dead come to life. Because of love, the king becomes a slave.[22]
>
> Know that the revolution of the heavens is due to the waves of love. If it were not for love, the world would freeze and stand still.[23]

Rumi's *Divan-i Kabir* also contains many couplets that deal with this subject:

> Every part, every element of the world is in love. Every part of it is intoxicated with the reunion.
>
> But these lovers will not tell you their secrets because a secret is revealed only to one who is worthy.
>
> If the heavens had not been in love, its skies would not have been so clear and pure.
>
> If the sun had not been in love, there would have been no light, no brightness on its face.
>
> If the earth and the mountains had not been in love, there would have been not one blade of grass growing on them.
>
> If the sea had not been aware of love, it would not have been fluttering so much, it would have been frozen, standing still in one place.[24]

Iqbal, who gives as much importance to love as Rumi, pleads to love and says, "Come, O love! O secret meaning of our heart! Come! O our field, O our crop! Come, these human beings that are made of clay became old and worn out. Come make a new man of our clay."[25]

According to Iqbal what makes us find ourselves in ourselves and makes us discover the "I" is not only love. It is also to love the Prophetic Tradition that says, "Poverty is my pride." What this

Prophetic Tradition refers to is not material poverty. It means, rather, not to value wealth and money and to fulfill one's obligation. To be in need of nothing, to depend on no one, and to own the world with this kind of poverty is Iqbal's ideal. This point should not be misunderstood. The opposite of lawful income is not poverty but beggary. Instead of requesting even the slightest thing from anyone else, one should be content with whatever one has. The human being is not to worship anyone except God. This state will lower one's value. A person who bows before this or that person is even lower than a dog. In his poem called "Slavery" Iqbal says, "Man became slave to a man because of the lack of intelligence and insight. He had a very valuable ore. He sacrificed it for Kubad and Jamsheed. With his habit of slavery, he became even lower than a dog. I have not seen a dog that bows before another dog."[26] According to Iqbal, requesting something from someone weakens the 'I': "Your 'I' falls into pieces when you present your need to someone and ask for something. Then in the tree of the Mount Sinai of the 'I', light does not manifest. How happy is that thirsty person who is under the burning sun and does not request a glass of water even from Khidr."[27]

In Iqbal's view, those brave people who develop their human attributes with love and faith will find a way to the 'I'. These fortunate people are cleansed of all vices and flaws since they are lovers of God. Rumi expresses the same truth: "Whosoever's dress has been torn due to love is cleansed from ambition, flaws, and vices. O our love that is so pleasant to feel, live long! O the doctor of all illnesses of ours!"[28] People who are cleansed with love and have attained perfection find God in themselves by finding themselves in themselves and finding what is in themselves. From that time on the person who found God should not raise his or her voice while praying and intoning and call out to far places. In a couplet from the *Mesnevi*, Rumi says, "O God, when you are closer to me than my jugular vein, how can I call out to you saying 'O, O' because the address of 'O' is used for those who are at a distance."[29] The atomic, *Rahmani* self is not separate from the universal God. As one gnostic put it, "Men of God are not God but they are not far away from God either." Another poet says, "I am not talking of a reunion with the Beloved since I have never been away from the Beloved."

But Iqbal maintains that by feeling the *Rahmani* self, the *Rahmani* atom that is in human beings, it becomes easy to find a way to the whole. This state cannot be explained with logic, this is matter of feeling and sensing. In a quatrain Rumi says, "Man reaches such a place, such a rank that without his material eyes he can see the Friend at every moment." One cannot imagine a greater spiritual joy in the world than feeling what is in one's self. How beautifully Rumi explains this spiritual state: "If you find yourself close to the Beloved for one moment, in that moment you will have obtained your share from life. Do not let that moment pass by because such a happy moment cannot always be experienced."[30]

Iqbal discovered in Rumi's books aspects that paralleled his spirit, inclinations, and beliefs. There is a constant activity, motion, and dynamism in Rumi. In Rumi exists the notion of discovering the Divine Entrustment, the *Rahmani* self in one's self and falling in love with it. Iqbal became fascinated with these views. He also thoroughly embraced Rumi's understanding of *insan al-kamil* (perfect human being). Rumi was a lover of God. He says, "Leave the negation and start the word with affirmation. To negate the existence of something is to affirm its existence."[31] Iqbal took Rumi as a spiritual guide to himself. "I gained respect because of the blessings of Rumi.[32] I received a share of his light and warmth. My night has become day due to his star."[33] In another quatrain he says, "In Rumi there is a sorrow, a burning that is not strange to us. His union talks of going beyond the separations. One feels the beauty of love in his reed and receives a share, a blessing from the Greatness of God."[34]

The great scholar and great poet Iqbal, who knew the greatest poets, writers, scholars, scientists and philosophers of the East and the West, read their books, and was familiar with their ideas and feelings, found himself in Rumi. Rumi became a mirror to him. As seen in the examples presented above, in all his books, Iqbal expresses the love and admiration he feels toward Rumi on every occasion: "Rumi turned the soil into an elixir. He has in me, who is as valuable as dust, many, many manifestations. It was as if a particle from the desert soil set out on a journey to obtain the light of the sun. I am a wave. I settled in his sea in order to obtain a bright pearl. Rumi, who is not separate from God, has manifested himself to me. It was that Rumi who composed a Qur'an in the Persian language. He told me, 'O bewildered lover! Take a sip from the pure wine of divine love.'"[35]

In all his books beginning with the *Asrar-i Khudi* (*Secrets of the Self*) to his last book that was published after his death, *Armaghan-i Hijaz*, Muhammad Iqbal has took Rumi as his spiritual guide, and he was inspired by him. In *Javidname*, which is accepted as his masterpiece, Iqbal calls on Rumi's spirit by reciting one of his odes, and in Rumi's company he ascends to the heavens on a spiritual journey. In the *Divine Comedy*, the Italian poet Dante (d. 1231) takes the famous Latin poet Virgil as his guide on the imaginary journey that he makes to the underworld to find his beloved. Together with him he visits hell, purgatory, and paradise. In his spiritual ascension to the heavens, Iqbal takes his beloved Rumi as guide, and with his blessings they ascend to the Divine Presence. In his masterpiece, after passing through many levels with Rumi, they eventually arrive at the seventh gate, the highest level of paradise. In paradise, they meet and speak mainly with Eastern scholars, poets, and rulers. Iqbal's soul cannot find peace even in paradise. He does not listen even to the sweet words of the beautiful houris. No one can prevent him from going into the presence of God. The spiritual ascension of Iqbal, the lover of God, ends in the presence of God.

Iqbal asks Rumi a question and with the inspiration he gets from Rumi, he answers it from the tongue of Rumi: "Once again I asked, 'What is it like to walk to God? How can one crush the mountain of water and earth?'" The poet asks how Rumi's words are going to be realized. How can the density of this body that is composed of water and earth be eliminated? How can one reach the spiritual world from the physical world? The Commander and the Creator is outside of the physical and spiritual worlds. We are stuck in the web of the world. How can a relationship be possible between God, who creates everything and commands every happening, and the human being, who is created and is now a prisoner in the web of the world? He says, "If the sultan (power) comes to your hand, you can readily crush the heavens." Here, the word "sultan" refers to the Qur'anic verse: "O community of humans and demons! I dare you to transcend the boundaries of the earth and the heavens if you can, which without a power you cannot."[36] If the divine sultan or power is granted to a person, in that moment he can perform extraordinary things that defy logic. At that time, this body, a hill of clay, will not interfere with the ascension into the heavens.

Be aware that this universe is naked and removes the dust of the dimensions from your skirts! A person realizes his or her self in the Divine Light, in his or her view this universe will be saved from the dimensions of time and space; that is, he or she will be free from the laws of physics and enter the timelessness and spacelessness of the Divine Order. If human beings do not join the power of this Divine sultan, they are not above animals and insects. They die like animals before attaining real humanity and cannot obtain everlasting life. O good person, you came to this world with four directions from the path of birth. You can exit it again with the path of birth and you can eliminate your bonds yourself. But this second birth is not from water and clay. Only a possessor of heart knows it. In his book *Reconstruction of Religious Thought in Islam*, Iqbal bases his notion of the second birth on the Qur'anic verse, "Say: Travel on the earth and observe how He brought creation into being. Then God will create a later creation (resurrection in the hereafter) because God is Omnipotent."[37] In this verse, Iqbal reads the word *akhirah* (hereafter) as *akhir* (another). Thus, he translates it as, "He will give another birth."[38]

A COMPARISON BETWEEN RUMI AND PLATO

Epictetus, the Greek philosopher, likens humankind to slaves who have run away from their masters without permission in order to watch some theatrical play. A wonderful play is being presented on the stage. While the slaves are watching what is being performed, their eyes keep turning back to the door because they are afraid that at any moment their master might come in, and they will be punished. Therefore, they cannot fully enjoy the play. Their anxiety and fear take the joy out of their pleasure. According to this philosopher, the world is like a great theatrical stage. A beautiful and grand play is being presented. At the same time, this world is like a museum full of beautiful works. We human beings, although living in this magnificent museum, are unable to examine it minutely. We are unable to penetrate into the fine points in the wonderful works kept in this museum because all of us are too busy with our daily work. We all have duties that we have to perform. We have to make our living, and this causes us to be slaves to life. For this reason we are unable to think about the life drama that is being presented on the stage, the masterpieces around us, and the Creator of it all.

Were we to take our minds and hearts as our guide in the light of science and knowledge, we would stand in wonderment at what we see, from the smallest atom to the greatest being either in what we see in our own world or in the infinite vacuum of the heavens, those other worlds, other stars and other suns going round and round . . . We do not need to look far. We have only to turn our eyes to our own bodies. Every human being is a universe composed of billions of cells. Unknown to ourselves these billions of cells in us work on our behalf. And our minds? All the cities we visit, the valleys we pass through, the mountains we cross, the human

beings we know, the books we read are all photographed and compiled in our minds. What a wonderful archive that is! Even the copy
of the voice of a friend whom we have not seen in years is stored
in our minds. We can recognize the voice of that friend even when
we do not see his face. Our brain, our most precious possession, is
placed inside a strong case, carefully folded and packed by a master's hand. How many architects, how many chemists, how many
engineers and physicists could have worked together to prepare the
plan of this mysterious laboratory of the human body, and have put
together this masterpiece of the human being?

The world is not made up of human beings only. There are
millions and millions of living beings from microscopic germs and
microbes to elephants. Each creature, like the human being, has
been created in a wondrous way. The fineness and art in a mosquito's wing is not to be found in the wing of a giant airplane. The
bees make their honeycombs so precisely. The young of a duck
know how to swim as soon as they come out of the egg. The horses carried over to America by Christopher Columbus knew how to
distinguish between the good and the poisonous plants in a strange
land examples of which they had never seen in Europe.

Plants, too, are innumerable. They are tied to earth by their
roots and they cannot move about, but they can feed, they can
breathe, they reproduce and eventually die. The order in their
leaves serving as lungs, the beauty, color and taste in their fruit—
what is all this? There is motion and liveliness even in things that
we perceive as lifeless. Atomic science and new discoveries have
proven that the smallest particle of every substance revolves around
a nucleus at a dazzling speed. Where is the Artist who made all
these beings in accordance with these very fine calculations? Who
created this art and who caused us to stand in wonderment before
the beauties He created? Who is the owner of all this work we see?
Who created all these beings? I remember the following two verses we had to learn by heart when I was a child:

When you read a book,
You ask who the writer is.
When you see a nice building,
You wish to know who the builder is.

Have the heavens and the earth no owner?
When one thinks of it, one understands,
That everything proves to us
That there is a great and Almighty God.

Where, then, is the great Creator who has calculated everything precisely, thought of everything thoroughly, and who rules the universe by unchangeable rules? How should we look for God who demonstrates great art in every single atom? The peerless Creator who has adorned the whole universe, including our own earth, with magnificent beauty is hidden behind His works. Making these works a veil to Himself, he does not show Himself.

The great philosopher Plato and the great saint Rumi put the same great effort into searching, finding, understanding and making others understand the Being who created the universe. They expressed their ideas and feelings in a very similar manner. However, Plato made his thought and feeling a guide in attaining the truth and discovering the secrets of the universe while the great Rumi took his own faith and inspiration as his guide in his search.

How can we explain the fact that the thoughts of Plato and those of Rumi were identical on some points? The truth has been manifested to human beings since Adam. Therefore, who knows, Plato may have been influenced by the great religions and philosophical currents that came before him. The fragments of truth in his books may have come out of the sources of these great religions. The heavenly religions agree on the faith in One God. As a matter of fact, certain Muslim thinkers have considered Plato possibly as one of the Prophets whose name is not mentioned in the Qur'an. One wonders if Rumi saw Plato's works. He possibly did. Even if with his knowledge of the Greek language he did not understand and comprehend these works, the works of the great

Greek philosophers like Plato and Aristotle had been translated into Arabic since the time of the Abbasids.

Let us consider briefly some of the ideas and beliefs Rumi and Plato have in common in their books. Both Rumi and Plato have declared that the present life in which we are living must have origins. Both of them thought that our spirits dwelt in some other world before we came to exist on earth. This, Plato explains, is the "World of Ideas," the "World of Examples," while Rumi calls it the "World of Spirit." According to Plato, in the world where our spirits were before we came into this present world, there were the best, the most beautiful and perfect of what we see in the present world. The things we have seen and liked in this world such as a pretty face, a beautiful sight, a good work, lovely music, and so on, remind us of the beautiful things that we have seen in the world of spirit. The beautiful things that we saw in that world have left traces of memory in our spirit. For this reason, Plato says, "To know is to simply remember that which was known before."

According to Rumi, our real motherland is that universe which is the "World of Absolute Beauty." We are strangers on earth. All human beings are strangers in this world. That universe which Plato calls the World of Ideas is our paradise lost. We have been exiled from that world into this one. Rumi explains in his *Mesnevi*:

> The man who lives in a city (many) years, as soon as his eyes go asleep, beholds another city full of good and evil, and his city comes not to his memory at all, to that (he should) say, "I have lived there (so many years); this new city is not mine, here I am only in pawn." No, he thinks that in truth he has always lived in this very city and has been born and bred in it. What wonder (then) if the spirit does not remember its ancient abodes, which have been its dwelling place and birthplace aforetime, since this world, like sleep, is covering it over as clouds cover stars?[39]

This place is like an exile for us and our spirits are prisoners in our bodies. Rumi says in one of his poems, "Where am I, where is the prison? Whose property did I steal so that I was locked up in the prison of body?" We are troubled because we are separated from our own land, which is the world of spirit. There is a deep complaint on this account in the beginning of the *Mesnevi*. We are in trouble because we have been separated from our origin.

What is death according to Rumi? Death is deliverance from this world of suffering, returning into our real homeland. For this reason death is a release. It is the release of the soul from the prison of the body, the return to the world of spirit to unite with the Absolute Beauty, and this causes death to cease to be dreadful and to become sweet. This is the reason why the night on which Rumi passed away was called *shab-i 'arus* (the wedding night). "On the day of my death, when my coffin is carried away, do not suppose that I have any of this world's troubles and pain. When you see my funeral being performed do not cry 'Separation! Separation!' The day of death is the day when I shall attain union with the Beloved."

It is the same faith that caused Mansur al-Hallaj to give his life without regret on the gallows. It is the same faith with which Farid al-Din 'Attar infuriated the Mongol soldier who wanted to sell him as a slave, facing death in full knowledge. The same faith caused Sayyid Nesimi to have his body flayed as he uttered no complaint. It was the same faith that allowed Plato's teacher Socrates to drink his hemlock poison cheerfully and go to his death feeling no anxiety. This story given in Plato's book called *Phaedon - the Immortality of the Soul* is worth reading as a warning.

According to Plato everything we see in this world is subject to permanent change. Everything is not perfect and faultless in this world. The best of the beauty that enchants us in this world, the best of the good things that capture our hearts in this world is in the World of Ideas, that is, in the World of Examples. Therefore, we should not be troubled about the beauties that perish in this world. Rumi, in a poem touching on this matter, says, "The original of every substance, or every picture you see in this world is in the World of the Spirit. Do not worry that the picture is gone. Do not be troubled that every pretty face you have seen, every subtle saying you have heard has vanished since the truth does not consist of what you see and what you know in this world."

According to Rumi, after being exiled to this world, God has given us possibilities to be delivered. Without waiting for death to come, we can be lifted toward the world of spirit by killing our passions and getting rid of our worldly desires. A ladder of love is being placed before us so that we may be able to go up higher: "Since the day you came to this world of being, a ladder has been placed before you so that you may escape." Rumi very often thinks of our spirit as locked up in the prison of the body and imagines ways of deliverance. On a spring day as Rumi goes around among the gardens he notices that the dry branches that looked dead in winter have come to life, have given forth buds and leaves. The buds are breaking their hard shells and are like flags of triumph bursting out in joy and excitement. The great thinker and poet Rumi asks the leaves, "O leaf, you must surely have found strength to force the branch to burst open so that you could emerge. What did you do to become free from the prison? Speak, speak, so that we may do what you did in order to become free from this prison."

Rumi often reminds man who has been exiled from the world of the spirit into the present world to try to understand what he is, from where he came, and that it is necessary for him to tear himself away from this earth and return to his original home: "Think on your condition, try to understand yourself. Get out, go traveling and search for your real homeland. Get yourself far from the prison of the material world, journey to the world of the spirit. You are the bird of the holy world of the spirit. Alas, if you should appropriate this mortal world and wish to remain in it." Here we see the real matter: We should not become bound to this world and to things of material benefit, to the mortal beauties and ephemeral delights, but we should look for the eternal beauties, to remember God, Creator of all the universe, to find Him in our hearts and consciousness and to love Him truly.

This is the real love, the platonic love called after Plato. It is easy to love not the perishable beauties, the beautiful who lose their beauty in one way or another, but the Most Beautiful of all beauties, who hides Himself behind His own creations and works, to love Him who is known but not seen, Him who is infinite and immortal. How are we to find the Greatest Being who created not only the beauty and the beautiful but everything, the only God? How are we to love Him? Everyone sees God from their own angle. God is expressed according to everyone's thought, understanding, and comprehension. Are we to look for God like the shepherd who was found by Moses? A well-known story in the *Mesnevi* illustrates this concept: "One day, Moses met a shepherd on his way. He heard him talking to God as follows: 'O God who chooses whoever You will, where are You that I may become Your servant and sew Your shoes and comb Your head? That I may wash Your clothes and bring milk to You, O Worshipful One, that I may kiss Your little hand and rub Your little foot (and when) bedtime comes, I may sweep Your little room. O You for whom may all my goats be sacrificed. O You, in remembrance of whom are my cries of ay and ah!'" Moses scolded the shepherd for his candid speech, and he was reproached by God. Every person will understand and feel God according to his own mind and capacity and according to God's grace bestowed on him. God shows His power in everything, in every atom. One cannot help but remember Sadi's famous couplet: "In the sight of the wise, every leaf of plants and trees is a book telling of God and His art."

Plato searched for God a great deal and acted according to his mind and logic. Rumi's way, on the other hand, is that of the heart: "The inside and outside of my heart is He. He is the soul, the vein, the blood in my body. How can there be infidelity and belief in such a place? My being has become non-existent, because He has become all my being." Rumi sensed the Most Beautiful of all beauties first of all in his own being; then he found Him in everything, in every atom. "Do not say He is here or there. Tell the truth where is He? He is in the whole universe. But where is the eye that will see Him?" In another verse Rumi says, "Can there be a more beautiful friend than Yourself? Can there be anything more beautiful than seeing Your countenance? God forbid, certainly not! O my beauty, O my Beloved, it suffices me that You do exist in the two worlds. Wherever there is a spot of beauty it is the reflection of Your light." When the power and the greatness of God are felt in every atom, in every being, it is natural to find Him, the All-Present, the All-Seeing: "Wherever I lay my head He is the only one in whose presence one prostrates. He is the only God in six directions and from the six directions. The vineyard, the rose, the nightingale, and the beautiful beloved are all pretexts. The purpose of all these is only He."

Plato's *Prosperity* contains a parable about a cave: According to Plato, we are like the slaves who are imprisoned in a large cave and sit with their backs to the cave door with their hands, arms, and feet tightly bound. At the door a great fire is burning. As we watch on the walls of the cave the moving shadows of laborers carrying their loads on their backs and talking together, we understand nothing from the confused and smothered noises that come to our ears. Likewise, we see beings and things existing in this world like images. For, just like the slaves, our hands and feet are tied. We cannot go out and we cannot see the truth. We see only images. In this parable what Plato means by the slaves is the spirits that are imprisoned in our bodies. The spirit bound within the prison of the body imagines the shades and images reflected on the walls of the cave by Plato (like the pictures we see today on the screen of a movie theater) to be the truth and thus deceives itself. In order to find the true life, we must find not the shades but those whose shades are reflected or Him who causes the reflections to appear.

Emerson, the well-known thinker, says, "If we consider this visible world a symbol of the real world, the visible things are the images of the unseen things." This is repeating in different words what Plato and the great Rumi have said. However, among the images reflected from the world of the spirits into this world, or in this world which receives the visible images of the invisible world, the superior being is humankind because in man's spirit there is something entrusted to man for safekeeping, a divine spark, from the Supreme Being who has created the universe. Caliph Ali said, "You consider yourself a small thing, but in you the greatest universe is hidden." Shaykh Ghalib also says, "Take care of yourself, for you are the quintessence of the universe, you are a human being who is the pupil of the worlds." Truly in the human being, who is the most honorable of all creation and the quintessence of the universe, is a spiritual essence, a divine spark that is not to be found in any other being. This divine spark struggles passionately to meet its origin, it runs and hurries without us beyond our material being, trembles, burns, and jumps and spiritually it searches for Him. Rumi tells of the good news that in humans there is a pearl from His mine in these words: "There is something in you that, without your awareness, seeks Him. There is a pearl in your soul which is from His mine." Therefore, a human being is the most honorable creature in the universe and the most sublime.

Because of the Divine Entrustment that was rejected by other beings and given to humans in the end, humans have beautified the world and invented wondrous and wonderful things. Rumi, praising the superiority of humankind, says: "We are the treasure of God's secrets. We are the infinite sea full of pearls. What exists in all beings, from the moon to the fish, is our self. It is we who sit on the throne of sovereignty. We are the most exalted of all beings." When humans comprehend and discovers what is in them, they will find the truth. But humans are not able to find the truth of their own being. They are unable to enter the city of their body. In one of his poems, Yunus Emre says:

> Into the city of my body
> I would like to enter for a while
> The face of the Sultan therein
> I would like to witness.

It is not easy to enter the city of the body and to witness the Sovereign therein. Rumi says, "Master, travel from yourself to yourself and search for yourself in yourself." Thus, Rumi leaves behind Plato, who seeks for the truth by the dexterity of intellect, and goes down deep into man's very heart. This way he discovers humankind and the substance that is in humankind. "O soul, who is your beloved, do you know? O heart, who is your guest, do you know?" For a person who has found the Guest within himself or herself and loves Him, there can be no separation. While others struggle to attain the union and while they burn with the desire to meet the Beloved, Rumi says, "I do not talk of meeting the Beloved, I do not mention a union because I have not been separated from the Beloved."

There are many verses in the Qur'an telling of man's superiority among all creatures and that he was created with the best qualities and superior virtues: "We have honored the children of Adam"[40] or "Verily we have created humans in the best pattern."[41] Let us consider the meaning of these verses to see God's great favor to us and the infinite gifts he has bestowed upon humankind: "We are nearer to him than his jugular vein."[42] What a wonderful thing it is to think that God is nearer to us than our jugular vein! "God is the light of the earth and the heavens," and we do not need any telescope or anything else to detect Him. He demonstrates His Existence in every atom, in everything. May God open our hearts so that we may feel His Existence in ourselves without the need for telescopes. May we find Him in our souls and hearts. We do not need to look around, neither on earth nor in the heavens, to find Him, for He is nearer to us than our jugular vein. Niyazi Misri says,

I looked around, left and right,
In order to see the face of the Beloved,
I searched for Him outside
When He is the Soul within my soul.

Again in the Qur'an, we read, "He is with you wherever you are and God sees whatever you do."[43] What glad tidings are in this verse for those who believe! The great Rumi was moved by the good news in this verse and his heart was gladdened greatly. In one poem, he says, "The good news that He is with you wherever you are comes from God. This news fills one's heart with gladness and hope. You have not found peace and joy because you have not known yourself. Were you to know yourself, were you to know who your guest inside of you is, you would never see discontent and lack of peace coming your way."

Plato searched for the truth through reason and dialectics. Since Rumi knew that reason is unable to comprehend the superior truths and likened it to "a donkey that got stuck in the mud," he left the path of reason, and, through inspiration, through God's grace, he found himself in himself and fell in love with himself: "I wish to go far away hundreds of stages from the place where the intellect is. I would like to be rid of the existence of good and evil. There are such beauties behind this curtain. My real existence is there, too. O you who are short of comprehension, I would like to fall in love with myself."

For Plato it was necessary for man to know himself and discover that which is in him so that he may conform to this example. It was necessary for man to know from where he came and who is the guest within himself. Then man would know that he was different from the animal that was not different from him materially, and he would value himself. Rumi brought this truth to a deeper level. Man searched for and found the ways in which to recognize the Guest that is within him, to love Him and become worthy of Him, and to be loved by Him. This was the human way, the way of perfection and the way of love.

According to Rumi, since man has within him a Divine Entrustment he must appreciate his entrustment as well as his own value; in fact, he is to show respect for his own humanity. Truly, since man has accepted the Divine Entrustment granted to him by God and become His vicegerent on earth, even though he may resemble animals in his flesh and blood and bones, he must not consider himself as equal to animals but must believe in his own superiority and consider the fact that he is the most honorable of creatures. For this reason, he must withdraw himself from the states his carnal existence forces him into, such as human uncleanness, falsehood, hypocrisy, passion, and lust, and he must seek after the truth with a pure heart. He must in truth love man and humanity. Then he would not be unfaithful to God's entrustment; then he would become His honorable vicegerent as stated in the Qur'an and would have the right to bear the title of human being. If he acts in this way, man will kill (overcome) his human passions and weaknesses, find his origin while still living on earth, and no will longer be a stranger.

RUMI'S INFLUENCE IN THE WEST

As widely known, Islam attaches a high value to science and knowledge. The Prophet said, "Seeking knowledge is an obligation upon every Muslim."[44] In another tradition, he said, "Wisdom is the lost property of the believer. He takes it wherever he finds it,"[45] encouraging Muslims to seek knowledge and wisdom wherever or in whatever country it may be. It is for this reason that during the reign of Caliph Mansur, the founder of the city of Baghdad, the Muslims took *Kalila and Dimna* which is among the greatest masterpieces of the world from the East and translated it into Arabic, just as they translated the works of Plato, Ptolemy, Porphyry, Aristotle, Hippocrates, and Galen from Greek into Arabic. Islamic scholars have written commentaries on and criticisms of these Western works. They could be said to have preserved these books for humankind, for before the Renaissance, these ancient Greek texts had been banned in Europe by the clergymen who had turned their backs on true science. For this reason, it can be said that after the Renaissance European scientists learned Greek philosophy from the works of the Muslim scholars who truly loved scientific thought.

Science and knowledge or rather civilization, is not the possession of a single nation or religion. No nation can claim that civilization belongs exclusively to it. Civilization is the common product of all humankind. From the Stone Age up to today, humans of
different colors and different religions have lived in different parts
of the world and spoken different languages, and all have contributed to civilization. Islam and Islamic scholars have made many
contributions to the Western civilization of which Westerners are
proud.

The biggest mistake of the West was that it lacked love and
mercy. In an open letter to Jesus written by Süleyman Nazif, a modern Turkish poet, Nazif complains of the exploitation, oppression,
and injustice that Westerners were committing against weaker nations
that could not protect themselves. Iqbal mentioned that the spirit
of Jesus was crucified everyday by Westerners. Just as there have
been people who loved justice and truth in all parts of the world,
even if few in number, there have been also such noble-spirited people in Europe and America. For example, Washington Irving in
America, Thomas Carlyle in England, and Goethe in Germany
saved themselves from religious intolerance and showed sympathy
toward Islam. When the American historian Washington Irving
was in Spain as an ambassador, he was fascinated by the artwork
that remained from the Andalusian Muslims of Iberia. After deep-
ening his knowledge about Islamic history, he wrote books on
Muhammad and his Companions. In his book *Heroes*, the English
historian Thomas Carlyle wrote sections praising the Prophet of
Islam that reflect the truth. To those who did not understand the
Prophet because of religious bigotry, he said, "Humanity should
listen to the voice of Muhammad. His voice is God's voice."

Goethe, who not only is one of Germany's but also the world's
greatest poets, was more courageous. He thoroughly studied Islamic
history and literature. He brought forward the Prophet Muhammad's character in many of his books, criticisms, and poems. In his
works, Goethe compared the East and the West and tried to show

that they complement each other. Goethe's interest in Islam and his being inspired by Islam until the end of his life was possible in particular because of the direction of Herder, a scholar, philosopher, and literary man. Goethe carefully studied the Latin and German translations of the Holy Qur'an and explained some of the verses according to his understanding, and hence he took pleasure and inspiration from it. Goethe also wrote a play called *Muhammad* in the year 1773. The play began with a prayer called "Muhammad's Supplication." In the play Prophet Muhammad is depicted in his youth. The Prophet has retired to the desert, praying under the stars in the open sky. The supplication of Muhammad ends with these words: "O heart that is renewed and revitalized with love! Ascend toward your Creator! O Lord, you are my only God. You are the love that encompasses everything. O my God, you are the One who created the sun, the moon, the stars, the earth, the sky, and me." Goethe, who was a poet as well as a natural scientist and philosopher, saw the truth, showed interest in the East, and had respect and love for Islam and the Prophet of Islam. He was not only a great scholar but also a man of gnosis. A vivid example of his gnosis is that he did not distinguish people as being Easterners or Westerners, viewing all humanity as one: Goethe says, "A person who duly knows his identity and human nature knows that the West and the East are interrelated, and it is impossible for them to be separate."

If this view of Goethe and the view of Rumi, who viewed all human beings as siblings, were adopted by the administrations of the stronger nations that rule the world today, wars would stop and people would not massacre each other. Hunger, oppression, tyranny, imprisonment, exile, and massacres would be erased from the face of the earth. The rights of the people with black skin in South Africa would have been recognized earlier. Guerillas would not slaughter innocent people. The Turks in Bulgaria would not be tortured because of their beliefs. Bombs would not rain down on the towns and villages in Afghanistan. Just as America and Russia worked hand in hand to save a whale that was stuck in the ice at a cost of two billion dollars, they would also feel compassion toward and save the oppressed people that armed soldiers kill and torture by beating them with sticks, which we watch on television almost every night like a sporting event.

Understanding that Islam is a religion of love and affection that sees all as equal regardless of their skin color, or race, Bernard Shaw (d. 1951) said, "The future religion of humanity is going to be Islam." Goethe had understood this truth before Bernard Shaw when he said, "If Islam means to submit to the will of God, then we all live and die with Islam." Goethe, who was so sympathetic to Islam and the Prophet of Islam, was of course destined to discover Rumi, the lover of humanity and the lover of God. In his book entitled *The West-Eastern Divan*, Goethe quotes the following quatrain from Rumi:

> You are seeking peace and comfort in this world.
> But this world passes like a dream.
> You want to travel and see many places.
> But destiny makes you trip and it will not let you.
> You can tolerate neither heat nor cold.
> And the flowers you attempt to smell wither at once.[46]

Until the end of the eighteenth century, very little was known about Rumi and the Mevlevi order in Europe. Toward the end of that century, a French ambassador named J. de Wallenbourg, who lived in Istanbul for some time, translated the complete *Mesnevi* into French. Unfortunately, there was a fire in Beyoğlu in 1799, and this important work was burnt to ashes. Hammer, who was a very well-known German Orientalist in Turkey and author of *The Ottoman History*, was also interested in Rumi's work.[47] Indicating the importance of the *Divan-i Kabir*, Hammer writes,

> By separating from the exoteric differences and world affairs of all the positive religions, Rumi found the Supreme and Everlasting Being, and on the wings of highest spiritual joys

and pleasure, he rose to levels that other poets (including
Hafiz) could not reach. Rumi not only transcends the sun and
the moon but also time and space, creation, the Assembly of
Alast, and the Judgment Day and reaches infinity, and from
there he attains the Absolute Being that is Everlasting and
Everpresent and represents the ultimate servant, the infinite
love and lover.

Unfortunately, Hammer's translations of the *Mesnevi* and the
Divan-i Kabir are not as beautiful and eloquent as his translations
of Hafiz. But although these translations did not reflect the wonderful, deep meanings of Rumi's poetry, they were very important
because they introduced Rumi to the West. Hammer also came to
live in Turkey for some time. It can be said accurately that during
his time in Istanbul, he regularly visited libraries and attended ceremonies in Mevlevi lodges, where he also collected couplets and
quatrains that were recited during these ceremonies. The following
couplet is among these poems that he collected and appears in
Rumi's original Persian: "Alas, love, its states and its pain! The fire
of love has burnt my heart."

In those years the odes of Friedrich Ruckert (d. 1866) were
published in Germany. These odes all expressed divine love. Ruckert,
who is regarded as the most well-known German Orientalist, tried
to introduce the divine love that Rumi expressed in his poems to
the Germans by employing the ode form for the first time in
German. In fact, Friedrich Ruckert was not only a great German
Orientalist but also a great Sufi. With the encouragement and help
of Hammer, he learned Arabic, Persian, and Turkish. He was a
lover of God in spirit. He fell in love with Rumi after reading the
honorable *Mesnevi* and the *Divan-i Kabir*. He found himself in Rumi.
He translated forty-four of Rumi's odes into German verse. He
published these translations that he composed with love and feeling, their deep meanings in his heart, in Stuttgart in 1820 under
the title *Odes*. Two years later, Ruckert's selections were published in
Leipzig under the title *Östliche Rosen* (Eastern Roses). Afterwards

he translated in verse form poets like Sadi, Hafiz, and Jami. With his work, Ruckert wanted to show Europeans the greatness of the Sufis of Islam and make them feel the divine love that these Sufis express. In order to give an idea about the poems that this great poet and Sufi chose to translate, here is the poem 'The Rose' selected from the *Divan-i Kabir*. This poem smells of roses:

> Today is a spring day, a day of joy and happiness. This year where the roses bloom more than usual is the year of the roses.
>
> In this season of spring our state and condition are very good. May the state and condition of the rose be good as well.
>
> Help has arrived from beyond, from the rose garden of the Friend's face. Therefore, our eyes won't see the rose wither and its petals falling.
>
> Everybody's eyes are in awe before the rose's beauty, elegance, magnificence, color, and smell. In the garden it is smiling with its beautiful mouth. It is whispering the secrets of the nightingale's love and the virtues of the rose into the ear of the cypress tree.
>
> In order to do us a favor, to make us sense its fragrance better, the rose has come to us running and tearing its clothes. We, too, are tearing our clothes because we have reunited with the rose, and we want to be closer to the rose.
>
> The rose has come from beyond; it is from the other world. That's why this world cannot encompass the rose.
>
> The rose is so graceful, so elegant that the world of dreams is too narrow to dream of the rose.
>
> Who is meant by "the rose"? A messenger from the garden of the intellect, from the grove of spirit? What is "the rose"? A document that describes the beauty and the highness of the rose of truth that neither turns brown nor withers.
>
> Let us hold onto the rose's skirt and be its fellow traveler so that we may journey happily to the origin of the rose, the everlasting rose shoot.
>
> The origin of the rose, the everlasting rose shoot, has sprung from the sweat of Mustafa, peace and blessings be upon him, and has grown from His grace.

Thanks to that Gracious Being, it turned from a crescent to
a full moon. You may pluck the rose's petals and break its
branches and yet they grant it a new spirit, a new life, they
bestow it with hands and wings.

See how the rose has answered the invitation of the spring.
Just like Abraham's, the Friend of God, four pigeons that were
resurrected after being killed and returned to their master.

O Master, be silent! Don't open your lips. Sit in the rose's
shadow and just like the rosebud, secretly smile with your lips.[48]

This poem, every line of which smells of roses, was translated
into German by Ruckert, a lover of Rumi and a lover of God.

Through Ruckert's odes, Rumi became known in Germany,
and with this book the *divan* form entered German literature. Soon,
another German translation of *Divan-i Shams-i Tabrizi*, which contains selected poems from Rumi's *Divan-i Kabir*, appeared. Toward
the end of the last century scholars and intellectuals all over the
world began to show interest in Rumi and his works. In one of his
books, *Ethe*, a famous German Orientalist described Rumi as "the
greatest Sufi poet of the East and at the time." In Germany, Rumi's
work has been studied extensively by Helmut Ritter, who also is
very well known in Turkey. This great scholar produced very valuable studies about Rumi's life, poetry, the reed flute, and whirling
ceremonies that were based on the oldest manuscripts. With his
studies on the history of Sufism, he helped us to understand better
many aspects of Rumi. One also should not forget the great poet
and lover of Rumi, Hans Meinke (d. 1974), who was influenced
very much by Rumi. Meinke, who first got to know Rumi through
the works of German Orientalists, was fascinated by the Divine Love
in Rumi and dedicated all his poetry to Rumi. He also traveled to
Konya to rub his face against the threshold of Rumi's tomb. Although
this poet did not know Persian, he felt Rumi's spirit and especially
the infinite Divine Love in Rumi's poems and reflected it surpris-
ingly well in the hundred odes that he wrote in Rumi's name. As

an example, I am presenting one of his poems translated from German into English:

> O Rumi, since I became you,
> The turmoil stopped . . .
> O Rumi, since I became you,
> North has become south and south has become north.
> One pole has created the other pole.
> Chaos has melted in harmony.
> At the shore of the pulsating sea,
> Tell me if there has remained any silent gulf.
> Tell me if in your sight,
> There has remained any meaningless word.
> Is there a man who doesn't dance?
> O Rumi, I am the center of the circle of the heavens,
> Till I became you.

We also should remember the famous orientalist and an admirer of Rumi, Professor Annemarie Schimmel with respect.[49] Of the orientalists in the West, Schimmel wrote the largest number of books and articles about Rumi. She not only wrote about Rumi in German, English, and Turkish but also has translated Iqbal's *Jawidname* into Turkish and wrote a commentary on it.

Just as different people understand and value Rumi according to their own personal views, talents, inclinations, perceptions, and thoughts, different nations have approached Rumi in their own ways. A careful study will show that among all European nations, the Germans and the British are the nations that have concentrated most on Rumi. The disciplined, hard working, skillful German nation has at the same time a mystical spirit. For example, Martin Luther (d. 1546), who began the Reformation, is a German. Since Germans are inclined to faith and religion in spirit, they have identified themselves with Rumi and have worked on Rumi's books more than any other nation in Europe, except for the British.

As for the British interest in Rumi, Hippolyte Taine (d. 1893), an expert in English literature, maintained that the inhabitants of the British Isles, which are separated geographically from continental Europe and surrounded with thick fog and high waves, were not content with their surroundings and feeling the urge to open up to the outside world, they sought out something overseas. Unlike the French, who are theoretical, and Italians, who are artistic and ponderous in nature, the determined and pragmatic British also have a strong inclination toward mystical thought. Their love of experimentation, dislike of concepts imposed on them, and more logical approach to emotions have lead the British to understand Rumi more deeply and study him thoroughly.

We shall end this section with the British admirers of Rumi. In 1881, Sir James W. Redhouse translated in verse the first volume of the *Mesnevi* into English. He also included a number of stories from Aflaki's *Manaqib al-Arifin* at the beginning of his translation. E.H. Whinfield studied all six volumes of the *Mesnevi*. He then translated in verse selected passages and published them in 1898 under the name *Mesnevi-i Manavi*. In his shortened *Mesnevi* in verse, Whinfield summarized the stories and then diligently translated into English the portions about spiritual matters in rhyme and meter. The fact that this *Mesnevi* translation was republished twice in 1979 and 1984 shows how positively this translation was received. In 1898, in the foreword of the first edition, E.H. Whinfield introduced the *Mesnevi* to English readers, writing, "The *Mesnevi* addresses those who leave the world, try to know and to be with God, efface their selves and devote themselves to spiritual contemplation."

E.H. Palmer, who is known in England for his remarkable studies in Sufism, published selected poems of Rumi in a work titled *Song of the Reed*. With this publication, Rumi was introduced not only to a British audience but also to all the people in the English-speaking world. In a periodical published in 1886, a scholar named J. Scherr wrote about Rumi, "I swear that there has appeared no lover of God sweeter and more charming than Rumi in the world." R.A. Nicholson, regarded as one of the greatest Orientalists and Rumi scholars, produced his first work on Rumi with the translation of a number of selected poems. In this book titled *Selected Poems from the Divan-i Shams-i Tabriz* there are forty-eight poems selected from the *Divan-i Kabir*. The original text of each ode is included in the book as well as its translation, which is placed on the following page. There are also explanations at the end of this book. One should confess the fact that in Turkey, there is no Rumi anthology published that is as well prepared, as tastefully and carefully selected, nor as inclusive of the original text.

One also should note that the mentioned earlier Orientalists—the British scholar Graham, the German Orientalist Hammer, and the German Sufi poet Ruckert—declared that all the poems in the copies of the *Divan-i Shams-i Tabrizi* and *Divan-i Shamsu'l-Haqa'iq* to which they had access were authentic poems by Rumi. Since the edition of the *Divan-i Kabir* that was put together carefully by the Tehran University Professor Furuzanfar and published in Tehran did not exist at that time, these works that contain poems that do not belong to Rumi have misled Western Orientalists.

This great lover of Rumi worked all his life and with Rumi's inspiration and spiritual influence translated many invaluable works of other Sufis and other poets into English and showed the path to many people with a taste for gnosis. But the most important work of Nicholson is the translation of and commentary on the six volumes of the *Mesnevi*. In this work that was published in eight volumes beginning in 1925, Nicholson produced the *Mesnevi*'s most reliable text as well as its translation and commentary. Nicholson was not only a great Orientalist and a renowned scholar but also a great lover of God. As related by his friends and students, he would shed tears during *Mesnevi* lectures, becoming enraptured. In a room of his house decorated in oriental fashion, he would prepare the explanation of the *Mesnevi* dressed in Eastern clothing and wearing the long, round Mevlevi hat on his head. It is said that Nicholson completed this commentary in forty years.

A.J. Arberry who headed the Oriental Languages Department at Cambridge University after Nicholson, followed the same path as his predecessor and continued to translate Rumi's works into English. In addition to translating Rumi's quatrains and *Fihi Ma Fih* into English, he also published a selection of tales from the *Mesnevi* in two volumes. A few years prior to his death, Arberry said to a close friend, "I will devote the remaining years of my life exclusively to studying Rumi's work because it is possible to find spiritual cures and consolation for the miseries of our time in it."

I should also quote these sentences from a speech by E. W. F. Tomlin, former chairman of the Turkish - English Cultural Committee, that he delivered at the memorial celebrations for Rumi in 1960: "In spite of the elevation of Rumi's thought there is also a phenomenon called concrete imagination. This infiltrates the reader's spirit and attracts him to itself. Whenever I read passages from Rumi, it reminds me of Chaucer. But Chaucer (d. 1400), who is one of the most distinguished personalities of English literature, does not have religious views as deep as those of Rumi. One cannot reach the truth immediately. As Rumi says in the first book of the *Mesnevi*, 'God has set up a ladder in front of us. We have to climb it step by step.' I find the truth that Rumi has brought not only to his home country but also to us all in the fourth book of his *Mesnevi*: 'The believers are many but men are one.' I will conclude my speech with a quote from Rumi that points to the same truth and is an example of the above-mentioned concrete imagination: 'The sunlight from the sky is thousand-fold with respect to the courtyards that it illuminates. But if you remove the walls from in between, all these fragmented lights are one and the same thing.'"

Although in the last few centuries Turkey has had the strongest contact with the French people among the European nations, the French did not exhibit the same interest in Rumi as did the British and the German. However, the French explorers who traveled through the Ottoman Empire were very interested in the whirling ceremonies in the Mevlevi lodges. They included these ceremonies in their memoirs, and some painters painted whirling dervishes, which increased this interest. C.L. Huart, a French Orientalist who visited Konya in 1897, wrote a book on Konya. He later translated Aflaki's *Manaqib al-Arifin* into French under the title *Whirling Dervishes*. This translation led Maurice Barres, a famous literary figure and a French Academy member, to visit Konya. Barres, who visited Rumi's lodge and shrine in Konya in 1919, took notes which in 1923 he published under the title *An Interview in the Eastern Countries*. Mehmet Önder translated some sections from this book in 1969 under the name *In the Presence of Rumi*.

Maurice Barres, this lover of Rumi, begins his memoirs as follows:

> I can't wait. I want to see Rumi's lodge, whirling hall and shrine, experience his Divine rapture and hear the melodies of his poetry. He is such a genius that odor, light, music, and a little bit of bohemianism emanate from him. His original expressions in the poetry are vivid and divine. It enraptures the reader. Only the reader? No. Jalal al-Din Rumi himself is in rapture and whirling in his poems. He placed a book in our hands so as to draw us into his magical atmosphere. If I am fortunate I will see the Mevlevi dervishes, the followers of his path, who very proficiently perform his music. His memory has been living for seven hundred years from generation to generation, and his name is mentioned around his tomb more enthusiastically every day. How fortunate am I![50]

In Asaf Halet Çelebi's translation of the same book, Barres confesses, "In my opinion, the life of no poet, whom I consider to be the messengers of the world of enthusiasm, light, and joy, compares to the life of Rumi. After seeing the dervishes whirling and singing to his rhythm I noticed that there is something lacking in Dante, Shakespeare, Goethe, and Hugo."[51] Barres' book received much attention in France and many French scholars, literary personalities, and poets were introduced to Rumi. Also Mme Myriam Harry published a book entitled *Mevlana Jalalu'd-deen* in 1956. Today in Paris Professor Eva de Vitray has been studying Rumi and his works, and has completed a work titled *Rumi and Sufism*.[52] Professor Irene Melikoff, a lover of Rumi, also works in this area.

In Italy, too, there are admirers of Rumi. We must remember the Rome University professors Alessander Bausani and Anna Masala. In Holland, Professor Brakell Busy and Dr. Carp, in Denmark, Professor Asmussen, and in Switzerland, Professor Burgel, all are among the admirers of Rumi. In recent years there is increasing interest in Rumi in Russia. The broad research done in 1972 by Radi Fis in Moscow on Rumi's life, views, and books is an example of this interest.

In the United Stated there is great admiration for Rumi. He earns the title of the most read poet in America. His influence is evident in academia as well as Sufi circles. There are many names who have written on Rumi. William Chittick, Kabir Helminski, Coleman Barks, and recently Franklin Lewis are some examples. Also, there are institutions dedicated to the teachings of Rumi.[53]

CHAPTER IV

Rumi's Sufi Order and His
Approach to Orders

THE MEVLEVI ORDER

C ontrary to popular misconception, the Mevlevi order, named after Rumi, was actually not established by Rumi. The foundations of this order were laid by Husam al-Din Celebi and Rumi's son Sultan Valad. So then which path or which dervish order did Rumi follow when there was no Mevlevi order? As is commonly known, *tariqah* in Arabic means path, way, path of God, and the path taken during the spiritual journey. So, then, which path did Rumi follow to find the truth, attain God, and became Rumi?

Risale-i Sipehsalar, one of the most reliable historical accounts of Rumi's life, tells us that Rumi followed his father's path, charac-ter, and order.[1] From this account it is understood that Rumi's first spiritual guide and shaykh was his father Sultan al-Ulama Baha al-Din Valad. Afterward, Sayyid Burhan al-Din al-Tirmidhi, one of Sultan al-Ulama's deputies, became Rumi's spiritual guide and shaykh. Both Sultan al-Ulama and Burhan al-Din Tirmidhi were members of the Kubrawiyyah order. Hamdullah Musevfide writes that Rumi's father, Sultan al-Ulama, was one of the deputies of Najm al-Din al-Kubra who was the founder of the Kubrawiyyah order.[2] In addi-tion, there is an account in *Nefahatu'l-Uns* that Sultan al-Ulama was one of the deputies of Najm al-Din al-Kubra.[3] Similarly, in his book *Hadiqatu'l-Awliya*, Hoca Zade Ahmed Hilmi relates Sultan al-Ulama to our Prophet through the following *silsila*.[4] The well-known saints in this *silsila* are as follows:

1. The Beloved of the Lord of the Worlds: Muhammad Mustafa, peace and blessings be upon him.
2. Hadhrat Ali
3. Hadhrat Husayn
4. Maruf al-Karhi
5. Junayd al-Baghdadi
6. Ahmad al-Ghazali
7. Shaykh Ismail Kasri
8. Founder of the Order: Najm al-Din al-Kubra
9. Sultan al-Ulama Baha al-Din Valad (may God be pleased with them and exalt their secrets)

There are also those who relate Sultan al-Ulama's *silsila* through Hadhrat Abu Bakr. Professor Furuzanfar, contradicting an account by Aflaki, relates Sultan al-Ulama's attachment to Najm al-Din al-Kubra, the founder of the Kubrawiyya order. Just as Baha al-Din Valad was a deputy of Najm al-Din al-Kubra, who was martyred in 1221 while fighting against the Mongols, Sayyid Burhan al-Din was also Sultan al-Ulama's deputy. Sipehsalar narrates Sayyid Burhan al-Din's attachment to Sultan al-Ulama Baha al-Din Valad as follows:

> Sayyid Burhan al-Din was not in Konya when Sultan al-Ulama passed away (1231). When he received the news of the passing of his shaykh, he became so sad that the dirt of sorrow was spread over his head. His heart burned, and he mourned a long time. For one complete year he melted like a candle because of his shaykh's death. One night he saw Sultan al-Ulama in his dream. He angrily addressed him: "Burhan al-Din! How is it possible that you have left my Muhammad (Muhammad Jalal al-Din) alone and made a mistake in his custody?"[5]

Because of this dream, Sayyid Burhan al-Din came to Konya. He worked for the guidance of the young Rumi for nine years. Sayyid Burhan al-Din not only granted deputyship to Rumi but also to Salah al-Din, the jeweler. As Aflaki relates, Burhan al-Din Tirmidhi expresses the fact that he is a disciple of Sultan al-Ulama when he says: "I received two bestowments from my shaykh, Sultan al-Ulama: One is the ability to speak well, and the other is the beauty in spiritual states. Since Rumi has beauty in spiritual states I granted my ability to speak well to Salah al-Din."[6] Sultan Valad expresses his love and devotion to his father's shaykh and spiritual guide Burhan al-Din Tirmidhi beginning with the following couplets:

> Rumi was with Sayyid Burhan al-Din for nine years. He was in his service. Then he became his equivalent in terms of both knowledge and spiritual maturity.
>
> Since their hearts were one in the spiritual world, they were one on the outside as well as inside. Afterward Sayyid Burhan al-Din migrated from this world, from the world of non-existence to eternity, the world of existence. Jalal al-Din became an orphan. He worshipped God day and night. For this, he abandoned sleeping, eating, and drinking. He raised the flag of search for a spiritual guide. In this way he spent five years in devotion to his spiritual guide with mourning, heartfelt crying, lamentation, and self-mortification.[7]

RUMI AND ISLAMIC LAW

It is wrong to associate Rumi with a single order and view him as strictly confined within the rules of a single order. We have discussed Rumi's order before the Mevlevi order. Four or five years after Rumi lost Sayyid Burhan al-Din Tirmidhi, he met Shams of Tabriz. Shams became Rumi's "shaykh of company," but not his spiritual guide. But he took him from the scholastic path to the path of Divine Love. Rumi was no longer a scholar in the university busy with lecturing and educating students. He began to view the path of the Prophet as a path of love, unlike some university scholars who were stuck in formalities and thought of the path of the Prophet as a path of Islamic Law (*shari'ah*): "The path of the Prophet is the path of love. We are born of love, and love is our mother. O our mother hidden within our physical existence composed of flesh and blood! O our Creator, concealed beyond our faithless nature that cannot grasp the truth! Rumi proceeded ever further, leaving behind all orders and religions to attain the truth and God: "The religion of love is different from all other religions. The religion and creed of the lovers is God."[8]

This view should not be misunderstood as Rumi denouncing all religions and creeds. On the contrary, he saw the essence of religions and creeds. He expressed that no matter to what religion or to what creed people belonged, they all sought God according to Divine Predestination and Divine Manifestation. Some go to mosques, some to churches, and some to synagogues, but they all plead with God in their own language and according to their own religion. As a gnostic poet says, "O God! Sometimes I go to the church and sometimes I stay in the mosque. That is, I seek you house by house."

Referring to the subject of particular orders, Rumi says in the *Mesnevi*:

> Islamic Law is like a candle. It sheds light and shows the way. One cannot reach the destination solely by taking the candle in the hand, but one cannot start walking down the path without taking the candle in hand either. Once you start walking on the path in the light of Islamic Law, your walking is the Way (*tariqah*). And when you reach your destination, then that is the Truth. Therefore, it is said that if the truths were revealed, the Laws would have been invalidated. Indeed, if copper is turned into gold with alchemy, then there remains no need for alchemy. In other words, the processing of copper according to alchemy is not needed anymore. It is for this reason that they said, "It is inappropriate to seek a guide after one has reached a destination under guidance. But it is also inappropriate to abandon the guide before reaching the destination for which one needs a guide."
>
> In short, Islamic Law is like learning the science of alchemy from a teacher or from a book. The Way is like obtaining the elixir and treating copper with the elixir according to alchemy. And the Truth is copper becoming gold with the effect of alchemy. Those who know alchemy are happy that they possess this knowledge. The practitioners of this craft are happy that they

do things that not everybody can do. And those attaining the truth are happy to have attained the truth and say, "We have become gold. We are free from the knowledge of alchemy. We do not have to treat copper with the elixir anymore. We are free servants of God. We have no attachment to anything." Every group is happy with what they have attained. Everybody is pleased with the path they are on.[9]

In another analogy, Islamic Law is likened to learning the science of medicine. The Way is using medication and dieting according to the knowledge of medicine. And Truth is attaining everlasting goodness and health and hence deliverance from the need of medicine. When a man passes away from this world and dies, the jurisdiction of Law and the Way is lifted from him, but the truth remains in the following senses.

Islamic Law is likened to a candle, a source of light, that shows the way. After stressing the importance of the Law by saying that "one cannot start walking the path without taking the candle in hand," he states that the Way is the walking on the path in the light of the Law, and Truth is when one reaches the destination walking the Way in the light of the Law. Expressions, such as "if the truths were revealed, the Law would have been invalidated" and "it is inappropriate to seek a guide after one has reached a destination under guidance, but it is also inappropriate to abandon the guide before reaching the destination for which one needs a guide," can be very misleading. Therefore, we must be very careful and reflect deeply in order that these statements not mislead readers to invalid conclusions. Is one supposed to throw away the Law and its commandments just like an outdated lamp after attaining the truth? Will it be inappropriate for one to seek the Law once one has attained the Truth to which the Law had been the guide? These words of Rumi should not be taken in the wrong sense.

My dear readers, please think about this statement. Are the daily prayers, which our utmost beloved Prophet counted as "the ascension of the believer" and described as "the light of my eye" an enjoyable duty for the believer or a burden and unnecessary task? A person who annihilates his existence in God with voluntary death is the happy person blessed with attaining the secret "Die before you actually die." Is such a person supposed to abandon his obligatory worship prescribed by Islamic Law? Is he not going to perform daily prayers, fast, or remember God anymore? No, my readers, no! Such a person will be closer to God since he now knows the truth and will be attached to the commandments of Islamic Law with even more love and enthusiasm. Such a person will be saved from the kind of worship that is confined to form and ostentation and performed with little or no understanding. He will be attached to God with love, saying, "I perform my duties neither to enter Paradise nor to escape Hell." Such a person will raise his faith from the level of imitation to the level of realization and, as Yunus Emre pleads, "They all say 'Paradise, paradise!' But it has a few houses and a few houris. Give them to whomever wants them. All I want is You, none but You!" Although our Great Prophet had attained the truth of truths, he used to pray all night long and his holy feet used to swell due to his extraordinarily long worship.

I find it useful to turn to the views of early Sufis concerning the subject of Law and Truth. In his *Risala*, Qushayri writes, "What is Law? The Law is doing whatever is necessary to be a true servant of God and diligently obeying the commandments of God. The Truth is observing the Greatness, Power, Creation, and Art of God in awe. No Law is acceptable other than that supported and approved by the Truth. And no Truth can be accepted other than that which is attached to the Law. Indeed, worshipping God is the Law and observing His Power and Art in His Creating and feeling Him in the heart is the Truth."[10] Hujwiri writes, "We see no difference between the Law and the Truth. Both are one. What is the Law is the Truth and the Truth is the Law."[11] Has Yunus Emre not said, "The Law and the Way are paths for those who reach (the destination). The Truth and Gnosis is further inside them"? Nimatullahi Kirmani summarizes Rumi's view in the following quatrain:

Knowing what the religion prescribes is the Law. Practicing the religion according to its rules is the Way. And if you combine religious knowledge and good deeds with sincerity, i.e. perform your acts of worship with the knowledge you acquired, not for any self-interest but only for the sake of God, then that becomes the Truth.

If we express all these views in brief, we reach the following conclusion: The main idea behind all these discussions is to walk with the guidance of Islamic Law on the Way and thus attain the Truth and enjoy the pleasure of knowing God. It is to love God truly from the heart and to be close to Him. Rumi tells us to take the love of God to the forefront, to abstain from being attached to the letter of the law rather than the spirit of it, to find the essence of the faith, and to raise our faith from the level of imitation to the level of realization.

Since Rumi, who honored the world seven centuries ago, saw this division among believers, he disapproved of the dervish orders. In his view, there is but one order. And that is the order of Muhammad (*tariqat al-muhammadiyyah*) and the Way of Divine Love (*tariqat al-'ashq al-ilahi*). It is for this reason that Rumi never mentioned the names of dervish orders nor saints associated with dervish orders in the *Mesnevi* nor in *Divan-i Kabir*, nor his other works.

In Rumi's time there were Qadiriyyah, Rufaiyyah, Suhrawardiyyah, Kubrawiyyah, and Akbariyyah orders. Rumi mentions the names of saints who are not associated with any particular order, such as Bayazid Bistami (d. 848), Dhu al-Nun al-Misri (d. 859) and Mansur al-Hallaj (d. 921), but never mentions the names of saints who were associated with an order, such as Abd al-Qadir al-Jilani (d. 1165), Ahmad Rifa'i (d. 1182), Muhy al-Din Ibn al-'Arabi (d. 1239), and even the spiritual guide of his father and the founder of the Kubrawiyyah order, Najm al-Din al-Kubra (d. 1221).

As Rumi always avoided showing-off, ostentation, and fame, he never established an order and never opened a dervish lodge. He had seen the "spiritual kingdoms" of some shaykhs in the dervish lodges. There used to be lodges with many servants and doorkeepers. Rumi did not want to be distinguished from the common folk and to seem superior. He always remained far from exploiting those who loved and revered him, and he distributed the donations from the sultans, state officials, and other rich men to others and spent them for the poor. He was not someone who enjoyed boasting as a shaykh, having his hand and feet kissed, and having others prostrate before him. His distinguished modesty and his Muhammadi character kept him away from shaykhdom and the "dervish lodge kingdom." It is for this reason that he led a poor man's life while being a unique king of spirituality in his time. He did not become a king of a dervish lodge that was bound to be ruined in time, but he became the king of hearts. Although he was a distinguished personality with knowledge, morals, and gnosis who showed the way for the lovers of God, and although he was a living example of virtue, grace, and love of humanity, he considered himself nothing: "They have determined a value for my turban, robe and head, all three together. They valued them under one dirham. Have you heard my name in this world? I am nothing, nothing, and nothing."

Why would peerless Rumi who views himself as nothing, but in fact is a unique personality, need an impermanent dervish lodge bound for destruction? He entered the hearts of the lovers of God with the tunes coming from the depths of the heart and became the sultan of the lodge of hearts. The first dervish lodge was established in Ramlah, Syria in the eight century of the Christian Era. After the formation of the dervish orders, dervish lodges spread all over the Islamic world. Initially dervish lodges were built for no purpose other than piety, asceticism, morality, knowledge, gnosis, arts, music, virtues, manners and humanity. The dervish lodges served as purification places and refuges for the travelers on the path of God, and they performed many great services for the believers. Like many other institutions, dervish lodges degenerated and became places of exploitation and asylums for the idle. Maybe it is because Rumi knew what was really going on in the dervish lodges that he did not establish one. In a passage from the *Mesnevi*, Rumi says the following through the words of a young boy who was bothered in the dervish lodge, "I could not find comfort or safety even in the dervish lodge which is supposed to be the safest place. The dervishes who survive on a cup of wheat soup looked at me with lust and expressed their dirty intentions."[12]

Elsewhere in the *Mesnevi*, Rumi woefully complains about the dervish lodges of that time which had lost their morals, manners, virtues, and spiritual strengths:

> These disciples of the lodge have left aside hundreds of elements of knowledge, maturity, virtue, manners, and humanity and submerged themselves in fraud, hypocrisy, lying, ostentation, and show. This is their state.
>
> They view all kinds of sins as permissible and see no reason to abstain from them. These vices that are not considered a sin anymore have spread around as if there has been a permission issued to commit sins.
>
> Where is the path of our Prophet and His Companions? Where are prayers? Where are beads? Where are the manners of the saints?[13]

To summarize what has been said up to this point: The main reason that Rumi did not establish an order or a dervish lodge was his intent not to disturb the unity of the believers and not to lead believers to different paths other than the Muhammadi path (*tariqat al-muhammadiyyah*). Rumi, who said, "Our *Mesnevi* is a shop of unity," did not want the believers to be divided by details. Furthermore, he did not hold a high opinion of being the "shaykh of a dervish lodge," which had lost its initial purity.

Rumi himself did not establish an order or a dervish lodge, but he did not belittle the saints who did so. He did not see himself as superior to them and did not criticize them. He furthermore loved them with his superb tolerance. This is because all saints love each other no matter what differences there are in the details of their approaches. They exchange ideas and views. Indeed, Muhy al-Din Ibn al-'Arabi liked very much the ode that Rumi recited in Arabic for his grandson, Ulu Arif Chelebi,[14] and included the second verse of the ode at the beginning of the *kalima al-muhammadiyyah* section of his famous *Fusus al-Hikam*, which deals with the issue of love: "His spirit is my spirit. My spirit is his spirit. Who has seen two spirits living in one body? The public understood that I am in love. Only they did not know with whom I was in love."[15] It is a very important fact that Muhy al-Din Ibn al-'Arabi quoted Rumi's poem in his book. However, Rumi never mentions Ibn al-'Arabi's name in his works since he was the founder of a dervish order. He became, however, close friends with Ibn al-'Arabi's stepson, Sadr al-Din al-Konavi, who is the most well-known shaykh of the Akbariyyah order founded by Muhy al-Din Ibn al-'Arabi. They were so close that Rumi willed that he lead Rumi's funeral prayer when he passed away.

Thus Rumi knew that all the orders and creeds were paths that lead to God, and he did not denounce the founders of orders although he did not found an order himself. As Prophet Muhammad tells us, "The paths leading to God are as many as the creatures of God." Rumi also said in the *Mesnevi*: "In this world there are hidden stairs that climb all the way up to the heavens. These stairs lead to the heavens step by step. Every group has its own stairs. All like their own stairs. They are unaware of the other stairs. However, all of them lead to eternity in one way or another."[16] If the followers of the Law and the followers of the Way had attained the truth and had thought like Rumi, they would accept each other and love each other because they all share the same faith. The Prophet has said, "The believers are not other than brethren."

EPILOGUE

This concludes the book on Rumi's life and personality that I prepared with the help of God using many different books. It took years to complete because I spent a lot of time on each section of the book, as if I were writing a small booklet. This is not meant as a boast. I do not have any claim. I am just a poor literature teacher. Being a human being, there might be places where I am wrong. But I love all the saints and my love for Rumi grew as I studied his works. This book has ended up being more than a book exclusively on Rumi's life and views. It also can be seen as a book on Sufism since it deals with many subjects of Sufism while at the same time explaining Rumi's views. Before concluding the epilogue of this book, I have to confess that even though I have been studying Rumi's works for decades I have not been able to understand this great saint properly. It is for this very reason that I am unable to explain him properly to my readers. However, we should not be pessimistic. Let us listen to what Rumi, this great person that we love, this great saint, whose ideas we cannot quite understand, this sultan of lovers of God says about himself. Let us not say anything about this great saint. He will be kind enough to tell us his views and feelings through his poems from *Divan-i Kabir*. Therefore, I selected some poems from *Divan-i Kabir* that best explain Rumi's views and feelings. Let us concentrate on these poems, let us carefully absorb the divine tunes and spiritual meanings echoing from a saint's heart. In his own words, these poems are the "holy light of the sea of Unity of God, springs of spiritual joy, light of hearts, and flowers of the garden of hearts."

Please read again and again the section on *Divan-i Kabir*. The selections are from a total of 43,561 couplets that comprise *Divan-i Kabir*, which Rumi himself named "the divan of the lovers of God," and are "true words accepted by the lovers of God and gnostics." Let us not give our minds but our hearts to these words because these poems are poems of the heart. Rumi did not compose these poems like other poets by taking a pen in his hand. He sang the divine tunes that arose in his heart. And people around him recorded his poems. We shall find Rumi with Rumi's love and feelings. Let us try to find in our hearts an echo of these tunes.

My dear readers, while selecting poems I have not limited myself to my own preferences. I have looked at the selections of Nicholson, Schimmel, Gölpınarlı, and Midhat Bahari. I marked the most beloved poems. I took as a reference the edition of *Divan-i Kabir* published by Professor Furuzanfar. I have excluded poems not found in Furuzanfar's edition since these poems are unreliable and may not be authentic. However, my selections are not an independent Rumi anthology. It is only a section added to a book on Rumi's life and personality. They are diamonds beautifying a poorly written book. Each of these diamonds is worth thousands of books. If you happen to attain the bliss of feeling these poems in your heart, I plead that you remember well Şefik Can, this poor servant of God, who selected these poems, overlook his mistakes, and recite the *Fatiha* for his soul.

My dear readers whom I know and do not know! Friends who love wisdom and truth! Lovers of God! I leave you alone with the poems of Rumi and retreat. I greet all of you with respect and love and wish you ample health, peace, and spiritual joy.

Şefik Can
The servant of Rumi's devotees

BIBLIOGRAPHY

al-Aflaki, Shams al-Din Ahmad. *Manaqib al-Arifin*, ed. Tahsin Yazıcı. Ankara: Turk Tarih Kurumu Basimevi, 1959.

Ankaravi, Ismail Rusuhi. *Risalah Hujjat al-Sama*. Istanbul: Rıza Efendi Matbaası, 1869.

————. *Şerh-i Kebir-i Ankaravi ber Mesnevi-yi Ma'navi-i Mevlevi*, tr. Ismet Settarzade. Tehran: Chapkhaneh-e Mihan, 1970.

Bursalı Mehmed Tahir. *Osmanlı Müellifleri*. Istanbul: Matbaa-i Amire, 1333.

Çelebi, Asaf Halet. *Mevlana Hayatı ve Şahsiyeti*. Istanbul: Kanaat Kitabevi, 1939.

Furuzanfar, Bediüzzaman. *Mevlana Celaleddin,* tr. Feridun Nafiz Uzluk. Ankara: Milli Eğitim Bakanlığı, 1986.

Gölpınarlı, Abdülbaki. *Mevlevilik Adab ve Erkanı*. Istanbul: Inkılap ve Aka Kitabevleri, 1963.

————. *Mevlana Celaleddin*. Istanbul, 1959.

Ibn al-'Arabi, Abu Abd Allah Muhy al-Din Muhammad b. Ali, *The Wisdom of The Prophets (Fusus al-Hikam,* tr. Angela Culme-Seymour. Wiltshire: Beshara Publications, 1975.

Hilmi, Hoca Zade Ahmed. "Silsile-i Meşayih-i Mevleviyye", in *Hadikat al-Evliya*. Istanbul: Şirket-i Mürettibiye Matbaası, 1318.

al-Hujwiri, Ali b. Uthman. *Kashf al-Mahjub,* tr. Reynold A. Nicholson. Karachi: Darul-Ishaat, 1990.

Ibn al-Farid, Abu al-Qasim Sharaf al-Din Omar b. Ali. *Ta'iyyah al-Kubra*. Cairo: al-Maktabah al-Azhariyyah, 1319.

Ibn Hibban, Muhammad al-Tamimi. *Sahih*, ed. Shuayb al-Arnaout. Beirut: Muassasah al-Risalah, 1993.

Iqbal, Muhammad. *Esrar ve Rumuz*, tr. Ali Yüksel. Istanbul: Birleşik Yayıncılık, 1996.

————. *Cavitname*, tr. Annemarie Schimmel. Ankara: Kültür Bakanlığı, 1989.

Izmirli, Ismail Hakkı. *Yeni Ilm-i Kelam*, Istanbul: Evkaf-i Islamiyye Matbaası, 1339.

Jami, Abu al-Barakat Nur al-Din Abd al-Rahman b. Ahmad b. Muhammad. *Nafahat al-Uns Min Hadarat al-Quds*, tr. Mahmud b. Osman Lami'i Çelebi. Istanbul: Marifet Yayınları, 1289.

Köprülü, Mehmed Fuad. *Türk edebiyatında ilk Mutasavvıflar*. Ankara: Gaye Matbaacılık, 1981.

Lewis, Franklin D. *Rumi Past and Present, East and West*. Oxford: One World, 2001.

Al-Munawi, Muhammad Abd al-Rauf. *Faydh al-Qadir*. Beirut, 1972.

Muslim b. al-Hajjaj, Abu al-Husayn al-Qushayri. *al-Sahih*. Cairo: Dar Ihya al-Kutub al-Arabiyyah, 1954.

Najm al-Din al-Kubra. "Majmuat al-Resail", manuscript in Ayasofya Kütüphanesi, Istanbul, n.d.

Nicholson, Reynold A. *The Mesnevi of Jalalu'ddin Rumi*. Lahore: Islamic Book Service, 1989.

Önder, Mehmet. *Hazret-i Mevlana Hayatı ve Eserleri*. Istanbul: Tercüman Yayınları, n.d.

al-Qushayri, Abu al-Qasım Zayn al-Islam Abd al-Karim. *al-Risalah al-Qushayriyyah*, eds. Abd al-Halim Mahmud and Mahmud Ibn Sharif. Cairo: Dar al-Kutub al-Hadithah, 1973.

Rumi, Muhammad b. Muhammad b. Husayn Mevlana Celal al-Din. *Fihi Ma Fih*, tr. Meliha Ülker Ambarcıoğlu. Istanbul: Milli Eğitim Basımevi, 1969.

————. *Divan-i Kabir*, tr. Bediüzzaman Furuzanfar. Tehran: Daneshgah-e Tehran, 1957

————. *Mesnevi*, tr. and commentary by Olgun Tahir Mevlevi. Istanbul: Ahmet Said Matbaasi, 1967.

Sipehsalar, Faridun b. Ahmad. *Risale-i Sipehsalar*, tr. Mithat Bahari Beytur. Istanbul: Selanik Matbaasi, 1331.

Shams al-Din Muhammad Tabrizi. "Maqalat", manuscript in the Fatih Library, Istanbul, n.d.

————. *Maqalat*, ed. Muhammad Ali Muwahhid. Tehran: Chapkhaneh-e Diba, 1349/1970.

Shabastari, Sa'd al-Din Mahmud b. Abd al-Karim b. Yahya. *Gulshan-i Raz*, ed. Ali Muhammadzade Qurban. Baku: Ferhengistan-i Ulum-i Jumhuri, 1972.

al-Tabarani, Sulaiman bin Ahmad bin Ayyub. *al-Mu'jam al-Kabir*. Mosul: Maktabat al-Ulkm wa al-Hikam, 1983.

Taşköprüzade, Abu al-Khayr Isam al-Din Ahmad. *Mawdhuat al-Ulum*, tr. Kemaleddin Mehmed Efendi. Dersaadet: Ikdam Matbaası, 1895.

Tirmidhi, Abu Isa. *al-Sunan*. Beirut: Dar al-Ihya al-Turath al-Arabi, n.d.

Tirmidhi, Muhaqqiq Husayn Sayyid Burhan al-Din. *Maarif*, tr. Abdülbaki Gölpınarlı. Ankara: Türkiye İş Bankası, n.d.

Valad, Baha al-Din Muhammad Sultan. *Ibtidaname*, tr. Abdülbaki Gölpınarlı. Konya: Konya Turizm Derneği, 1976.

————. *Ma'arif*. Tehran: Kitabkhaneh-e Tahuri, 1977.

de Vitray-Meyerovitch, Eva. *Rumi and Sufism*. Sausalito, CA: Post-Apollo Press, 1977 French; 1987 English.

Yavuz, M. Hakan, and Esposito, John L., eds. *Turkish Islam and the Secular State: The Gülen Movement*. Syracuse, New York: Syracuse University Press, 2003.

AUTHOR'S BIOGRAPHY

Şefik Can was born in 1910 in the village of Tebricik near Erzurum, an eastern province of Turkey. During his childhood, he learned Arabic and Persian from his father. He graduated from Kuleli Military High School in 1929 and from the Academy of War in 1931. He began working as a teacher at a military high school in 1935. He retired from the army with the rank of colonel in 1965. In addition to his native Turkish, he spoke French, English, and Russian, along with Arabic and Persian. Until he passed away on January 24, 2005, he was the *ser-tariq* (head) of the Mevlevis (the most authoritative spiritual figure of the Order). He was also the latest *Mesnevihan* (*Mesnevi* reciter) who received his *ijazat* (special certificate in the recitation of the *Mesnevi*) from his spiritual master Tahir al-Mevlevi. Şefik Can authored nine books on Rumi as well as on poetry and classical mythology.

AUTHOR BIOGRAPHY

NOTES

FOREWORD

1   Majnun is a legendary personality of love found in Islamic literature.

2   Buraq is the name of the horse that carried Prophet Muhammad during his Ascension into Heaven.

3   Qur'an, 5:54.

CHAPTER I

THE POLITICAL AND PHILOSOPHICAL SITUATION OF THE ANATOLIAN SELJUK EMPIRE DURING RUMI'S LIFE

1   Turkish: Alaeddin Keykubad

2   Qur'an, 2:285.

3   Those who elected Abu Bakr as Caliph later would be called "Sunni" Muslims, or those who followed the way (sunna) of the Prophet. Those who had given their hearts completely to the Prophet's family (ahl-al-bayt) and wanted to make Ali the Caliph later were called Shi'ites. Sunni Muslims make up 85% and Shi'ites 15% of the Muslim population today.

4   Muhammad Abu Isa al-Tirmidhi, *al-Sunan*, Beirut: Dar Ihya al-Turath al-Arabiyyah, n.d., vol. 5, p. 51.

5   Muhammad b. Muhammad b. Husayn Mevlana Jalal al-Din Rumi, *Fihi Ma Fih*, tr. Meliha Ülker Ambarcıoğlu (Istanbul: Milli Eğitim Basımevi, 1969). p. 265; For further discussion on this see Franklin D. Lewis, *Rumi Past and Present, East and West* (Oxford: One World, 2001), p. 317 – 24.

6   The term suggests a respect for the deceased among Mevlevis.

7   Qur'an, 55:19.

8   Turkish: Gevher Hatun

9   *Mumine* means "faithful."

10   Baha al-Din Muhammad Sultan Valad, *Ibtidaname*, tr. Abdülbaki Gölpınarlı (Konya: Konya Turizm Derneği, 1976), p. 242.

11   Muhammad Iqbal, *Esrar ve Rumuz*, tr. Ali Yüksel (Istanbul: Birleşik Yayıncılık, 1996), p. 26.

12   Faridun b. Ahmad Sipehsalar, *Risale-i Sipehsalar*, tr. Mithat Bahari Beytur (Istanbul: Selanik Matbaası, 1331), p. 98.

13   Qur'an, 2:26.

14   Bediüzzaman Furuzanfar, *Mevlana Celaleddin*, tr. Feridun Nafiz Uzluk. (Ankara: Milli Eğitim Bakanlığı, 1986), p. 218.

15   Ibid., 114.

16   This commentary has been completed by the author and its publication is forthcoming.

17   Bediüzzaman Furuzanfar, *Mevlana Celaleddin,* p. 222.
18   Bursalı Mehmed Tahir, *Osmanli Muellifleri* (Ottoman Authors) (Istanbul: Matbaa-i Amire, 1333). v. I, p. 105.
19   *Jabarut* is a higher realm of being.
20   Muhammad Baha al-Din Valad, *Ma'arif* (Tehran: Ketabkhaneh-e Tahuri, 1977). An original copy of this work can be found in the Persian Manuscripts section of Istanbul University's library.
21   It is a custom in Islam that whenever one mentions the name of one of the Companions of the Prophet or of a saint, he/she adds the Arabic phrase, *radiya Allahu'anh/'anha,* meaning may God be pleased with him or her.
22   *Risale-i Sipehsalar,* p. 164.
23   Shams-i Tabriz, *Maqalat,* manuscript in the Fatih Library in Istanbul, Folio 45a. Cf. Shams al-Din Muhammad Tabrizi, *Maqalat,* ed. Muhammad Ali Muwahhid. Tehran: Chapkhaneh-e Diba, 1349), pp. 274 – 75.
24   *Risale-i Sipehsalar,* p. 171.
25   *Ibtidaname,* pp. 61 – 65.
26   Turkish: Kimya
27   *Risale-i Sipehsalar,* p. 179.
28   Qur'an, 7:54.
29   Abdülbaki Gölpınarlı, *Mevlana Celaleddin Hayatı,* p. 84.
30   *Ibtidaname,* pp. 64 – 65; see also pp. 249 – 251.
31   Baha al-Din Valad, *Ma'arif,* (a manuscript at Istanbul University Library), Folio 38b.
32   The source of this poem in Professor Furuzanfar's *Divan-i Kabir* (Tehran: Majles, 1954), No. 2648.
33   Abu al-Qasim al-Qushayri's (d. 1072) *al-Risalah* is one of the earliest books written on the subject of Sufism.
34   Qur'an, 57:4.
35   Muhammad b. Muhammad b. Husayn Mevlana Jalal al-Din Rumi, *Mesnevi,* translation and commentary by Olgun Tahir Mevlevi (Istanbul: Ahmet Said Matbaası, 1967) v. II, no. 96, 99-101, 103.
36   Muhammad b. Muhammad b. Husayn Mevlana Jalal al-Din Rumi. *Divan-i Kabir,* tr. Bediüzzaman Furuzanfar (Tehran: Danishgah-i Tehran, 1957) vol. V, no. 2364.
37   *Ibtidaname,* p. 141.
38   *Mesnevi,* vol. III, following couplet no. 3103.
39   *Divan-i Kabir,* vol. VII, no. 3172.
40   *Divan-i Kabir,* vol. V, no. 2573.
41   *Divan-i Kabir,* vol. III, no. 1353.
42   *Divan-i Kabir,* vol. II, no. 656.
43   When God created all the human spirits and asked them "Am I not your Lord?" they responded "Yes." (Qur'an, 7:172).
44   *Divan-i Kabir,* vol. II, no. 972.
45   *Divan-i Kabir,* vol. IV, no. 2039.
46   *Risale-i Sipehsalar,* p. 154.
47   Ibid., p. 156.
48   Ibid., p. 158.
49   A phrase in the Islamic tradition used when a reference is made to someone who has died.

CHAPTER II

RUMI'S PERSONALITY AND VIEWS

1 *Mesnevi*, vol. II, no. 95.

2 *Mesnevi*, vol. V, no. 2467.

3 Qur'an, 2:285.

4 Qur'an, 2:253.

5 *Mesnevi*, vol. V, no. 2556.

6 We have to give a lot of thought to this quatrain. Along the same lines, the well-known Turkish poet Mehmet Akif says, "It is the statue of himself that man worships. But this strange love affair is not publicized."

7 Furuzanfar, *Mevlana Celaleddin*, p. 191.

8 Shams al-Din Ahmad al-Aflaki, *Manaqib al-Arifin*, ed. Tahsin Yazıcı (Ankara: Türk Tarih Kurumu Basımevi, 1959), vol. I, 613.

9 Ibid., 405.

10 Ibid., 267.

11 Qur'an, 31:28.

12 Aflaki, *Manaqib al-Arifin*, vol. I, 438.

13 Ibid., vol. I, 516.

14 Ibid., 446.

15 Ibid., vol. I, 582.

16 Qur'an, 4:77.

17 Aflaki, *Manaqib al-Arifin*, vol. I, 578.

18 Ibid., vol. I, 582.

19 Qur'an, 39:22.

20 A title given to the wife of the Prophet.

21 Aflaki, *Manaqib al-Arifin*, vol. I, 585.

22 Ibid., v. I, 397. Rumi and Sadr al-Din were two well-known saints living in the same town. Both lived at the same age, guiding the lovers of God. It was impossible not to admire the love and respect they showed each other. We always should remember these peerless saints who left envy and jealousy to small shaykhs, with respect and gratitude. One day one of Rumi's friends was depressed. Rumi told him, "All the depression of this world is due to loving this world. Once you know yourself as detached from this world and as a stranger in this world, and that all the colors and beauties that you know and look at and the delights that you enjoy are not going to remain forever and everything is temporary and that you will go to another place, you will be relieved from the depression. How fortunate is the person who sits with people of wisdom and not with arrogant people, and spends time with people who see themselves as lowly and unworthy." Rumi continued, "The free man, mature person is the one that is not hurt by someone hurting him. The brave man is the one who does not hurt the one that deserves to be hurt." (Aflaki, *Manaqib al-Arifin*, vol. 1, 432.)

23 Ibid., vol. I, 164.

24 Ibid., vol. I, 324.

25 Qur'an, 33:45.

26 Aflaki, *Manaqib al-Arifin*, vol. I, 424.

27 Ibid., vol. 1, 424.

[28] This famous book, *Risale-i Sipehsalar*, written in Persian by Majd al-Din Feridun, son of Ahmed, also called Sipehsalar, literally meaning commander, because he was actually a military commander in the Seljuk times, was translated into Turkish by three proficient persons. First by my teacher, Midhat Bahari, and by Ahmed Avni Konuk who is among the Mevlevi Gnostics and commentator to the *Mesnevi* and *Fusus* and more recently by Tahsin Yazıcı. The first two translations are in Turkish printed with Arabic letters while the translation of Tahsin Yazıcı was published in 1977 by the *Tercüman* newspaper's 1001 Main Books series. Sipehsalar Feridun who died in 1312 is buried in Konya in Rumi's shrine next to Rumi's blessed father. Since Sipehsalar was in Rumi's service for forty years (Midhat Bahari's translation, p. 11) his book is very important in getting to know Rumi and explaining him. Therefore, let us study Rumi from this prime reference work that was written seven centuries ago and is still bringing Rumi's holy fragrance to our day and let us not make up wrong tales about Rumi in our mind.

[29] A Prophetic tradition whose wording belongs to Muhammad, peace be upon him, and whose meaning comes from God.

[30] *Risale-i Sipehsalar*, p. 37.

[31] *Divan-i Kabir*, vol. IV, no. 2406.

[32] *Risale-i Sipehsalar*, p. 43.

[33] *Divan-i Kabir*, vol. III, no. 1438.

[34] Ibid., vol. II, no. 890.

[35] Ibid., vol. V, no. 2492.

[36] Ibid., vol. VI, no. 2831.

[37] *Risale-i Sipehsalar*, p. 22 (Persian edition).

[38] *Divan-i Kabir*, vol. VI, no. 3038.

[39] Ibid., no. 3238.

[40] Ibid., no. 3238.

[41] Qur'an, 53:9.

[42] *Divan-i Kabir*, vol. III, no. 1135.

[43] Ibid., vol. VI, no. 2978.

[44] Ibid., vol. III, no. 1282.

[45] Qur'an, 39:22.

[46] *Mihrab*: the place in the mosque where the prayer leader is positioned

[47] *Divan-i Kabir*, vol. V, no. 2336.

[48] Ibid., vol. I, no. 395.

[49] Ibid., vol. V, no. 2470.

[50] Ibid., no. 2627.

[51] Ibid., vol. III, no. 1129.

[52] Ibid., vol. I, no. 455.

[53] Qur'an, 17:22.

[54] *Mesnevi*, vol. I, no. 2842.

[55] *Divan-i Kabir*, vol. III, no. 1414.

[56] Ibid., vol. III, no. 1526.

[57] *Qutb*: (literally pole) the highest stage of sanctity amongst Muslim saints

[58] Ibid., vol. III, no. 1576.

[59] Ibid., no. 1459.

[60] *Risale-i Sipehsalar*, p. 90

61 Qur'an, 17:44.
62 Qur'an, 38:18-19.
63 For the Hadith see Sulaiman bin Ahmad bin Ayyub al-Tabarani, *al-Mu'jam al-Kabir* (Mosul: Maktabat al-Ulum wa al-Hikam, vol. II, 245.
64 *Mesnevi*, vol. III, no. 1019.
65 Ibid., vol. III, no. 1011-1016.
66 Ibid., vol. I, no. 2154.
67 Ibid., vol. IV, no. 2827.
68 The event is called Hani al-Jiz' (the moaning of the date trunk). The Prophet used to give his a sermon leaning on a date trunk. The Companions cut a new one which the Prophet used to replace the other. During the sermon the old one mourned because of its separation from the Prophet. The story is narrated in its entirety in the collections of Hadith (See Muhammad bin Hibban al-Tamimi (d. 354 AH) *Sahih Ibn Hibban*. Ed. Shuayb al-Arnaout. (Beirut: Muassasah al-Risalah, 1993), vol. XIV, 435).
69 Ibid., vol. I, no. 2113.
70 Qur'an, 36:79.
71 Qur'an, 36:82.
72 Qur'an, 2:286.
73 *Divan-i Kabir*, vol. III, no. 1576.
74 Ibid., vol. III, no. 1535.
75 Ibid., no. 1540.
76 Ibid., vol. VI, no. 3020.
77 Ibid., vol. VI, no. 3020.
78 *Mesnevi*, vol. VI, no. 971.
79 Ibid., vol. I, no. 111.
80 Ibid., vol. III, no. 14-15.
81 Abu Abdullah Muhy al-Din Muhammad b. Ali Ibn al-Arabi, *The Wisdom of The Prophets (Fusus al-Hikam),* tr. Angela Culme-Seymour (Wiltshire: Beshara Publications, 1975), pp. 116 – 33.
82 Al-Munawi, Muhammad Abd al-Rauf, *Faydh al-Qadir* (Beirut: al-Maktabah al-Tijariyyah, 1972) vol. VI, p. 180.
83 *Mesnevi*, vol. I, no. 333.
84 *Mesnevi*, vol. I. no. 3-6.5.
85 Qur'an. 16:15.
86 Qur'an, 15:29.
87 Qur'an, 26:38.
88 *Divan-i Kabir*, vol. I, no. 188.
89 *Mesnevi*, vol. I, no. 112 – 15.
90 *Divan-i Kabir*, vol. I, no. 207.
91 See Michael H. Hart, *The 100: A Ranking of the Most Influential Persons in History* (New York: Kensington, 1992).
92 *Divan-i Kabir*, vol. II, no. 901.
93 Ibid., vol. II, no. 1137.
94 Ibid., vol. I, no. 882.
95 *Mesnevi*, vol. IV, no. 3844 – 3846.
96 Ibid., vol. VI, no. 167 – 171.

97   Ibid., no. 816.
98   Ibid., vol. III, no. 3110 – 3129.
99   *Divan-i Kabir*, vol. II, no. 1135.
100 Ibid., vol. II, no. 792.
101 Ibid., vol. I, no. 490.
102 *Mesnevi*, vol. V, no. 2556 – 2557.
103 *Divan-i Kabir*, vol. V, no. 2578.
104 *Mesnevi*, vol. I, no. 1824.
105 Ibid., vol. I, no. 1997.
106 Qur'an, 57:4.
107 *Divan-i Kabir*, vol. III, no. 1098.
108 *Divan-i Kabir*, vol. V, no. 2508.
109 *Mesnevi*, vol. I, no. 2882.
110 *Divan-i Kabir*, vol. I, no. 441.
111 *Mesnevi*, vol. II, no. 1416-1426.
112 Ibid., vol. I, no. 316.
113 *Rubaiyat in Divan-i Kabir*, vol. VIII, no. 664.
114 Ibid., no. 1473.
115 Ibid., no. 1828.
116 Ibid., no. 1249.
117 *Mesnevi*, vol. II, no. 1361 – 1363.
118 Ibid., vol. I, no. 333.
119 *Rubaiyat* in *Divan-i Kabir,* vol. VIII, no. 418.
120 Ibid., no. 311.
121 *Mesnevi*, vol. II, no. 1083 – 1086.
122 Ibid., no. 1353.
123 Ibid., no. 23.
124 Ibid., vol. II, no. 1614, 1619 – 1624.
125 *Mesnevi*, vol. II, no. 1170 – 1186.
126 *Mesnevi*, vol. V, no. 3340.
127 Ibid., vol. IV, no. 1947.
128 Ibid., no. 2301.
129 Ibid., no. 2557.
130 Ibid., no. 1984 – 1989.
131 Ibid., no. 2188.
132 Ibid., no. 2181.
133 Ibid., no. 2265.
134 Ibid., vol. III, no. 2570 – 2588.
135 Ibid., vol. I, no. 2329.
136 Ibid., vol. IV, no. 1255.
137 Ibid., no. 1408. Refers to the Qur'anic verse that addresses the Prophet, "If they turn away from you, say, 'God is enough for me.'" (Qur'an, 9:129).
138 Ibid., vol. II, no. 2328.
139 See Qur'an, 18:65.
140 *Mesnevi.*, vol. II, no. 3262.
141 Ibid., vol. IV, no. 3311 – 3313.
142 Ibid., no. 3649.

143 Ibid., vol. V, no. 3233.
144 *Divan-i Kabir*, vol. III, no. 1082.
145 Ibid., vol. VII, no. 3134.
146 Ibid., vol. III, no.1185.
147 Ibid., vol. I, no. 172.
148 Ibid., no. 464.
149 *Mesnevi*, vol. VI, no. 3181.
150 Ibid., vol. VI, no. 3708.
151 Ibid., no. 3753.
152 Qur'an, 23:14.
153 *Mesnevi*, vol. V, no. 3278.
154 *Divan-i Kabir*, vol. VI, no. 2927.
155 *Faydh al-Qadir*, vol. II, p. 224.
156 Qur'an, 2:228.
157 *Mesnevi*, vol V, no. 3881.
158 Ibid., no. 3890.
159 Ibid., no. 3947.
160 Ibid., no. 1333.
161 Ibid., no. 1365.
162 For the whole story see, ibid, no. 957.
163 Ibid., no. 3999.
164 Qur'an, 95:4 – 5.
165 *Mesnevi*, vol. I, no. 2426 – 2435.
166 *Risale-i Sipehsalar*, p. 97.
167 The term *Sharif* means noble and is used as an honorific title for the *Mesnevi* in Turkish culture.
168 *Mesnevi*, vol. V, no. 2279.
169 *Divan-i Kabir*, vol. IV, no. 1791.
170 Years ago in a magazine, I read of the will of an English poet who said, "My most beautiful poem has been recorded on a gramophone record. It shall be played fifty years after my death." This record was kept in the university library. Fifty years later, the newspapers announced that the record would be played. Lovers of poetry filled the university's conference hall to listen to the most beautiful poem of this famous poet, many of whose poetry books have been published. The record, which had been carefully sealed and stored for fifty years, was put on a gramophone to be played for thousands of people holding their breath in the conference hall. But there was no sound from the record. A check of the record revealed that there was nothing recorded on it. After making everybody wait for fifty years, the poet wanted to say that the most beautiful poem is the one that is not verbalized but remains in the heart. He wanted to say it with a tongue that is beyond words and beyond letters. Rumi also maintains that the most beautiful poem is not the one that pours from the lips but the one that is felt at heart.
171 *Mesnevi*, vol. I, no. 733.
172 *Mesnevi*, vol. I, no. 1341.
173 Qur'an, 31:19.
174 Abu al-Khayr Isam al-Din Ahmad Taşköprüzade, *Mawdhuat al-Ulum*, tr. Kemaleddin Mehmed Efendi. (Dersaadet : Ikdam Matbaası, 1895), vol. II, 549.

322 *Fundamentals of Rumi's Thought: A Mevlevi Sufi Perspective*

175 Related in Abu al-Husayn Muslim b. al-Hajjaj al-Qushayri, *al-Sahih* (Cairo: Daru Ihya al-Kutub al-Arabiyyah, 1954), vol. II, 193.

176 Abdülbaki Gölpınarlı, *Mevlevilik Adab ve Erkanı* (Istanbul: İnkılap ve Aka Kitabevleri, 1963), p. 50.

177 Ismail Rusuhi Ankaravi, *Risalah Hujjat al-Sama* (Istanbul: Rıza Efendi Matbaası, 1869), p. 26.

178 Ibid., pp. 13 – 14.

179 Abu al-Barakat Nur al-Din Abd al-Rahman b. Ahmad b. Muhammad Jami, *Nafahat al-Uns Min Hadarat al-Quds*, tr. Mahmud B. Osman Lami'i Çelebi (Istanbul :Marifet Yayınları, 1289), p. 404.

180 See Gölpınarlı, *Mevlevi Adab ve Erkanı*, p. 53.

181 *Risale-i Sipehsalar*, p. 91.

182 Aflaki, *Manaqib al-'Arifin*, vol. I, p. 89.

183 Najm al-Din al-Kubra, *Mecmuat al-Resail*, Ayasofya Kütüphanesi (Istanbul), Manuscript, no: 4821.

184 *Divan-i Kabir*, vol. I, no. 338.

185 Ibid., no. 339.

186 *Divan-i Kabir*, vol. III, no. 1295.

187 Ibid., vol. V, no. 2515.

188 Qur'an, 52:48.

189 *Mesnevi*, vol. V, no. 3678.

190 Ibid., no. 3676 – 3697.

191 *Divan-i Kabir*, vol. VI, no. 2675.

192 In Turkey

193 Ismail Hakkı İzmirli, *Yeni Ilm-i Kelam* (Istanbul: Evkaf-i Islamiyye Matbaası, 1339 AH), 98.

194 Ali ibn Uthman al-Hujwiri, *Kashf al-Mahjub* (Istanbul, 1982), p. 87.

195 Qur'an, 4:79.

196 *Mesnevi*, vol. I, no. 89.

197 Abu Isa al-Tirmidhi, *al-Sunan* (Beirut: Dar al-Ihya al-Turath al-Arabi, n.d.), vol. IV, 448, hadith no: 2139.

198 *Mesnevi*, vol. I, no. 601.

199 Qur'an, 8:17.

200 *Mesnevi*, vol. I, no. 615 – 619.

201 Ibid.

202 This line refers to the Prophetic Tradition: "If you come across a scholar, a mature man, you have met a tree of paradise. Sit under that tree and eat from its spiritual fruits."

203 *Mesnevi*, vol. I, no. 939 – 943.

204 Rusuhi Ismail Ankaravi, *Şerh-i Kebir-i Ankaravi ber Mesnevi-yi Ma'navi-i Mevlevi* tr. Ismet Settarzade (Tehran: Chapkhaneh-e Mihan, 1970), vol. I, 308.

205 *Mesnevi*, vol. I, no. 1480 – 1482.

206 Ibid., vol. I, no. 1487 – 1493.

207 *Mesnevi*, vol. I, no. 1496 – 1499.

208 Ibid., vol. VI, no. 407 – 415.

209 Ibid., no.1438 – 1443.

210 Qur'an, 17:44.

211 *Mesnevi*, vol. IV, no. 3636 – 3638.

212 *Arganun*: organ, a musical instrument played especially in churches.

213 *Mesnevi*, vol. IV, no. 3901 – 3906.

214 Qur'an, 53:9. In the account of the Mi'raj.

215 Mehmed Fuad Köprülü included this in his *Türk Edebiyatında ilk Mutasavvıflar* (The First Sufis in Turkish Literature) (Ankara: Gaye Matbaacılık, 1981), pp. 217 – 30.

216 Qur'an, 24:35.

217 *Divan-i Kabir*, vol. VI, no. 2778.

218 *Mesnevi*, vol. II, no. 1613.

219 Abu al-Qasim Sharaf al-Din Omar b. Ali Ibn al-Faridh, *Ta'iyyah al-Kubra* (Cairo: al-Maktaba al-Azhariyyah, 1319), no. 652 – 54.

220 Sa'd al-Din Mahmud b. Abd al-Karim b. Yahya Shabastari, *Gulshan-i Raz*, ed. Ali Muhammadzade Qurban (Baku: Ferhengistan-i Ulum-i Jumhuri, 1972), no.98 – 105.

221 *Mesnevi*, vol. I, no.1121 – 1135.

222 Qur'an, 6:103.

223 *Mesnevi*, vol. VI, no. 2356 – 2357.

224 Ibid., no. 2353 – 2355.

225 *Mesnevi*, vol. I, no. 601 – 602.

226 Dear readers, I had to write so much on this issue, making it quite involved, in order to prove that Rumi did not believe in reincarnation. For this matter to be understood better, I briefly mentioned the belief of *dawriyya* and *wahdat al-wujud*. I gave examples from Rumi and other poets. All these different issues and illustrations are for the sole purpose of eliminating un-Islamic beliefs that are very misleading. If I have erred, I ask God and you to forgive me. (ŞC)

227 Shabastari, *Gulshan-i Raz*, no. 362 – 63.

228 See Qur'an, 36:26.

229 See Qur'an, 51:22; *Mesnevi*, vol. V, no. 1734 – 1743.

230 See Qur'an, 36:78.

231 *Mesnevi*, vol. V, no. 1772 – 1779.

CHAPTER III

RUMI'S INFLUENCE

1 *Divan-i Kabir*, vol. I, no. 316.

2 Ibrahim Hakkı, *Marifetname* (Istanbul: Matbaa-i Amire, 1892) p. 315.

3 *Divan-i Kabir*, vol. I, no. 595. Abu Jahl was a doubter and unbeliever in the Prophet.

4 *Marifetname*, p. 435. Abu Lahab was an uncle of the Prophet who rejected his mission.

5 *Divan-i Kabir*, vol. III, no. 1353.

6 Qur'an, 58:39.

7 Muhammad Iqbal, *Payam-i Mashriq*, p. 62.

8 *Divan-i Kabir*, vol. III, no. 1142.

9 Qur'an, 2:30.

10 Muhammad Iqbal, *Armagan-i Hijaz*, p. 173.

11 *Divan-i Kabir*, vol. III, no. 1426.

12 Qur'an, 57:4.

13 Iqbal, *Esrar-i Hodi*, p. 19.

14 *Divan-i Kabir*, vol. I, no. 188.

15   *Mesnevi*, vol. V, no. 3340.
16   Muhammad Iqbal, *Armagan-i Hijaz*, p. 154.
17   Muhammad Iqbal, *Cavitname*, pp. 119, 426.
18   Qur'an, 50:16.
19   *Divan-i Kabir*, vol. I, no. 213.
20   Muhammad Iqbal, *Esrar-i Hodi*, p. 19.
21   *Mesnevi*, vol. V, no. 2014.
22   Ibid., vol. II, no. 1529.
23   Ibid., vol. V, no. 3854.
24   *Divan-i Kabir*, v. VI, no. 2674.
25   Iqbal, *Payam-i Mashriq*, 56.
26   Ibid., 157.
27   *Esrar-i Hodi*, 25.
28   *Mesnevi*, vol. I, no. 23.
29   Ibid., vol. VI, no. 668.
30   *Rubaiyat in Divan-i Kabir*, vol. VIII, 1667.
31   *Mesnevi*, vol. I, p.. 640.
32   *Armagan-i Hijaz*, p. 107.
33   Ibid., p. 105.
34   *Armagan-i Hijaz*, p. 106.
35   *Esrar-i Hodi*, p. 8.
36   Qur'an, 55:33.
37   Qur'an, 29:20.
38   In different books written on Rumi's life and works, sections have been assigned to Sufism and *wahdat al-wujud*, and these subjects have been discussed in depth. Since I hold the view that these subjects cannot be understood with the intellect and through logical reasoning, in this book I did not reserve sections for these issues. I tried not to make my dear readers understand these difficult subjects but to let them feel them by giving examples from Rumi whenever appropriate. Also by taking examples from Iqbal's books, who found his views and feelings in Rumi, I strived to make my readers understand these difficult subjects. This is the reason for my lengthy elaboration in this section.
39   *Mesnevi*, vol. V, no. 3628.
40   Qur'an, 17:10.
41   Qur'an, 95:4.
42   Qur'an, 5:16.
43   Qur'an, 4:57.
44   Haythami, *Majma' al-Zawa'id*, 1:119, 120.
45   *Kashf al-Khafa*, vol. 1, p. 435, no. 1159.
46   *The West-Eastern Divan*, 46.
47   This valuable scholar, who knew Arabic, Persian, and Turkish very well, translated the *Divan* by Hafiz of Shiraz into German. In his book *Persian Literature*, published in 1818, Hammer discusses Rumi's works extensively (pages 163 – 98) and describes the Honorable *Mesnevi* as a book that should be read by all Sufis from the Ganges River to the shores of the Bosphorous.
48   *Divan-i Kabir*, vol. III, no. 1348.

49 Schimmel (d. 2003), who was also a poet, was born in Erfurt, Germany in 1922. She showed interest in Arabic early in her youth, and in addition to Arabic she also learned Persian and Turkish. After graduating from Berlin University at age 19, Schimmel fell in love with Rumi, reading his poetry in its original language. She began translating Rumi's poetry. She came to Turkey for the first time in 1952 and lectured in Ankara University's Department of History of Religions in the School of Theology for five years. Afterward she joined Bonn University. In 1967, she began lecturing at Harvard University. Many universities awarded her honorary doctorate degrees. Her book on Rumi is *The Triumphal Sun: A Study of the Works of Jalaluddin Rumi* (Albany, NY: State University of New York Press, 1993).

50 Mehmet Önder, *Hazret-i Mevlana Hayatı ve Eserleri* (Istanbul: Tercüman Yayınları), p. 232.

51 Asaf Halet Çelebi, *Mevlana Hayatı ve Şahsiyeti*, (Istanbul: Kanaat Kitabevi, 1939), p. 50.

52 Eva de Vitray-Meyerovitch, *Rumi and Sufism* (Sausalito, CA: Post-Apollo Press, 1977 French; 1987 English Translation).

53 The Washington-based Rumi Forum for Interfaith Dialogue is one of them. There is also an annual Rumi Festival held in North Carolina.

CHAPTER IV
RUMI'S SUFI ORDER AND HIS
APPROACH TO ORDERS

1 *Risale-i Sipehsalar*, pp. 30 – 91.

2 Furuzanfar, *Mevlana Celaleddin*, p. 13.

3 Jami, *Nafahat al-Uns*, p. 480.

4 Hoca Zade Ahmed Hilmi, "Silsile-i Meşayih-i Mevleviyye" published in *Hadikat al-Awliya* (Istanbul: Şirket-i Mürettibiye Matbaası, 1318), p. 6. (I could not locate this reference in *Hadikat al-Awliya,* but I found a list of Mevlevi Masters in Abu al-Barakat Nur al-Din Abd al-Rahman b. Ahmad b. Muhammad Jami, *Nafahat al-Uns Min Hadarat al-Quds*, tr. Mahmud B. Osman Lami'i Çelebi (Istanbul: Marifet Yayınları, 1289)p. 64. (ZS).

5 *Risale-i Sipehsalar*, p. 160.

6 Aflaki, *Manaqib al-'Arifin*, vol. II, p. 705.

7 Muhaqqiq Husayin Tirmidhi Sayyid Burhan-Din, *Maarif,* tr. Abdülbaki Gölpınarlı (Ankara: Türkiye İş Bankası n.d), p. 15.

8 *Mesnevi*, vol. II, no. 1770.

9 Qur'an, 23:53.

10 Abu al-Qasim Zayn al-Islam Abd al-Karim al-Qushayri, *al-Risalah al-Qushayriyyah*, ed. Abd al-Halim Mahmud and Mahmud Ibn Sharif (Cairo: Dar al-Kutub al-Hadithah, 1973), vol. I, p. 261.

11 Hujwiri, *Kashf al-Mahjub*, p. 383.

12 *Mesnevi*, vol. VI, no. 3856.

13 Ibid., no. 2063-2067.

14 *Divan-i Kabir*, vol. V, no. 2127

15 Ibid.

16 *Mesnevi*, vol. V, no. 2556.

INDEX